The Trial of Queen Caroline

The Trial of
Queen Caroline

Roger Fulford

B. T. BATSFORD LTD London

First published 1967

© Roger Fulford, 1967

Made and printed in Great Britain by
William Clowes and Sons Ltd, London and Beccles
for the Publishers B. T. Batsford Ltd
4 Fitzhardinge Street, London W.1

Contents

The Illustrations

Line illustrations in the text

*The author and publishers wish to thank the National Portrait Gallery,
London, for permission to reproduce fig. 14.*

Introductory Note

There are several verbatim reports of the proceedings in Parliament about Queen Caroline. I have used the one compiled by Joseph Nightingale, which was published in three volumes in 1821. I have also consulted *Hansard* and the very full transcription in the *Annual Register*. Throughout I have relied on the splendid edition of King George IV's letters edited by Professor Aspinall.

Whether Queen Caroline was guilty or innocent, whether the case against her was sufficiently or insufficiently proved, whether the proceedings against her by parliamentary bill were wise or foolish are questions for each individual's judgment. I have not tried to answer them. Rather I have attempted, by recounting the details of the evidence, to show what life was like for the European traveller a century and a half ago, to show something of the consequences of royal behaviour, and to recapture the effects of an episode, which was dramatic and unparalleled, on the diverse characters who, in the House of Lords, were endeavouring to discharge the obligations of their order.

Roger Fulford

The Brunswick Princess

✦⊃◦⊂✦

'*Elle n'est pas bête.*' If we were to give these words the most favour-able twist in translation which is possible, they remain a forbidding commendation. They were weakened by the three terse sentences which followed. 'She has no judgment. She has been strictly brought up. It was necessary.' Such was the description of the bride chosen by the Prince of Wales in 1794; spoken by the bride's father the words could not be dismissed as an ill-informed verdict.

The speaker was that renowned Duke of Brunswick—Charles William Ferdinand—who thundered across Europe in the Seven Years War, winning the admiration and affection of his difficult uncle Frederick the Great and drawing words of praise from the elder Pitt in England—'his days are precious to Europe'. Two years before the winter of 1794, which found him speaking sternly of his daughter, he had spoken equally sternly to the citizens of Paris threatening them 'with never-to-be-forgotten-vengeance' unless they ceased to molest their royal family. That threat was uttered but never fulfilled. To the man who believed such things (and could say them) the marriage of his daughter was of secondary importance; his mind was absorbed with the safety of northern Europe which, as 1794 progressed, was seen to be increasingly threatened by the advance of the guilty rebels of Paris. To the old soldier the capture of Brabant and Bergen-op-Zoom by the revolutionary armies of France was a more engrossing topic than a distinguished royal marriage in his own family—a family well accustomed to such honours.

The contempt of the average Englishman for the dynasties of

Europe is an endearing part of the character of John Bull: an examination of this feeling would make a fascinating expedition down one of the by-paths of history—not creditable to native good sense but curious and amusing. On the sombre side are the national prejudices which made Englishmen criticise the Hanoverian dynasty as German, although in a thousand years of history there has never been a purely English one: on the lighter side are the delightful insular prejudices, such as the belief of a prime minister that Hanover lay to the north of Great Britain, or—from information provided by Lord Rosebery—that the princes of Germany endured ponderous dalliance with unattractive mistresses because such was the rule of life laid down by their prototype '*Le Roi Soleil*'. To the average Englishmen the states of Germany, their courts, their manner of living were completely insignificant—at most magnets drawing the hard-earned gold of England to stimulate their martial ardour against the French. Of Brunswick, that diminutive duchy lying to the south of Prussia with its capital city roughly half way between Berlin and the Dutch frontier, such gibes were superficially true: they are blunted by an acquaintance with the facts.

Duke Charles, whose words about his daughter have been quoted, was a pattern for benevolent despots—a fearless soldier abroad and a popular, prudent and enlightened sovereign at home. His family connexions were illustrious. At the beginning of the eighteenth century a Brunswick princess married the heir of Peter the Great and another Brunswick princess was the mother of Maria Theresa. Frederick the Great married a princess of this house as did his successor. Frederick the Great's sister married the reigning duke of Brunswick and their son, Duke Charles, married the eldest sister of King George III. At the time with which we are concerned, in the last decade of the eighteenth century, the court at Brunswick managed to combine remarkable domestic felicity with acknowledged infidelity. A royal biographer of olden days, Mr. Robert Huish, said that Duke Charles forgot the toils of war 'in the glance of the lustful eye' and that the dangers of war vanished 'when the midnight kiss is stolen'.[1] But there did not seem any need to steal the kiss for Duke Charles lived openly with a remarkable camarilla of ladies. First

[1] *Memoirs of Queen Caroline*, 1821.

there was his mother, the Duchess-Dowager, burbling away about long forgotten squabbles between her father, King Frederick William of Prussia and her uncle King George II. Then there was her daughter—the splendidly endowed Abbess of the Protestant Abbey of Gandersheim. This lady, no doubt disappointed in love, was fond of inveighing against the treachery and faithlessness of men. But neither this nor her sacred calling prevented her from making eager overtures to gentlemen who happened to be visiting her brother's court. The third lady was the Duchess herself—George III's sister. She had a good heart, little dignity and all her brother's flow of inconsequential chat. Her beliefs were simple. She thought that if a wife was afraid of her husband during pregnancy, the child could be marked with a likeness of the husband in the same way that it could be marked with anything else, such as a spider or a cat, which caused fright. Her anecdotes were not always seemly. She used, as a child, to share a bed with George III and she reported that he had not lost one trick of babyhood, but that her father cured him of his habit by making him wear a blue ribbon. She explained that to this ribbon was attached—not the George—but a piece of china. The fourth member of the camarilla was the Duke's mistress Madame von Hertzberg who was, according to Mirabeau, the most reasonable woman at Court. Possibly observers would accept the fact that the competition was not severe.

No doubt life at the Brunswick court was distinctly unexpected, a little different from the respectable tedium of an evening at the Windsor of King George III and Queen Charlotte; but it reflected real life—with the Duke taking people on one side to talk of grand alliances and spirited campaigns against the French and then settling down to a table of ombre at which Madame von Hertzberg was always one of the three players, with the Duchess prattling away in the background overjoyed at any opportunity of speaking English to a countryman visiting Brunswick. And about this flaxen-haired family there was, as Carlyle once noticed, a certain 'albuminous simplicity' which gave it charm.

But did this charm, did this albuminous simplicity extend to the younger generation, to the children of the Duke and Duchess? The answer to that question was clouded by a shadow of anxiety. 'The heart has nothing to do with royal marriages: the children are mostly cripples in mind and body.' The speaker is again Duke Charles and, unquestionably, he had in mind his own children. No doubt he would have made (and we should make) an exception for his youngest son 'Brunswick's fated chieftain' who fell at Quatre Bras. (But one of the fated chieftain's own sons was mad: the other was decidedly eccentric.) Of the other three sons of Duke Charles we can sense the quality by a comment of their too talkative mother. Although her nieces at Windsor were panting for husbands, the Duchess said that even these eager brides would reject her sons if they ever saw them. Two of them were said to be mad and the third was blind.[1] The elder daughter, the Princess Augusta, had married the heir to the duchy of Wurtemberg. Military duties took him to Russia where his wife accompanied him. He returned without her. She is believed to have misbehaved with a Russian grand-duke and to have been imprisoned and perhaps slaughtered by Catherine the Great.

And now the question arises whether the youngest member of the family had escaped the varying taints of her brothers and sisters. In appearance she had that striking albuminous look and, though short, she was not unattractive. As a girl in her early teens she attracted the tender and untouched heart of Lord Stanley of Alderley who, as a youth, was visiting Brunswick. He never forgot the Princess—outwardly the image of enchanting girlhood.[2] She had had several overtures of marriage, which included one from the Prince of Orange. History does not tell us why these negotiations stopped short of the nuptial bed. In 1794 she was 26. She was devoted to her father and used to say, in later life, with tears running down her face: 'I loved my father dearly, better nor any oder person.'

Was she one of those children of royal alliances who, in the words of her own father, are 'cripples in mind'? Many years later her mother was to say: 'Her excuse is, poor thing, that she is not right here,' tapping her forehead. But the good duchess, as we have seen, was always prone to shoot out anything that flitted into her mind without first submitting her thought to reflection. And this was precisely the trouble with her daughter. '*La parole en elle devance toujours la*

[1] Lord Edmond Fitzmaurice *Charles Duke of Brunswick*, 1901.
[2] J. H. Adeane, *Early Married Life of Maria Josepha Lady Stanley*, 1899.

pensée', observed that very wise mistress of the Duke—Madame von Hertzberg. With alarm the Englishman, who was sent to fetch her away, noticed that she was free and easy in her manner and that she did not wash: but what really worried him was this reckless speech. 'My eternal theme to her is—*think before she speaks.*' The Princess and the English envoy fell to discussing the infidelity of Princesses of Wales: he brought this edifying topic to a close by telling her that in England such infidelity was punishable by death. 'This startled her.'[1]

Could Princess Caroline, with her good nature marred by glaring faults, have made a success of any royal marriage in England? That is of course difficult to say but she had to an exceptional degree the one fault—indiscretion—which is fatal in royal persons. Had she been several years younger it might have been possible to mould her character, to smother some of the characteristics which she had absorbed through her long youth at Brunswick among the camarilla. One thing is capable of a clear answer because it is indisputable. Anyone realising the character of Princess Caroline and seeing it against the background of her bridegroom must have known that the marriage was foredoomed.

George, Prince of Wales—Regent in the future and King George IV still further ahead—was five years older than his bride. As was true of his father he was a man of strong sexual passions; unlike his father he had indulged them. However, when he was 23 he had established a regular connexion with Mrs. Fitzherbert, a widow of 29. He had parted from her, on account of her bad temper, a few months before negotiations were opened for his marriage with Princess Caroline. Although he was greatly liked in the narrow circle of the Whig aristocracy and by all who knew him well, he was not generally popular with the public who did not know him personally —unpopularity which is partly explained by the knowledge that he was extravagant and partly explained by his attachment to the Whig Party whose politics (especially when relations with France became more threatening) were antipathetic to the middle class. Consequently (and this is an important point) any appeal to public opinion over his behaviour in private life was likely to find him at a grave

[1] *Diaries and Correspondence of Lord Malmesbury*, 1844.

disadvantage. He could not afford indiscretion from within his private circle: a little trickle of malicious tittle-tattle outside the sentried walls of Carlton House or of the Pavilion at Brighton could—because the ground was ready to receive it—rapidly swell into a torrent.

The character of the Prince was curious. Unlike the forbears of his house he was not, by nature, a fighting man nor was he endowed, as some of them had been, with political aptitude. He was rather a man of taste and intellect: well-read, extremely amusing and gifted with a highly developed appreciation of the arts. He was kind-hearted but apt to be plunged into the depths of despair in the face of any difficulty. This is his own account of his afflictions in an early love affair: 'I have spit blood and am so much emaciated you would hardly know me again . . . in short my misery was such that I went under the promise of the greatest secrecy and threw myself at my mother's feet and confessed the whole truth to her. I fainted.'[1]

No one would pretend that married life with the Prince of Wales could have been easy: nor would anyone suggest that he could have proved what is called a 'good' husband. But one thing was paramount for even the possibility of a successful marriage: he would expect that his wife would fill her position with dignity. Everything else— looks, temper, disappointment in child-bed—might have been for- given: the one thing which was unforgivable was a lack of decorum which might, in turn, raise laughter against him. And it was just that lack of decorum which the Princess Caroline brought with her from Brunswick.

Why then did he choose her? He must have known perfectly well what the Brunswick family was like. Though different from other mortals in some respects, royal persons share the common human curiosity about their uncles, aunts and cousins. Moreover he would have known a great deal about them from his next brother, the Duke of York, who had spent seven years in north Germany and knew the whole family well. There seem to have been three influences which determined the Prince's choice.

The first was the absence of any other suitable princess. The only

[1] *Correspondence of George Prince of Wales*, edited by A. Aspinall, vol. i, 1963.

other name seriously suggested was the Princess Louise of Meck-
lenburg-Strelitz. She was niece to Queen Charlotte and another
marriage, in succession, with that insignificant family would have
been scarcely welcome in England. 'I had scarce found it with a
magnifying glass', wrote Horace Walpole of the diminutive duchy.
In fact this princess was to be the lion-hearted Queen Louise of
Prussia and had she been chosen by the Prince she would have
brought to the sequence of the Princesses of Wales a personality of
charm and distinction which might well have given stability to the
marriage. The second influence was that it was welcomed by the
King, his brother the Duke of Gloucester and the family generally—
though not of course by the Queen who was hoping for her niece.
The King told the Prince of Wales that it was indeed the one he
should have wished for in all respects.[1] The third influence was
perhaps the strongest. The Prince had, to a high degree, feelings of
pride in the English monarchy and in the distinction and lineage of
the royal house of Hanover. Both Brunswick and Hanover were
famous royal houses sharing a common ancestor: both carried the
white horse as their armorial emblem. In addition, as has already
been mentioned, the Brunswick family was recently connected by
marriage with the great dynasties of Europe—Romanoff, Hohen-
zollern and Habsburg. Moreover the Princess's father was a renowned
European personality. Writing to the Prince, his brother the Duke
of York said: 'I like the Duke of Brunswick exceedingly . . . he
behaved to me . . . with a degree of affection which one seldom finds
in such great people.'[2] No doubt none of these influences should
have weighed against the personality of the Princess in the eyes of
her suitor. Unhappily they did.

After a hazardous journey across northern Europe dodging the
French troops, Princess Caroline of Brunswick sailed up the Thames
and landed at Greenwich on 5 April 1794. The marriage took place
three days later at the Chapel Royal, St. James's Palace. This marriage, without courtship, must have been singularly embarrassing to
bride and bridegroom. Neither seemed conscious of physical attrac-
tions in the other. 'Harris, I am not well; pray get me a glass of

[1] Aspinall, *op. cit.* vol ii 454.
[2] Aspinall, *op. cit.* i, p. 96.

brandy' was the observation of the bridegroom on being introduced to his bride. '*Je le trouve très gros, et nullement aussi beau que son portrait*', said the bride on the same occasion. This first, frosty meeting between husband and wife was followed three days later by an evening wedding in the Chapel Royal, the ceremonial set off by the light of candles and the sound of trumpets and drums. Perhaps in that three day interval the relations between the happy pair were a shade less unfriendly, but there is evidence that the Prince was enquiring—as King Henry VIII had enquired when confronted with Anne of Cleves—'Is there no remedy then that I must needs put my neck in the yoke?' Alas! there was none.

Immediately after the wedding the Prince and Princess went to Carlton House. Their short married life was spent chiefly there with 'a honeymoon' at Kempshott Park near Andover, and with visits to Windsor and Brighton. Of this strange nuptial bed it is happily difficult to speak with certainty. The general belief among the aristocracy at the time was that Princess Charlotte, the only child of the marriage who was born on 7 January 1796, was the result of a single connexion between her parents and that there was something physically disagreeable about the Princess.[1] Whether this was the case or not is immaterial—and such details can best be left to the imagination. To the Prince it was not imagination, but reality. He said something on this delectable topic to Lord Malmesbury—the distinguished diplomat who had escorted the Princess from Brunswick—'the very day after or the very day but one after I was married.' To his mother he alludes to the Princess's 'personal nastiness' and his letters to his father contain hints of the same thing.[2]

What is incontestable is that the Prince and Princess had a conversation, when they were staying at Brighton some months before Princess Charlotte's birth, as the result of which they agreed to live separate lives within the establishment of a royal household. This meant that appearances would be kept up though the marital bed would not. After the Princess Charlotte's birth the Prince put the

---

[1] Some years ago an elderly lord, who was well placed for acquiring information of this kind, assured the present writer of the truth of both of these assertions.

[2] Aspinall, *op. cit.*

terms of this arrangement into writing. 'Nature has not made us
suitable to each other', he wrote, 'but tranquil and comfortable
society is, however, in our power.' He therefore decreed that they
should thus limit their relations and never resume 'a connexion of a
more particular nature'. Whether such suggestions were wise,
whether they were kind, whether they were practicable must remain
a matter of individual opinion.[1] A dynastic marriage, designed for
the succession, was to become a *mariage blanc.*

In this plight the Princess was not friendless. To the last the King,
her uncle, remained sympathetic. More importantly, the public,
which dearly loves a royal marriage and royal babies, espoused her
cause. If members of the public had known of the *mariage blanc,*
which they did not do until much later, they would not have liked
the sound of it. The Princess on the other hand tasted popularity;
she loved it.

The Princess quickly realised that although she might have lost
the battle for her husband, she could win for herself the sympathy
of public opinion and, in the process, discomfit the Prince. In
those times princes and princesses of the blood—even the aged
spinster Princess Amelia (George II's only surviving child)—maintained a splendidly impressive court. Members of these courts were
a cloud of witness, expected to reflect the glory of the personage and
to preserve it from a too scrupulous attention by the public. Such
were the public functions of a court. In private they were subject to
all the opinions, the prejudices and the partialities of any other con-
glomeration of human beings. The court of the Prince of Wales,
allowing for his financial stringency, was large. While we should be
right in discounting the lower members of the establishment—the
clerk of stables, the coachman, the sempstress, the housekeeper and
the porter, those, like doctors and apothecaries, who were infrequent
attendants and those, like the clerk of the closet and the chaplains
whose services were irregularly required by the personage there were
more than sixty, though these of course were not all in attendance at
the same time, grooms of the stole, chamberlains, gentlemen of the

[1] These were the terms on which Frederick the Great lived with his Brunswick
princess, and they did not perhaps greatly differ from the married life of the
Prince's next brother, the Duke of York.

bed-chamber, secretaries, comptroller of the Household, Master of the Robes, Grooms of the Bed-Chamber, Gentlemen Ushers, Equerries, librarians, pages of the back-stairs and pages of the presence, they reached a formidable total. In addition the Princess had her much smaller court—ladies in waiting and bedchamber women—about a dozen in all. And it was among these honourable, well-intentioned but sometimes opinionated people that the Princess attempted her first appeal to public opinion.

Here it is necessary to go back somewhat in the story. Some six months before his marriage the Prince had parted from Mrs. Fitzherbert—that 'wife' whom he had 'married' with protestations of eternal devotion (after an attempt at suicide) in a London drawing-room. No doubt Mrs. Fitzherbert had much to endure from the Prince: on his side he was tried by her temper. Though peppery towards the Prince Mrs. Fitzherbert was charming and friendly within the court. She had her supporters there. One of the gentlemen of the bedchamber, Lord Hugh Seymour, was a devoted partisan of Mrs. Fitzherbert. Lord Darnley, later the Groom of the Stole, was another. Within this court and almost certainly sped on its way by Mrs. Fitzherbert's friends the whisper grew that the Prince had transferred his affections to Lady Jersey, that she had supplanted Mrs. Fitzherbert, that she had picked an impossible bride for the Prince so that her own sway should remain unchallenged. The story was familiar to newspaper readers of the day and has been accepted ever since. It has always been highly unlikely.

Lady Jersey was older than Mrs. Fitzherbert, a grandmother and her husband and family were devotedly attached to the Prince. She was the daughter of an Irish bishop, vivacious and extremely amusing —her charms reputedly only blemished by thick legs. She was the first of those middle-aged ladies (Lady Hertford and Lady Conyngham were others) who were favoured—though not necessarily physically loved—by the Prince. He obviously delighted in her vivacity and wit, and encouraged by Queen Charlotte, with whom she was friendly, she was an important influence in deciding the Prince to marry. Before she left Brunswick, the Princess saw an anonymous letter from England shown to her by her mother 'with her usual indiscretion'. The letter animadverted against Lady Jersey 'in the most exaggerated terms': it was thought to be the work of a man 'who claimed to be in the daily society of Carlton House'.[1] Probably—though naturally this cannot be proved—it was the work of a Fitzherbert partisan. However the anonymous letter combined with the Princess's recollection of Madame von Hertzberg encouraged her, in her reckless fashion, to speak to the Prince about Lady Jersey as 'your mistress'. The Prince was furiously indignant. This was said in the interval between her arrival in England and the marriage. Such blunt language would hardly have been used by Queen Catherine to King Charles II: no doubt it would have been among the conjugal pleasantries of the German courts but in the circumstances the remark was unseemly and—more to the point—extremely unwise. It would be tedious to follow the wrangle between husband and wife and it would be profitless to attempt to decide where right lay. The marriage was doomed in the first few days: the *mariage blanc* was likewise doomed in the first few weeks after the Princess Charlotte's birth. The reason for this was that the Princess at once began to seek support within the Court and—what was far worse—from the public outside. At the end of May 1796 she went to the opera—the Prince was not with her—the Fitzherbert faction set up a hullaballoo—and she was loudly cheered from the pit, and more decorously in other parts of the house. It was the first of countless similar scenes when the lonely and neglected wife was, for a generation, applauded by the mob. Excluded from the heart of her prince she satisfied herself by becoming London's sweetheart.

And it was that appeal beyond Caesar to the public which converted the Prince's disdain for her into burning hatred, and explains why he described her in a letter to his mother as 'this fiend'.

After some uneasy months the Princess withdrew from Carlton House or 'the matrimonial home', as it would be called in a twentieth century divorce-court, and settled in a small way at Charlton, then an agreeable village between Greenwich and Woolwich, where she occupied, not altogether appropriately, the Rectory. After two years she was appointed Ranger of Greenwich Park and, to mark this dignity, moved into Montague House, Blackheath.

[1] Malmesbury, *op. cit.*

Though living in Blackheath, which was then a country retreat, she went up to London and used Carlton House to dress for ceremonial occasions, to see her daughter and for what in royal circles would be called *representation*. Husband and wife used to meet formally on these occasions and at the end of 1797 occurred that painful scene when the Princess demanded to see the Prince privately; confronted by him she complained that he did not treat her as his wife, as the mother of his child or as Princess of Wales: she spoke in a medley of French and English ending up *'je me regarde comme n'étant pas plus long temps assujettie, ni à vos ordres, ni à vos rules'*.[1] This was an important declaration of war because it followed an attempt by the Prince to say whom she should see and whom she should not see. The King, her constant friend in the family, had tersely said that she would be wise not to receive any society but such as was approved by her husband. The partisans of the Prince declared with delight that this meant that she should receive no men, no ladies below the rank of countesses and that not a candle should be lit or a dish of tea drunk without his permission.[2]

The ladies who formed her diminutive court at Charlton and Blackheath were middle-aged and stamped by respectability. There was Miss Garth, niece of the King's equerry, General Garth, and she found favour in Queen Charlotte's eyes because she was not 'befeathered' and she had no inclination 'to get into the great world'.[3] Then there was Mrs. Harcourt, the wife of General Harcourt, who had served the King in varying capacities for 30 years: she was entertaining with a rattling style of talking: and there was an unmarried daughter of Lord Vernon, who was closely connected with the Harcourt family. Although there is no evidence that the Princess did not get on well with these ladies they were bound by the closest ties of friendship and relationship with the court at Windsor, and although they were not, so far as history records, informers against her she could have cried with the psalmist 'Thou art about my path, and about my bed: and spiest out all my ways'.

[1] Aspinall, *op. cit.*
[2] Aspinall, *op. cit.*
[3] D. M. Stuart, *Daughter of England,* 1951.

And there was plenty to spy. Excluded from the regular companionship of the members of the royal family and their friends and made somewhat inaccessible to the world of fashion by the distance from Piccadilly to Charlton she collected round her a strange assortment of naval men—not young but dangerous and experienced. First was the fine and forceful admiral, Lord Hood, a vigorous septuagenarian, who was at this time living nearby as governor of Greenwich Hospital; there was Lord Amelius Beauclerk, then in his middle twenties, who had commanded a ship under Hood; there was Sir Sidney Smith, the immortal defender of Acre, and the future Admiral Manby, at this time commanding a frigate. And among these jolly tars was a rising politician, George Canning, whose early friendship with the Princess was to cause a political difficulty when the Prince came to the throne as George IV. 'The thing is too clear to be doubted. What am I to do? I am perfectly bewildered.' So wrote Canning to a close friend soon after the Princess had left Carlton House; it is not unreasonable to suppose, from other evidence, that this cryptic sentence alludes to an amorous advance from the Princess.[1]

She had the simple accomplishments of those in her station and the Prince had encouraged this side of her life by arranging that she should have lessons in music and the harp, in painting, in imitating marble and in English from a gentleman rather surprisingly named—Mr. Geffadiere.

Like other royal ladies the Princess found in charity and good works a solace for her loneliness and neglect. Her fellow Brunswicker, Joachim Campe, has left the best account of her domestic life at Charlton. She grew, and sold in London, a large quantity of vegetables and with the proceeds she educated orphan children—the boys for the sea and the girls for housewifery. But when she brought one of these children into her house as part of her family circle the net had begun to close round her. The ill-chosen circle of gentlemen friends, the indiscriminate succour to very young children caused a breeze of gossip and whispers, which by the time it reached her husband in Carlton House and her mother-in-law at Windsor had risen to a wind. By the turn of the century it was blowing at gale force.

[1] See Dorothy Marshall, *The Rise of George Canning*, 1938.

As soon as a government was formed which included the political allies of the Prince (this was the Ministry of All the Talents formed at the beginning of 1806) a commission was set up to examine the conduct of the Princess. It was powerful, consisting of the Prime Minister, the Home Secretary, the Lord Chancellor and the Lord Chief Justice. Its deliberations were popularly known as the Delicate Investigation, and it is there that posterity can see most clearly the Princess as she really was. We see her walking across the Heath on a winter's day in a lilac satin cloak, yellow half boots and a small, lilac travelling-cap embellished with sable. In the course of this winter's stroll she went to call on a complete stranger, for no better reason than she heard that she was the mother of a beautiful child. For an hour she sat in the parlour of this lady, chattering to a fellow visitor—Lady Stuart, 'a West-India lady who was a singular character'. She did not know Lady Stuart from Eve. She caused some raising of eyebrows by driving out alone with Lord Hood's son in his whisky. Again it was noticed that in the evenings she enjoyed allotting the parts among her guests in a game of French proverbs which, with the jaunt in the whisky, seemed to give her an appearance which was more dashing than royal. One of the explanations which she herself gave for her friendship with Sir Sidney Smith was that he was helping her to decorate her rooms in the Turkish style—one was modelled on the tent used by the Egyptian commander, Murad Bey, in the campaign against Napoleon. Again, although the Near East was coming into fashion there was just a hint of the seraglio in these furnishings which might have made those sitting in them a shade uneasy.

Such were the trimmings of the case: the substance was more serious. The gravest charge—that the Princess had given birth to a son—rested on the evidence of Sir John and Lady Douglas. Sir John was an officer in the Marines, subsequently a major-general, who had come to live in Blackheath partly because the air was thought to be healthier than in London after his service in Egypt and partly because it was on the road to Chatham where he was called by his service duties. His wife was the daughter of Colonel Caesar Hopkinson of Gloucestershire who was alleged by her enemies to have assumed the christian name after reaching the rank of serjeant in the army. Lady Douglas was talkative, unwise and provincial—not a companion for royal personages. She was the stranger on whom the Princess had called during that winter's walk. Her evidence was designed to show that the Princess had confided in her—with a wealth of physical details—that she was pregnant and had in fact given birth to the boy, familiar to the inmates of Montague House as William Austin. Although it is possible that Lady Douglas was not mistaken in what she remembered of the Princess's talk, the conclusion to be drawn from it was different. William Austin was the son of a labourer in the Dockyard at Deptford and his wife—a simple creature who believed that since the baby had a birthmark on its hand it was 'marked with red wine'. The Austins were in distressed circumstances because, with the coming of peace, Mr. Austin had been discharged from the dockyard. The charitable heart of the Princess is admitted by even her sternest critics, and when the mother and baby arrived at Montague House petitioning her to use her influence to have Mr. Austin reinstated, the sequence of events which led to the child's adoption was perfectly logical. The Commissioners, reporting to George III on this part of the charges, spoke of 'our perfect conviction that there is no foundation whatever for believing that the child now with the Princess is the child of her Royal Highness.' No one reading the evidence could possibly challenge that verdict.[1]

There was, however, formidable evidence about her familiarity with her naval friends—especially with Captain Manby. There was also the evidence of one of the servants that she had seen the Princess and Sir Sidney Smith in such an indecent situation that she collapsed in a faint. On this part of the evidence the Commissioners were more guarded—'the circumstances must be credited until they receive some decisive contradiction'.

Even more formidable than the direct charges of immorality were the examples of the Princess's conversation because they were stamped by that recklessness and absence of premeditation which

[1] The Princess was later to claim that Austin was an illegitimate child of a nephew of Frederick the Great and that Captain Manby had been employed to bring the infant to England. That was possibly said to explain her association with Manby.

were characteristic of her whole life from Brunswick to Carlton House. She chattered and gossiped with abandon about the King's family and much of this tittle-tattle has been patiently garnered and accepted as gospel by twentieth-century writers about the Royal Family. Of the Prince: 'I should have been the man, and he the woman'. 'Prince William of Gloucester would like to marry me . . . he is the grandson of a washerwoman'. 'The Duke of Kent is a disagreeable man and not to be trusted'. The royal dukes had 'plum-pudding faces which I can not bear'. 'The Duke of Cambridge looked like a serjeant, and so vulgar with his ears full of powder'. On less exalted topics her talk was even more decidedly unbecoming. When she retailed exactly what Mr. Wyndham said on the occasion of his marriage to Lady Jersey's daughter, a married lady who was present had to ask her daughter to leave the room. On another occasion she prattled away—'I have a bedfellow whenever I like. All men like a bedfellow. But Sir Sidney better than anybody else.'

More than this, the Delicate Investigation revealed a course of conduct which, according to taste perhaps ill-became her sex, and certainly ill-became her position. William Cole, a servant who had been with her since 1795 said that he had observed the Princess 'too familar' with Sir Sidney Smith. He had seen Sir Sidney sitting 'very close on the sofa' to the Princess . . . 'they appeared both a little confused' when he came into the room bringing them some sandwiches. Going to lock up, when the Princess's portrait was being painted by Lawrence, he found the Blue Room door locked and heard 'a whispering'. In commenting on the evidence to the King, the Princess thought it very hard that she should be expected to recollect which corner of the sofa she had occupied four years previously. She also said that Cole was a very disagreeable servant— 'he talked French, and was a musician playing well on the violin'. And of course it is fair to remember that most of the evidence against her was derived from witnesses like Cole who were servants and had been in the employment of the Prince before his marriage. This could not, however, be said of one witness, Mrs. Lisle, who was sister of Lord Cholmondeley and a member of the Princess's household. Although she dismissed the suggestion that the Princess had had a child, she said that the Princess's behaviour with Captain Manby was such as might have been shown by any woman 'who likes flirting' and she added the severe words that she would not have thought any married woman was behaving properly who behaved as her Royal Highness did to Captain Manby. The Princess devoted much space in her letter to the King in attempting to soften these comments of Mrs. Lisle, enlarging on the difference between women of vivacity and want of caution and those of a graver character. She even urged that Mrs. Lisle had taken a gloomy view of her behaviour because, a few days before she gave evidence, she had had the misfortune to lose her daughter. Making every allowance for the desire of the servants to keep on good terms with the Prince, the reader will probably endorse the verdict of the commissioners that the particulars respecting the conduct of the Princess 'must, especially considering her exalted rank and station, necessarily give occasion to very unfavourable interpretation'. In 1807 the cabinet, which was still the Ministry of All the Talents and made up of the political friends of the Prince, advised the King that the investigation revealed no grounds to justify his refusing to receive his daughter-in-law but that he should give her 'a serious admonition' to be more circumspect in her future conduct. The Ministry fell a few weeks later and was succeeded by a government partial to the Princess which gave no advice to the king on the question of a reproof.

Apart from any question of the guilt or innocence of the Princess there is a subsidiary though important side to the Delicate Investigation which has been too easily overlooked. The enquiry threw the relations of Prince and Princess into the hands of the party politicians. In the same way that the Tories attached themselves to Frederick, Prince of Wales when he was at variance with George II and that the Whigs looked to the Princess's husband as their champion, when he quarrelled with his father, so the Tories in 1806 championed the Princess. Spencer Perceval, one of the Tory leaders in the Commons after Pitt's death and the future prime minister, was appointed legal adviser to the Princess. He was determined that the evidence should be made public and had it prepared in book form in the spring of 1807. Some 2,000 copies were printed, and perhaps the Tory was not in a minority of one who thought that the Princess had been so 'unguarded and truly German in her manners that publication would ruin her instead of the Prince'.[1] But when the book was printed (though not distributed) the situation dramatically changed: the Ministry of All the Talents fell and Perceval found himself Chancellor of the Exchequer. He immediately set to and burned the copies of the book in his garden in Lincoln's Inn Fields. He had however lent several copies to friends—including rather surprisingly his banker—and he is believed to have spent some thousands of pounds—not his own cash (as he had none) but money earmarked for the Secret Service—in buying back stray copies. Within two years the Princess was already veering to the Whigs against her former allies. She was essentially a talisman of opposition. 'Faction marked her for its own', said Canning in the House of Commons.

Had she learned the lesson of the 'Delicate Investigation'? There are signs that she had. While her conversation and behaviour were always ill-judged, she became a little less indiscreet, a little more circumspect. She was given rooms in Kensington Palace which then, as now, was the apartment house for the near relations of the sovereign. Although Blackheath remained her headquarters she was never frequently seen at London gatherings. Particularly while King George III (who was regarded as her champion) was still sane, dukes and marquises with powerful members of the governing class attended her parties. But when the King lapsed into final insanity such 'friends' came no more: as was well said by a member of her court 'the besom of expediency swept them all away'.[2] Perhaps the most agreeable side of her character, which was shown in the years immediately following the 'Delicate Investigation', was her pleasure in the society of men of learning. These were not the grand chams of literature, but rather the viziers of that subject—producing books, which were recondite and dependable and were concerned with the obscurer branches of learning. Such men are ever glad to bask in the comfort of a little royal sunshine. They included Richard Payne Knight, who wrote an important book on Taste and had a remarkable collection of bronzes which inspired Horace Walpole's description

[1] Quoted in *Spencer Perceval* by Denis Gray. (Manchester University Press, 1963.)

[2] Lady Charlotte Bury.

of him as 'the knight of the brazen milk-pot', Sir William Gell, who published much on the geography and antiquities of classical times and was known as 'topographical' Gell, M. G. Lewis, known after the title of his successful book as 'Monk', Mr. Keppel Craven, whose books on Italian travel were to be favourably received after the Princess's death, the clever and beautiful Mrs. William Lock of Norbury, the clever and frail Countess of Oxford, and Mr. Ward, afterwards Lord Dudley, of whom the Princess characteristically said 'in the ignoble necessity of eating and drinking he renders himself an unpleasant companion at table'. The Princess's circle was therefore more curious than brilliant, and she herself did little enough to make her parties distinguished. A guest, after enjoying a concert given by professional singers at Kensington Palace, tersely but not inaccurately said 'cats would do just as well'. The conversation on these occasions, which the music confused but could not drown, was led by the Princess and was described by a member of the circle as 'brilliant, evanescent and devoid of reflection'.

In 1812 the Princess was caught in the frenzy of political party warfare. She gained nothing from it save transient popularity: she lost the sympathy of the respectable: she enraged her husband and his circle: she prepared the ground for her own disaster. The relevant story can be briefly told.

> *Nought's permanent among the human race*
> *Except the Whigs not getting into place.*

So wrote Byron when the long exclusion of the Whig party from office had still a decade to run. For a generation before this, the Whig Party had looked to the Prince of Wales as their protector who, when he came to the throne, would conduct them out of the wilderness into the promised land. When George III lapsed into final madness, and the Prince became Regent hopes ran high. But from Carlton House came neither the pillar of cloud by day nor the pillar of fire by night. The Whigs stood fast in opposition. Their party— as is the fate of those long out of power—was rent by factions: to the left were a handful of men, driven by necessity or ambition or (here and there) a sense of justice who saw in the Princess a heaven-sent opportunity to vent their spleen on the Prince. Samuel Whitbread was their mouthpiece and his attacks were inspired from off-stage by Brougham and Creevey. From the spring of 1812 till the summer of 1814 the House of Commons, during the final chapter of the war with Napoleon, was pre-occupied with such domestic topics as 'Why is the Princess Charlotte kept apart from the Princess of Wales'? And 'Why is the Princess of Wales not received at court?' The Government was left with the somewhat feeble defence that the answers to these questions lay in the evidence of the 'Delicate Investigation'.

The reader will not overlook the point that as the Delicate Investigation was virtually an acquittal of the Princess from the charges brought against her, George III did not feel justified in refusing to receive her at court. The opposition were therefore justified in saying that she was being punished for supposed offences which six years previously had been proved to be unfounded. However the evidence and the findings of the Delicate Investigation were published in full under the title 'The Book' or 'The Genuine Book' in 1813. This publication did not diminish the popularity of the Princess with the mob—especially when she was excluded from any participation in the festivities which were held to mark the visit of the Allied Sovereigns in the summer of 1814. There are signs, however, that after the publication the official and respectable worlds viewed her with less enthusiasm. One victory she had however gained. Her champions in Parliament and her supporters outside had deeply and repeatedly mortified the Prince.

In the high summer of 1814—against the wishes and advice of her parliamentary advisers—the Princess determined to go abroad. 'The abroad' had been tantalisingly close—but out of bounds—for English travellers ever since her marriage, and now the overthrow of Napoleon had made everything different. We cannot, of course, exactly tell what influenced the Princess to leave England. The death of her mother in London, the seemingly permanent insanity of the King and the consequent ascendancy of the Prince Regent were powerful factors. Possibly a subsidiary point which determined her to go was the neglect shown to her by the Allied Sovereigns and Princes when they were in London earlier in the summer: with her mind, which was always swayed by a tit-for-tat,

bent on vengeance, she may well have thought that although the
rulers of Europe, acting on the known wishes of her husband, would
not receive her in London they could not deny her this civility if
she appeared in their country without the Prince. Above all she
wanted to be free—free from the boredom of her cautious political
advisers, free to choose her own friends and free to go exactly where
she liked—in other words to be royal without the restrictions of
royalty. She herself said as much 'Since de English neither give me
de great honour of being a Princesse de Galles, I will be Caroline,
a happy, merry soul'. That soon became only too obvious.

On 9 August 1814 the residents of Worthing, who for a few days
had enjoyed the spectacle of the frigate *Jason* lying off the Steyne,
became aware that an embarkation was about to take place and they
crowded towards the shore, respectable, bourgeois and inquisitive.
The Princess, in the late afternoon, drove past the crowd in a carriage
with her lady-in-waiting, Lady Charlotte Lindsay, and the boy
William Austin, and boarded the *Jason*'s barge at South Lancing.
She was strikingly dressed in a dark cloth pelisse with great golden
clasps and she wore a hat, which caught attention, of violet and green
with a green feather. It was modelled on the headdresses worn by the
Prussian hussars.

Some curiosity was roused among members of the general
public and some indignation among partisans of the Princess when
it was seen that the heads of the Bow Street police court were
stationed in a hotel on the sea front at Worthing. (They were presumably there for protection rather than for investigation.) The
Princess was respectably attended; in addition to Lady Charlotte,
Lady Elizabeth Forbes[1] was her lady-in-waiting. Of her gentlemen
the leader was Colonel Anthony St. Leger.[2] With him was that
rattling pair of gay oddities Mr. Berkeley Craven and Sir William
Gell. (The latter opened the ball with the Princess which was held

[1] Presumably Lord Granard's daughter. He was a strong Foxite.

[2] Anthony Butler St. Leger was the younger brother of Colonel John St.
Leger with whom he is constantly confused. The latter was painted by Gains-
borough in a familiar portrait and was the intimate friend of the Regent 'one of
ye best fellows yt. ever lived'. The former was a minor diplomat and remarkable,
according to Lord Malmesbury, for his dancing.

on board the *Jason* to celebrate the Regent's birthday.) These three gentlemen were somewhat oddly called chamberlains: lord chamberlains and vice-chamberlains are well known in English court life, and the description without prefix may have been used to designate their duties over travelling accommodation and particularly in providing bed-rooms. Her equerry was a short but handsome German—Captain Hesse—reputed to be the son of the Duke of York. Her doctor was Henry Holland, a young man fond of travel who was to marry Sidney Smith's daughter, become a royal physician and to be described at the end of his life as 'not fit to attend a sick cat'. In addition there was a small retinue of servants, stewards and messengers. The Princess travelled—to begin with—under the Brunswick name of Countess of Wolfenbüttel.

Within a few weeks almost all the English members of this little itinerant court had left her, and this was naturally a cardinal point in the case developing against the Princess. They left, it was argued, because they were outraged by her behaviour. She went straight to her old home at Brunswick and although Henry Holland made an excuse for the ebullience of the Princess's behaviour owing to 'the joyousness of early travel' he had to add that 'she was not altogether mindful of the wonted proprieties'. On the other hand the disappearance of her English court could be explained by the perfectly reasonable realisation that serving the Princess meant not so much foreign travel as banishment, not so much an excursion as exile. The weight of these points was of course carefully considered at the trial.

No doubt the conventional-minded and the Regent hoped that she would settle on the fringe of some German court, as her aunt—the separated wife of King Frederick William II of Prussia—had done, or her great-aunt, Frederick the Great's separated wife, had likewise done. The latter lived at Schönhausen near Berlin and won the warm eulogy of Carlyle because, although feeling herself neglected, 'she became *more* amiable'—an achievement which, as he wryly observed, is difficult for any Queen. But the cardinal virtues of patience, meekness and long-suffering formed no part of the Princess's character: she was determined to enjoy herself in her own way, regardless of what her enemies might imagine and regardless of what the foreigners might say. Again, although the world thought that her interest in naval officers, now general knowledge as a result of the publication of the Delicate Investigation, was physical it could be argued that their tales of travel, their description of the wonders of Africa and Sidney Smith's account of Acre touched some secret longing of hers for a life of adventure and discovery: in this (if it was the case) her wish ran parallel with that of Lady Hester Stanhope who had likewise left the shores of England on board the *Jason* and—impatient of the restrictions of English social life—sought freedom in the East. Whatever may be said for or against the Princess her interest in antiquities and in the civilisation of the Orient was held with tenacity and intelligence.

The Princess stayed only a few days in Brunswick, where her levity contrasted strongly with the gravity of her brother who within months was to lie on the field of Quatre Bras. She then travelled along the Rhine and through Switzerland to Milan. Here she made the controversial appointment of 'a cabinet-courier'—an Italian who was to fix the attention of the world at her trial. Bartolommeo Pergami, sometimes known in the more plebeian form of Bergami, was supposed to be a man of some family, and in support of this it was argued that his sisters were well married—one being a Countess Oldi. Pergami's family is supposed—like many another family in search of an explanation for obscurity—to have fallen from grandeur to penury, and he himself, in an effort to climb back to the heights from which his house had tumbled, adopted a military career, and served in the campaigns of 1812, 1813 and 1814. Pergami's origins and career were a source of infinite dispute and speculation but one thing about him was indisputable. He was just short of six foot, with a robust form: he had a military aspect and an agreeable countenance. But it was bold. 'A magnificent head of black hair and moustachios which reach from here to London' was the description of him by an English visitor to Italy. Association with this gallant called for the utmost discretion. But had the Princess been blessed with discretion there would have been no trial.

In the late autumn of 1814 she moved down to Rome and was received in audience by the Pope—Pius VII, who had re-entered Rome that year after having crowned Napoleon and been held prisoner by him. The Princess went on to Naples and then crossed to Tunis, where she took coffee with the Bey in his seraglio. From here she went by sea to Athens, visiting the Greek islands and then crossing to Constantinople. She then went by sea to Acre, visiting the strong-hold where Napoleon had been defeated by the Turks. With a suite of 25, swollen to a rabble of 200 by servants and camp followers, she entered Jerusalem on horseback in July 1815. She stayed some days, visiting with reverence and knowledge the holy places. To commemorate her visit to Jerusalem she instituted an order of chivalry—the knights of the Order of St. Caroline. Pergami was made Grand Master of the Order, and William Austin one of the Knights. After this flourish of originality she not inappropriately went to Jericho.

Before setting out for the East, the Princess had bought from an Italian countess a pretty little casino on Lake Como. This she enlarged, planting the two-mile-long avenue up from Como to the house, and renamed it the Villa d'Este after the illustrious family from whom both she and her husband were descended. (To-day it is the Grand Hotel Villa d'Este—a luxury hotel with 181 bedrooms.) In the Princess's day the property included a theatre on the stage of which the Princess often appeared 'in character'. But she was strangely restless. She went twice to Germany, visiting Munich, Innsbruck and Vienna between 1817 and 1819. At the end of that year she was wintering in Marseilles and moved down to Rome, at the very beginning of 1820, where she heard the news that King George III had died, and that her husband was King.

The reckless folly of the Princess's manner of life since she left England five and a half years earlier needs no emphasis here. It was the immediate cause of the trial, and the fierce light of legal examination beat on every corner of her life, illumining her folly and possibly her adultery with Pergami. Two things however deserve to be emphasised. She had shown herself a genuine and intrepid traveller, braving horrible storms in her polacca, facing long days of quarantine and all the discomforts of travel in the days before the bourgeoisie had subdued 'the abroad' to their own comfortable standards of civilisation. Her intellectual curiosity about the East was manifest and endearing. Nor should she be condemned (as has already been explained) because her English courtiers gradually disappeared. Exiles need something more than personal pity for fallen royalty to drag them from the routine of their homes and the society of their families. Even the Gells and Cravens had their sunny ruins and their excavations from which it was a real sacrifice to tear themselves away in order to caper across Europe with the Princess. Foreign attendants on the Princess were, in these circumstances, inevitable but it was the particular choice of a handsome Italian as a personal bodyguard which scandalised diplomatic Europe and affronted the European establishment—restored in all its power and prejudice after the overthrow of Napoleon. Perhaps inevitably but certainly mistakenly George IV made it clear to his brother sovereigns that his wife was to be given neither civility nor recognition. At Rome the Pope declined the request of the Queen, as she now declared herself, that the Guard customarily granted to sovereigns and their consorts, should be accorded to the house where she was staying. The refusal, drawn with characteristic deftness, explained that as the King of England and Hanover had not sent His Holiness any notification about the movements of the Queen 'he does not know that the Queen of England is in Rome'. Ever impetuous and eager for a foray against her husband, the Queen threw caution to the winds and decided to hurry across Europe to England to proclaim her innocence and, as it transpired, to face her trial.

2

In the House of Lords

One question remains to be asked—and answered. Why was some compromise, some *modus vivendi* seemingly impossible? Sufficient has already been said to show that the Queen (as she must now be called) was blessed with a nature which loved the dangers and dramas of existence. If she was in the centre of the stage, provided the auditorium was packed—never mind the quality of human beings there so long as they were excitable—she was happy. Such people are not swayed by accepting their lot, by deciding to make the best of the worst. But even for such a temperament as that of the Queen a generous, financial settlement might have deterred her from coming back to England, from the dark prospects of a rantipole life in London, with the huzzas of the mob as comforters and companions.

Moreover signs were not lacking that she might have been ready to negotiate and to accept voluntarily a financial settlement on condition that she stayed away from England. In order to understand this the reader must go back in the story to the year 1818. In that year the Regent sent to Milan a commission—or an inquisition (as it was called by partisans of the Queen)—to examine her conduct. This was arranged by a personal friend of the Regent, Sir John Leach, the vice-Chancellor, who sat as a judge in Chancery. He sent to Milan, William Cooke, a member of the Chancery Bar, J. A. Powell, a solicitor, and T. H. Browne, a distinguished Peninsular officer whose father had been British consul in Tuscany. They were appointed by command of the Regent and with the approbation of the Lord Chancellor and of the Prime Minister. The Government paid for the commission, but the Prime Minister made it clear that whatever was found the question of taking legal proceedings should remain 'an open question'.[1] The Commission, which had received every assistance from the Emperor of Austria, in whose territory Milan then was, reported in July 1819, after examining a number of Italian witnesses on oath. No one, who was not mad or blindly devoted to the Queen, could for a second doubt, after reading the evidence, that she had formed an adulterous connexion with Pergami.

Her principal legal and political adviser was Henry Brougham who, in 1820, was in his very early forties. An Edinburgh man, he devised for himself a mighty English pedigree so that he sat under one of the largest family trees in Christendom, but, as someone cruelly said, in the rapidity of its growth it resembled the Indian mango tree. From this it will be seen that he was a romantic, but in addition he brought to his public career the more solid gifts of wit, memory and unbounded self-confidence. His fame—and the word is not too strong—rested on his contributions to the *Edinburgh Review* in its heyday—contributions which were of astonishing versatility and diversity. By the time he was 30 he had made his mark in Whig politics and it might be fair to say that as an advocate he was a politician first and a lawyer second. Indeed did not someone say that if he had known a little law he would have known a little of everything? In 1820 he had been a member of Parliament, with a short break, for ten years. He was appointed by the Queen her attorney-general and took his seat by right of that office, within the bar among the silks in April 1820.

While the Commission was about its business Brougham sent out his brother, James Brougham, to the Princess, who dispatched back to England, a vivid and factual account of what he found. In conversation with James Brougham the Queen made it quite clear that she was prepared to remain abroad and that she would accept a title other than Queen in return for a handsome annual income—though it is fair to add that she was hopelessly vague about money and spoke of accepting a lump sum of £100,000 which was meagre in comparison with the £50,000 which the Government was prepared to offer her annually. But there was one shadow across these hopes.

[1] A. Aspinall, *The Letters of George IV*, ii, 282.

She did not wish for a separation by mutual consent. 'That is doing nothing'. For a divorce or parliamentary separation she would have to appear guilty of infidelity. 'That is impossible.'[1]

Almost at once the impossible became the actual. It was proclaimed to the world by a too hasty answer to an awkward question. How was the wandering queen to figure in the liturgy? Before the death of George III on 29 January 1820, the relevant passage in the prayer for the royal family ran thus: 'their Royal Highnesses George Prince of Wales and the Princess of Wales.' The new king insisted that his wife should be excluded from the prayers for the royal family. The Prime Minister and the Archbishop of Canterbury recommended caution, but the King—possibly reasonably—felt that her behaviour made it impossible to bring her personally before the Fountain of All Goodness. She was branded as guilty by this exclusion—and branded without being heard in her own defence. Unquestionably her fury and indignation at this treatment encouraged her to put matters to the test in England.

Whether she could have been stopped is an academic question on which space need not be wasted. Had the King or the Government foreseen the extent of the popular frenzy which she was able to arouse they would surely have moved heaven and earth not to irritate her. They would have been wise to leave her alone—to beat out one of the saddest lives known to mortal man—a royal exile in Europe.

One mistake the Government made; they placed too much reliance on Henry Brougham. Castlereagh, the foreign secretary, in a letter which he wrote, at the time of the Queen's return, to his brother who was ambassador at Vienna, said that if Brougham had gone to Geneva—as the Queen had wanted him to do—he might have sent her back to Italy with the greatest ease. 'But he said that he could not leave the House of Commons and that she must come near the coast.'[2]

An effort, which was bungled, was made by Brougham and by Lord Hutchinson to arrange terms with the Queen at St. Omer in June. 'Hutch', wrote Creevey, 'is by far the most interesting and

[1] Aspinall *op. cit.* 358.
[2] Alison, *Lives of Lord Castlereagh and Sir Charles Stewart*, 1861.

agreeable man I know'. He had been distinguished in the Army and in diplomacy and was anxious to do his best for the King and to prevent a disagreeable scandal. But he saw at once, in his own words, 'the Lady has other advisers besides Brougham'.[1] Chief among these was a Devonshire chemist whose fortune had flourished when he transferred his pestle and mortar to London: he was member for the City and had been Lord Mayor in the triumphant year—1815. He was faithfully described by Hutchinson as 'that enlightened mountebank Alderman Wood'.[2] Henceforth queen and mountebank were to entertain the crowds of London with the brittle skill of the performers in a circus or the puppets in a Punch and Judy show. She drove in to London, in an open carriage, on 6 June attracting cheers and crowds and went straight to the Alderman's house in South Audley Street. In response to the plaudits of the people she came out on the rather modest balcony of the house. The crowd cheered her lustily, and among their shouts—in allusion to her protégé—was heard 'God save Queen Caroline and her son, King Austin.'

Elsewhere more serious business was going forward.

At the time of the Milan Commission, Castlereagh had written: 'we must always recollect that the proceeding, if it be taken, must ultimately be a parliamentary one.' He meant by that remark that the King could not take action in a court of law. The High Court of Parliament alone could set him free.

Under English statute law, dating back to the shadowy times of King Edward III, high treason was defined by a famous statute which enacted, among other things, that the violation of the King's wife was treason. As Pergami was a foreigner and as the connexion had existed only on foreign soil, he and his actions were not of course subject to English law and consequently the laws of treason had no relevance in the case. She could not therefore be tried in the literal sense of the word. A different parliamentary proceeding had to be found. On the day following the arrival of the Queen in London the King sent a message to both houses of parliament. The message stated that he was communicating 'certain papers' about

[1] Aspinall *op. cit.* ii 318.
[2] Aspinall *op. cit.* ii 340.

the conduct of the Queen which 'he recommends to the immediate and serious attention of this House'. The message ended with the statement that the King had 'the fullest confidence . . . that the House . . . will adopt that course of proceeding, which the justice of the case, and the honour and dignity of his majesty's crown, may require.'

The Heart of Mayfair

A Cruikshank cartoon of 1820

The papers were contained in a green bag which was the subject of endless (and not very good) squibs, lampoons and caricatures. The House of Commons made an active attempt to persuade the Queen to negotiate, and the Duke of Wellington, on behalf of the King, and Brougham, on behalf of the Queen, opened negotiations which lasted for some days; they finally broke down on 24 June. The House of Lords, in the meantime, had elected a committee of scrutiny to examine the contents of the green bag. This committee was respectable, partly episcopal and partly Cabinet, wholly Tory, but not of course judicial. The committee reported that the bag contained documents with allegations 'supported by the concurrent testimony of a great number of persons in various situations of life which deeply affect the honour of the Queen'. The documents were described as attributing to the Queen 'conduct . . . of the most licentious character'. The Committee further stated that the charges affected 'the moral feeling and honour of the country'. They recommended that the charges should become the subject of 'a solemn enquiry' which they suggested 'may be best effected in the course of a legislative proceeding'. On the following day the Prime Minister, Lord Liverpool, introduced a Bill of Pains and Penalties.

A bill of pains and penalties is an act of parliament for punishing a person without resorting to a legal trial. Such a bill is not a judicial act, though in procedure it may have much in common with a legal trial. As with any other bill it must be passed by sovereign, lords and commons. The machinery is similar to an act of attainder, except that a bill of pains and penalties cannot impose the punishment of death. The most celebrated bill of pains and penalties was that introduced into the House of Commons concerning Atterbury, the Jacobite Bishop of Rochester, in 1721. The justification for a bill of pains and penalties was that it could be used where the proofs of wrongdoing were unlikely to secure conviction under the law. Many people—and they were not only partisans of the Queen— would have agreed with the historian Lecky that a bill of pains and penalties is an extreme, unconstitutional and justly unpopular measure. Liverpool's bill firmly confined the issue to Pergami whose relations with the Queen were described as 'a most unbecoming and degrading intimacy', 'a licentious, disgraceful and adulterous intercourse', 'scandalous, disgraceful and vicious conduct'. The Bill enacted that 'Her Majesty Caroline Amelia Elizabeth shall be deprived of the title of Queen' and that the marriage between her and the King 'shall be for ever, wholly dissolved, annulled and made void'.

Two points affecting the House of Commons must here be emphasised. The Commons did their utmost to arrange a settlement—their efforts culminated in Wilberforce and three other members, in full court-dress, attending the Queen and urging a compromise on the question of the prayer-book which was the only material difference remaining after a series of conferences between the advisers of both the King and Queen. But otherwise the Commons took no part in the proceedings at all. These were left to the Lords alone, because as Castlereagh—the Leader of the House—said: 'two investigations would have been indecent and inconvenient'. Had the bill passed the Lords, it would have come automatically to the Commons. When the examination of witnesses began in the House of Lords the Commons adjourned for four weeks, and then to 17 October and then to 23 November. (The case ended on 10 November.) The House met for a few hours before each adjournment and this enabled the Left to make a number of violent speeches on each occasion. A characteristic specimen of these orations was provided by one of the members for Westminster, John Cam Hobhouse —'My Friend H' as Byron called him.

'The degradation was not merely at home, but abroad . . . . And at last to complete the picture, the peers of England—the representatives of noble families, and the descendants of heroic ancestors—the pillars of the state—were sent to pry into foul clothes-bags and pore over the contents of chamber utensils. Was such the legitimate duty of a peer of parliament? Was this the mode in which the lawmakers of the greatest country in the world should be employed?'[1]

There is also a further point (though it is not connected with the Commons) which affected opinion. The second part of the Bill which divorced the King from the Queen was highly controversial. Possibly the King had dreams of a second marriage, of some spirited

---

[1] Hobhouse was in Italy at the same time as the Queen, and we have the advantage of knowing from his published diaries something of his private opinions. After saying that she must be mad he goes on to say that 'at an entertainment she gave she had an ass brought in to table, caressed it before the company and crowned it with roses'. 16 October 1886 (Lord Broughton, *Recollections of A Long Life*, 1909).

Anne Boleyn who would strengthen the succession at a time when the royal family consisted of many elderly princes and princesses and three babies. But it is more likely that he wanted a divorce so as to make a complete break with an association which he regarded as revolting and humiliating. Whatever the reason, the inclusion of the divorce clause was mistaken because it antagonised many of the bench of bishops and some of the strongest adherents of the Crown who still displayed, in a dark world, their shining faith in a commonwealth resting on church and state.

We should probably have to turn back the pages of history to the time of the trial of the Seven Bishops in King James II's reign to find an occasion comparable with the excitement, the frenzy and the sympathy for the accused shown at the Queen's trial. The words which Macaulay used of that occasion were certainly applicable to 1820. 'The agitation spread to the farthest corner of the island.' The clamour started in the west end of London. While the Queen was in South Audley Street at Alderman Wood's house she was the magnet for a seething, mischievous mob every night. After serenading its heroine the mob rioted through the streets smashing windows with indiscriminate glee. After a few days the Queen moved to a slightly more secluded part of the West End and occupied the house in Portman Square which belonged to her lady-in-waiting—Lady Anne Hamilton, daughter of the ninth Duke of Hamilton and sister of Lord Archibald Hamilton, an advanced member of Parliament who was a noisy supporter of the Queen in the Commons. Lady Anne was very tall, over 6 foot, and was said to look rather like one of Lord Derby's red deer. The Queen always referred to this giantess as 'My Joan of Arc'. As the summer wore on, the Queen moved out to a delightful seventeenth-century house on the river at Hammersmith, which had been built by an ardent royalist—Sir Nicholas Crisp. The house belonged to the Margravine of Anspach and was consequently known as Brandenburg House. The Margravine, by her first marriage, was mother of Mr. Keppel Craven—the Queen's chamberlain, and it was no doubt through him that she took the house. Every time the Queen moved from Portman Square to Brandenburg House or back she was the centre of a vociferous, wildly cheering mob and it is likely that she went to Hammersmith

to have some moments of peace without these affectionate demon-
strations. There was also the attraction here that it was possible for
deputations, with addresses of sympathy, to visit the Queen by water:
both roads and river could carry the curious to see her. Her company
was commemorated in some not inaccurate but not very compli-
mentary verses written by Theodore Hook and beginning 'Have
you been to Brandenburg—heigh ma'am; ho, ma'am?' The verses
went on to describe the trippers who enjoyed these excursions:

> *And who were your company—heigh ma'am; ho ma'am?*
> *And who were your company, ho?*
> *We happened to drop in*
> *With* gemmem *from Wapping,*
> *And ladies from Blowbladder—row—row*
> *And ladies from Blowbladder—row.*

There were in addition more impressive and more respectable
manifestations of feeling, which were shrewdly organised by her
advisers. These were loyal addresses—influential ones from the
City, from Exeter signed by 11,000, from the mechanics of London
signed by 29,500, from Liverpool signed by 30,000; less influential
ones from the ladies of Bath, Bristol, Exeter, Halifax, Leeds, Notting-
ham and Sheffield, and less serious ones from the married ladies of
Marylebone, the young men of Hereford, and the aldermen of Nor-
wich. All shades of importance were reflected in addresses that poured
in from Newcastle or Carlisle down to Chipping Sodbury. The peers
of the land, who were to try the case, needed the courage of their
order not to be swayed by this pressure of feeling. It mounted as the
preparations for the case went forward.

The preparations for the case—so far as the arrangements at the
House of Lords went—were in the hands of Black Rod. He was Sir
Thomas Tyrwhitt—greatly beloved by Queen Charlotte and George
IV who nicknamed him, on account of his diminutive stature, 'the
Twenty-third of June' meaning the shortest (k)night. To him fell
the duty of delivering the Bill of Pains and Penalties to the Queen,
after the first reading by the Lords—an embarrassing occasion since
they had last met when the Queen was living with her husband at
Carlton House. Receiving the bill she said, alluding to the King,

'We shall not meet in this world: I hope we shall in the next where justice will be rendered me.' In the middle of July the Government announced that the second reading of the Bill, which really meant the start of the trial, would begin on Thursday, 17 August.

The first important step was to collect the members of the court—after a careful search for precedents, the chairman of committees and deputy Speaker of the House of Lords decided that attendance should be compulsory and that absentees should be heavily fined—£100 for the first three days, and £50 for each succeeding one. Minors, Roman Catholics, invalids, those out of the country and anyone over 70 was excused from attending. All the judges except those on circuit had to attend. They did not vote but were present to advise the House on points of law. The death of parent, wife or child was accepted as a reason for absence, but every peer wishing to claim exemption had to write to the Lord Chancellor giving the reason 'upon his honour'. Bereavement did not of course prevent a peer from attending if he so wished and the Duke of York showed indifference to convention or a stoical attachment to duty by attending the trial three days after burying his wife. The rather surprisingly large total of 109 were excused. The bishops did well, producing 13 exemptions—two were sick, one was not instituted, two were dead and the rest were more than 70.

The next question was the accommodation of the 260 peers (or thereabouts) expected to be present. (There were at that time on the roll of the peerage 367 peers.) The House of Lords was a meagre building—completely lacking both the size and padded splendour of the present structure: it was not unlike a chapel without the pews. The woolsack, in front of the throne, was at one end with benches for the peers running down either side. The building was only 80 feet long, 40 feet wide and 30 feet high. On the walls was a remarkable tapestry of the Armada and above this were three semi-circular windows. At the lower end of the Chamber, below the bar, was standing room for about 150. It was therefore decided to increase the accommodation for peers by building temporary galleries above the benches normally used by them. The architect to the Houses of Parliament was Sir John Soane, but the speed at which things had to be done and the dinginess of the setting made it impossible for that gifted man to display any flourishes or conceits of his art in adapting the building for the case. Peers were allowed a single ticket to admit spectators to the space below the bar: tickets were allotted to peers on alternate days only—the barons one day and the higher orders on the next day.

More particular arrangements had to be made for the comfort of the principal personality—a woman in exclusively masculine surroundings. When she arrived she was to be conducted by Black Rod to the room set aside for her as a retiring room and normally used by the chairman of committees. The deputy housekeeper of the House of Peers was provided to wait upon the Queen in this room. Arrangements were also made that the Queen should bring with her one female companion (Lady Anne Hamilton). A chair and foot-stool in what would to-day be regarded as in the most splendid Regency taste was provided for the Queen immediately within the bar of the House. In this elegant chair the Queen sat through the case in an attitude in which ease and defiance were nicely blended. Sir George Hayter in his celebrated painting of the scene in the House of Lords has faithfully recorded the chair, the sitter, the pose.

Adjoining the House of Lords at this time, on the west-side, were the apartments of the officers of both Houses of Parliament known as Cotton-Yard. Here all the preliminary arrangements were being made for cooking the great coronation banquet which was to have been held in Westminster Hall. But instead of the great ovens, instead of all the paraphernalia of a *batterie de cuisine*, hurriedly arranged dormitories were made for the witnesses—most of them Italians. They came by water to Parliament Stairs and, awaiting the case, they enjoyed a cloistered existence with a lavish supply of ale and English victuals. Credit must be given to Black Rod for all the arrangements and especially for his success in keeping the House of Lords and its precincts immune from the clamour of the Queen's partisans, from the roaring London mob. The traffic was to be strictly regulated. All carriages, drays or carts travelling between Pall Mall and Abingdon Street were to keep moving in single file and to keep to the right. Though it is not clear why the ordinary rule of the road was reversed, this arrangement left the centre of the road free for the carriages of peers going to the House of Lords.

The crowd grew noisier as the time for the trial grew nearer. For the duration of the case the Queen took 15 St. James's Square—the second house on the west side of the square coming in from King Street. Her next-door neighbour was Castlereagh, and his house, barred, shuttered and emptied of its valuables, displayed an expectation of bombardment. Generally in the evening, she went down to Brandenburg House, coming back to St. James's Square at 10 in the morning. These progresses again gave every opportunity for the crowd to demonstrate—the listlessness of an August evening in London encouraged the lounger and loiterer to an exercise in bawling. From St. James's Square she drove to Westminster in a state carriage, which was specially built for the occasion, and was drawn by six bays. The coachman, postilions and footmen wore the sovereign's livery. In St. James's Square itself the press of human beings was immense. In the early morning a number of waggons were driven in: the horses were taken away, and standing positions in the waggons were sold for 1/– a head. Private carriages were also left in the square, and the throng of pedestrians gave the whole square an animated appearance. There were of course vociferous crowds between St. James's Square and Westminster. The Queen was given a royal salute as she drove past Carlton House—perhaps a little shamefacedly, but it was given more formally from the footguards stationed round the House of Lords. She was received at the entrance by Black Rod. He took her right hand and Brougham, in silk gown and long wig, with characteristic conceit put himself forward to take her left hand. Thus supported the unhappy lady moved to the room allotted for her private use. Although the raucous cries of 'The Queen, The Queen' did not disturb the tranquillity of the Palace of Westminster not a single member of the House of Lords could have been unmindful of public feeling. The Lords were asked to pronounce on right and wrong, but they started their task in an atmosphere of acclaim and jubilee. None the less they were well aware that the dark facts of the case remained dark for all the fervour and rejoicing on the streets of the capital.

The Lord Chancellor took his seat on the Woolsack at half past eight in the morning. Lord Eldon was a Newcastle man of great intellectual powers which distinguished him at Oxford. After a career at the bar and in politics he became Lord Chancellor in 1801, and was the member of the government most in the confidence of George III until that king lapsed into insanity. He knew the Queen well because he had been her closest adviser during the Delicate Investigation when he was out of office. He was in the amplest meaning of the word a conservative, a doughty supporter of everything established by time and tradition. In the conduct of the bill through the House of Lords even those who were not his admirers applauded his dignity and fairness. He was known affectionately to a wide circle, which included the royal family, as 'old Bags'.

Prayers were read by the Bishop of Llandaff as junior bishop: although also Dean of St. Paul's he deserves the affection of the Principality as the first prelate to reside in his wild diocese for many a long year. On the right and left of the Chancellor were the lord chief justices[1] and the judges. By 10 o'clock the House was crowded, and at that hour the names of every peer were called. The Duke of Sussex, at that time on bad terms with the King, asked and was granted permission to absent himself on the grounds of consanguinity to both parties. This was perhaps a rather craven request, and brought the Duke of York to his feet to say that he had stronger reasons—bereavement—and the fact that his wife and the Queen were related—than any of the family to claim exemption but 'he would do his duty, painful as it might be'. During the call-over the Queen entered. All the peers stood up in their places. She was wearing black sarsenet—the colour a tribute to the Duchess of York and the material a mark of attention to the warmth of high summer. She wore a large white veil which partially concealed her face and fell tastefully across her bosom. Her figure, thus draped, was described as 'interesting'.

A less flattering description of the Queen was given by that witty man of the world, Creevey. He said that her appearance in the House of Lords reminded him of a doll called Fanny Royds. This was a Dutch toy, with a round bottom weighted with lead, so that it always jumped erect in whatever position it was placed.

As soon as the proceedings began, the Duke of Leinster—though

[1] At this time there was a lord chief justice of the King's Bench and of the Common Pleas.

god-son of the king—moved that the order of the day for the second reading of the Bill of Pains and Penalties should be rescinded. Forty-one peers only supported him and that number may be taken as the hard core of the political supporters of the Queen. Most of the 41 were Whigs and they regarded the matter less as a verdict on the Queen than as one on the folly of the Government in agreeing to the proceedings in the first instance. There were over 200 in favour of continuing with the Bill, which was then read a second time.[1] The most influential of the Whig leaders, Lord Grey, raised the legal point whether the Queen 'if consenting to violation' by one who owed no allegiance to the crown was nevertheless guilty of high treason. The judges conferred for 20 minutes and delivered their opinion that this did not amount to high treason. Grey's motive in raising the point is a little obscure but he perhaps did it to stop the proceedings under the Bill of Pains and Penalties and encourage the Queen to negotiate if she saw herself faced with the more serious charge of treason.

At this time Grey was in his middle fifties, and represented during a long-drawn time of Tory power the finest tradition of Fox and the Whigs. He was never a party zealot in the sense that Creevey and Brougham were. One reason for this was that he obstinately preferred the wilds of Northumberland to the pavements of Westminster. He was never an enthusiast for the Queen and he once wrote to Brougham: 'we as a party have nothing to do but to observe the most perfect neutrality'. But he was no admirer of King George IV, and he perhaps knew that that sovereign once spoke scornfully of him as 'Grey with his dam'd cocked-up nose'. From this truly judicial independence he carried great weight in the proceedings—especially at their close.

In those days the Queen Consort had an attorney-general and a solicitor-general, not—as was the case with the King's legal officers —members of the government. Brougham, as attorney-general to the Queen, rose immediately, after the opinion of the judges on the point about treason had been made, to develop his objections to the principle of the bill. He began by distinguishing between an impeachment which had 'a quasi-judicial character' and a bill, designed

[1] Its terms will be found in Appendix A.

to meet a particular case—a mode of proceeding which was repugnant to every sound principle of jurisprudence. He made great play with the fact that the accusations against the Queen were all made when she was Princess of Wales and when she had, as he expressed it 'no immediate connexion with the diadem'. If it had been proposed to proceed against the Queen while she was Princess of Wales —and here the lawyer made a glancing blow at the King—the party claiming divorce would have had to come before the court 'with clean hands'. He suggested that this was the motive for waiting till the Princess had assumed the diadem because, once she was Queen, she could not be sued for divorce in the ordinary courts.[1] He then piously said, pointing to the Queen, that he had the solemn commands of this illustrious woman to abstain from recrimination. He brazenly went on that he was going to avoid all arguments designed to disprove the obvious truth that 'criminal intercourse—for why should I be afraid to use the term?' was fatal to the honour of the illustrious family governing the country. The reference to the King was palpable. He went on that he was dismissing for the present any question of the conduct or connexions of either party before marriage. 'Yet why should such things be overlooked in the stronger sex but punished in the weaker?' The poor, bereaved Duke of York was brought in. Why was no bill of pains and penalties introduced when in 1809, after the proof of his liaison with Mrs. Clarke, the House of Commons resolved that he had been guilty of most immoral and unbecoming conduct? He challenged his opponents to produce an instance when any marriage had been dissolved, except for adultery and on the application of the injured party. The procedure was, it will be remembered, by bill and not by the King's application. He closed with a threat to the House. He agreed that the committee of scrutiny had reported that there was evidence to support the bill but 'he is the greatest of all fools who consults his apparent consistency at the expense of his absolute ruin'.

Thomas Denman, who was the Queen's solicitor-general, was asked by the Chancellor to speak in support of Brougham's argu-

[1] Some six years before in an article in the *Edinburgh Review* Brougham had drawn attention to the extraordinary precautions taken by the law to safeguard— as he expresses it—'the approaches to the royal bed'.

ment. A handsome, carefree man with an exquisite voice Denman brought fervour and eloquence to the cause of the Queen. He was to coin the phrase, which caused some amusement, that his client was 'pure as unsunned snow'. On this occasion he said that his present state of health—he was suffering from incipient jaundice—made it difficult for him to speak, and the House accordingly adjourned. On the following day—18 August—the proceedings began with Denman's speech. He covered inevitably much the same ground as Brougham had but he was clearer. He was outspoken on recrimination, which he called 'the most important right belonging to a consort'.

Referring to the charge of adulterous intercourse Denman said that this turned on the evidence of 'some suborned wretch from among the perjured abject pack, dragged by bribes from among the dregs of society in those countries which the Queen had visited'. He ingeniously argued that a disputed succession might follow if the bill was passed. Was not the heir to the throne, the Duke of York, guilty of all that was imputed to the Queen and much more? Were the other royal dukes innocent of 'scandalous freedoms and adulterous intercourse'? He also referred to the possibility that the Queen herself might inherit the crown: she was, as Denman said, not so remote in blood, because of her descent from George II, as to make it impossible. On the fatal addition to the bill about a divorce he hoped that the Bishops might be allowed to explain to the House the sacred considerations affecting marriage. He ended: 'I will, for one, never withdraw from her those sentiments of dutiful homage which I owe to her rank, to her situation, to her superior mind, to her great and royal heart: nor, my lords, will I ever pay to anyone who may usurp her majesty's station, that respect which belongs alone to her whom the laws of God and man have made the consort of the King, and the Queen of these kingdoms.'

The Attorney-General then rose to reply and the Queen, with Lady Anne, left the House. The Attorney-General, Sir Robert Gifford, was a Devonshire man with a passion for the law which he had shown from the days when he was a grammar-school boy. He was sound rather than brilliant and Brougham, whose qualities were exactly the opposite, said that Gifford's career at the bar, supported in Brougham's view by few abilities, was the most extraordinary flight upwards of anything known to mankind, except a balloon. For all that, his coolness and good sense shone conspicuously at the trial. His answer was effective. He implored the lords to banish from their minds the impressions made by the eloquent addresses to which they had listened 'and in particular by that which they had just heard' (Denman's). He brought their attention back to 'the simple, dry question' whether the bill was sustained on principle. He went over the familiar ground that High Treason or impeachment was inappropriate, and he deplored the attempts of Denman to smirch the evidence against the Queen as 'tainted' before it had even been heard. He described this as 'acting in a manner as unjust and as partial as could be conceived'. They would complain if he were to enlarge on the evidence about to be produced. 'The pain of the task would be great enough, God knew, when the necessity arrived; but at present he refrained, both from a sense of what was due to the illustrious individual who was the object of the inquiry, and to their lordships, as well as from a conviction that the public ought to be kept unacquainted with such disgusting details.'

The Solicitor-General followed. He was Copley, the future Lord Chancellor Lyndhurst and, it would not be unfair to say that in the gay society of those a little careless of their virtue he was more at home than were his legal brethren. He scorned the genteel politeness of the Attorney, and referred to his opponents' aspersions on the witnesses as unfounded and foul. He dealt with the argument that the King should have appeared; 'it did not suit his high character and station . . . he was a consenting not a complaining party.' He flouted Denman's argument that the measure might endanger the succession because of the irregularities of the private life of the heir to the throne: an argument which he stigmatised as a cruel and wanton attack on a man of great talent and popularity. He pointed out that a bill of pains and penalties could not be applied to the Duke of York or his brothers since 'adultery in a man is in no way punishable'.[1]

---

[1] As a very old man, deep in his eighties, Copley made a great impression on this very point, by supporting in the House of Lords, the Matrimonial Causes Bill of 1857, which brought man's adultery within the province of the divorce courts.

The Queen came back after Copley had finished, interrupting Brougham, who was beginning to reply to the various points raised by Gifford and Copley. At the end of Brougham's speech Lord King, a clever, strange, left-wing lord, moved that 'it is not necessary to the public safety, nor the security of the Government to pass this bill.' He opened his speech on the following day—Saturday 19 August. He followed Brougham's argument that there was nothing to warrant the exceptional proceeding of a Bill of Pains and Penalties: he argued that Ministers had been prepared to allow the Queen to continue her life of licence provided she did not return to England and that therefore the Bill was aimed to punish what was past history rather than to vindicate the honour of the royal family or of the country by stopping something which was continuing. For a radical he possibly set too much store by social distinctions when he argued that the Queen, when abroad, had been 'thrown among persons of low rank' and among the vices and temptations prevalent in such circles. The Prime Minister, Lord Liverpool, made a not ineffective reply. He argued that a bill was the only possible proceeding: high treason had been ruled as inapplicable: it would be a matter of doubt if it would be possible, by impeachment, to deprive the Queen of her rights and privileges. A special act of parliament, such as the Bill, was the only way by which this could be done. He agreed that it was a great evil to leave her abroad committing adultery 'of the grossest kind' (meaning by that taking pride in wrongdoing) but this was a very much lesser evil than allowing her 'who had set at defiance all regard for morality' to enjoy the rights and privileges of her rank at home. He touched on the difference between men and women in the laws governing adultery, arguing that the improved reverence and respect paid to females distinguished modern from less civilised times, and that the severer law for women in cases of adultery 'supported that chastity which added so much to the attraction of personal charms'. He referred to the disgust with which he had listened to what the Queen's counsel had said of the Duke of York, and with regard to the King's remarriage he declared most solemnly that he believed that no such feeling had entered into the mind of his majesty. The divorce therefore was merely a corollary to the measure not its object. Here he evidently spoke with authority.

Lord Grey followed in a speech which, like the Prime Minister's, was moderate and therefore effective. He agreed that the provision about divorce was not important, and that if the Queen were degraded under the Bill it would not be possible, under any principle of propriety or justice, that she should remain the wife of the King. He went on that the feeling against the Bill of Pains and Penalties was 'almost as universal as the air'. He argued strongly, and with well-chosen precedents, in favour of impeachment and he moved that the Bill 'now before the House' does not afford 'the most advisable means of prosecuting the charges against Her Majesty'. This motion was defeated by a majority of 115, and the case then began. Such were the preliminaries to the proceedings.

3

Non Mi Ricordo

In an age when high significance was attached to natural phenomena a succession of loud peals of thunder, which greeted the Attorney-General as he opened the case, heightened the solemnity of the occasion. The speech of the Attorney-General can be briefly summarised because all the facts in it were to emerge in evidence, but it is important because it sets out in almost kaleidoscopic force the impression left by the Queen's surroundings and life. She arrived at Milan on 9 October 1814, and it was here that she engaged Pergami as *valet de place* or courier. At the time he was out of work but he had served under General Pino in the fighting against Napoleon.

Since the decision to employ Pergami went to the root of the case, it is fair to interrupt the Attorney-General and to give the Queen's own explanation for this in her own words.

'I arrived at Milan the 8th. Octr 1814. The Austrian Government received me very well [Milan was then part of the Habsburg empire] and Count Giziliere [Marquis Ghisiliari], Chamberlain to the Emperor, attended me everywhere .... I saw him frequently, and told him that it was my intention to settle in Italy for a few years. Count Giziliere then proposed that I should have a person who understood the arrangement of a large family—and how to keep it in a proper style of elegance and at the same time with economy .... I desired the Count to look out for such a person. He did so and recommended to me Mr. Pergami who had served in the army and was then with Count Peno [General Pino]; but that as peace was made, and Mr. Pergami would not serve the Austrian Government, he would accept of my situation (though inferior to what he had been accustomed to,) *on condition*, that if any vacancy occurred in my establishment, that I would then promote him to one more resembling that, he then held in Count Peno's family. This I promised to do—and accordingly he acted as my courier. But he was a superior kind of courier, more like an *ecuyer* whose province it is to keep near the Royal carriages by way of protection, and has nothing to do with posting horses, etc. A *courier de cabinet* has the rank of Colonel in the army and *that* was the situation Mr. Pergami held in my household.'[1]

The clearest account of Pergami is to be found in a description of him by James Brougham, who had gone out to Italy in 1819, as has already been explained, to report on the Princess's life. At this time the Princess was living on the Adriatic at Pesaro with a big establishment and a guard of soldiers allowed by the Pope. (Pesaro was in the Papal States.) James Brougham writes: 'The Baron [i.e. Pergami] is a chief person so I must give you a little history. I think him a plain straightforward *remarkably good sort of man*—assumes nothing, he has a great deal to do and is very active—quite a different man from what I expected. People all like him, except those who envy his situation . . . . He is neither a man of education nor talents, but understands figures very well and superintends everything— pays every shg., and nothing is got for which there is not a written order signed by him. All the books are as regular as possible . . . He is a tall, good-looking fellow about 35, *an Isaac* but more of a gentleman than the Dr's son or such like[2]—his grandfather was a physician, his father lived on his own property and was extravagant, the sons had to shift for themselves. He was in the service (*she* says aide-de-camp) to General Pino and at the battle of Moscow.'

Later James Brougham goes on to comment after a dinner at which they had dined off plate belonging to Pergami—'Nothing can appear more revolting to propriety than the P. of W., with her large fortune using another person's plate. Certainly the whole thing tells badly. *His* house and grounds, *his* plate, *his* ordering

[1] *Letters of George IV 1812–1830*, edited by A. Aspinall, 1938, pages 347–352.
[2] This is difficult to disentangle—possibly a family allusion. Obviously Pergami was gentlemanly; that his manners were better than might be expected from the son of a doctor could be a meaning of the passage.

everything, he even buys her bonnets, this I saw, and all his family quartered upon her.'

Then after he had been there a few days longer he wrote: 'In fact they are to all appearances man and wife, never was anything so obvious. *His room* is close to hers, and his *bed room* the only one in that part of the house. The whole thing is apparent to everyone. . . . '[1]

Going back to the Attorney-General's speech. He spoke of William Austin who, according to him, was six or seven but was in fact in his teens, and shared the Queen's bedroom though not the bed. The Queen arrived in Naples on 8 November 1814, and it was here that her sleeping habits changed. Austin was no longer permitted to share her bedroom though, if his correct age is remembered, this was not unreasonable. On the day after—or more exactly the night after—the Queen's arrival in Naples Pergami removed from the servants' sleeping quarters and went to a room joining the Queen's. Two people slept in Pergami's bed: no one slept in the Queen's bed. A few days later the Queen gave a masked ball to the King of Naples who was Napoleon's renowned general—Murat, married to one of the Emperor's sisters. The hostess at the ball appeared variously as a Neapolitan peasant, a Turkish peasant and the Genius of History. Though varied, the dresses, which she wore, were pronounced to be of uniform indecency. Pergami helped her into each of them. The intimacy continued. Servants saw and heard things. Thus matters progressed at Naples until the spring of 1815. Moving up to Genoa the Queen made no difference in her way of life. Her English courtiers had all left, and her household was composed of Pergami's family—mother, brother, sister and his child Victorine. On leaving Genoa for Milan the party was augmented by another sister of Pergami—the Countess Oldi 'a person of vulgar manners and totally uneducated'. The Count and his lady were not familiar figures in even the obscurer reaches of the continental nobility. The countess and Pergami lived in the society of their employer: the rest of Pergami's family lived with the servants. Thus they lived, travelling in Italy and Switzerland, till November 1815 when the Queen went by sea to Sicily, and on board ship Pergami dined with her at the Captain's table. After some time in Sicily the Queen sailed for

[1] *The Letters of George IV, op. cit.,* ii 272–285.

Tunis, convenient arrangements for Pergami to sleep near her on board ship being made. He was created a knight of Malta, and was thenceforward always addressed as chevalier by the Queen. In Tunis the Chevalier was allowed access to the Queen's bedroom in the early morning and, as the Attorney-General pertinently observed, 'her having raised him from obscurity to distinction could not furnish any ground for thus admitting him to her bed-room'. Thus companioned the Queen journeyed to Greece, and then across to Asia Minor.

When travelling in Syria the Queen slept in a tent. Pergami was observed coming from the tent in a state of undress, and was often the one of her servants chosen to attend her while she was in the tent. 'No woman', said the Attorney-General, 'would allow such a liberty to be taken with her, unless by a man to whom she had granted the last favour.' He instanced as one of the degrading offices performed by the Queen for Pergami—'she mended his clothes'. Here a lord laughed. On board ship sailing from Palestine to Italy the Queen had a bath prepared for her and when she went into it Pergami was the only person admitted to the precincts. 'Every man must be satisfied that the last intimacy had taken place.'

Back in Europe in 1817 the Queen did not change her course of conduct. Travelling to Germany in February of that year some of her clothing and other more decisive pieces of evidence were detected in Pergami's bed. And this year the Queen's travelling habits gave evidence of the same infatuation. Formerly the Queen had travelled in a carriage with Pergami, Countess Oldi and 'the little picaroon'—a rather strange use of language by the Attorney-General with its meaning of rogue or brigand. He applied it to Pergami's daughter Victorine. On the journey back from Austria to Italy the Queen travelled with Pergami alone—in a carriage made for two. Back at the Villa d'Este, she allowed a man, whose services she had enlisted in the east, to give exhibitions of 'dancing' to herself and Pergami. The servants attended these displays which were imitations, in the most indelicate manner, of sexual intercourse; these were characterised by the Attorney-General as 'not merely indecency but disgusting indecency'.

When she first went abroad the Queen had attended regularly the services of the Church of England, but with her increasing friendship with Pergami she accompanied him 'to a place of Catholic worship . . . kneeling down by his side.' Commenting on this and no doubt with a glance in the direction of the bishops the Attorney-General commented: 'Such was her abandonment of those religious feelings and rites which ought to be observed by all persons, under all circumstances'. He ended with a spirited defence of the witnesses, and poured scorn on the argument of the Queen's counsel that no credence could be attached to them because they were 'foreign'.

Before any of the witnesses were called Lord King raised the question whether they were liable to a prosecution at law for perjury, explaining that he raised the point because the House was sitting in a legislative and not in a judicial capacity. It was settled that the same rule should apply as in a case of impeachment—namely that the witnesses would be liable for prosecution if guilty of perjury. The Queen entered, while this question was being discussed, took her place and prepared to confront the witnesses.

The first witness was Theodore Majocchi, a man of middle height, decent appearance and well-dressed. The Queen fixed her eyes on him, and then exclaimed with a piercing cry 'Theodore, Theodore, oh no! no!' Some thought that she really cried 'Traditore, traditore'. The reports for all the newspapers gave the Theodore version, and it is likely that this was what she said—a warning cry of admonition to an old, confidential servant. She was immediately led out to her retiring room, looking—as a future Lord Chancellor remarked— more like a fury than a woman.

Nicholas Marchese di Spineto was first sworn as interpreter— the witness having no English—and Brougham made a rather graceless objection on the ground that the marchese was the nominee of the Foreign Office and the Treasury. He insisted on having his own translator as well—Binetto Cohen.

Majocchi said that he had first known Pergami in 1813 when they were both serving under General Pino. Pergami was *valet-de-chambre*. They had met again in 1815 when Majocchi was working in the stables of the King of Naples: he explained that he was, by profession, a rider or postilion. Through Pergami's good offices he was given employment and a better position by the Princess[1] after the Christmas holidays, becoming a livery servant. Here a lord interrupted to ask: 'Did you wear livery?' 'I did.' He was then asked to describe the sleeping arrangements of Pergami and the Princess. Pergami's room was separated from hers by a small corridor and a cabinet. On one occasion the Princess and the King of Naples (Murat) had gone on an expedition to a lake near by; on this trip Pergami was kicked by a horse and injured in the leg. Majocchi was told to wait on Pergami while he was laid up, and to sleep on a sofa in the Cabinet, which was between Pergami's room and that of the Princess. There was always a fire in the room. He slept here for five or six nights, and twice he saw the Princess come through after midnight on her way to Pergami's bedroom. The first time she stayed 10 or 15 minutes, and the second time 15 or 18 minutes. On both occasions he heard 'whispering conversation'. He gave evidence about the somewhat similar sleeping arrangements when the party moved on to Genoa and Milan. He enumerated the relations of Pergami, who joined the Princess at Genoa—his sister Faustina, his brother Louis and his mother. He added that there was also a child; it had a strange name. 'Was her name Victorine?' 'It was.' He also said that at this time the Princess rode a donkey. Pergami 'took her round the waist to put her upon the ass'.

At this stage there was some argument among counsel about the importance of no other witness on either side being present during the examination of any of the other witnesses. Brougham, at his most characteristic self, said that he could not say, until the close of the attorney-general's case whether he would even call any witnesses—'If he only heard such a witness as the present called, he certainly should not call any'. There was laughter.

The next hour or so of Majocchi's examination was taken up with details about the arrangements of the bedrooms during the Princess's travels. The arrangements were uniform. There was always a means of moving undetected from one bedroom to another though on one occasion, at Messina, access was possible only through the bedroom

---

[1] In the proceedings the Queen was referred to by her title at the time of which the witnesses were giving evidence, i.e. the Princess, and to avoid confusion that description has been followed here.

of the *dame d'honneur*. This lady was Pergami's sister, the Countess Oldi. At Messina Pergami asked the Princess if he might go into Messina to make some purchases. When permission was granted he took her hand, and kissed her lips. Majocchi often made the beds and observed that Pergami's bed had not always been occupied. When the Princess and Pergami were guests of the Bey of Tunis the two bedrooms were especially conveniently arranged—no doubt by a practised hand. After visiting Constantinople they travelled by sea to New Ephesus or Scala Nuova, just south of Smyrna. They did not stop here but went inland to see the grotto of the Seven Sleeping Men.[1] Near the grotto was a barrack or *caffè Turque,* and Majocchi remembered carrying the Princess's travelling-bed into the *caffè,* which had boughs of trees for a roof. Here Majocchi served dinner, the Princess sitting on the travelling-bed with Pergami on the ground at her feet. Possibly his most significant evidence concerned the domestic arrangements on the polacca (a three-masted type of sailing-ship, without a topmast or top-gallant mast) in which they travelled from Jaffa back to Italy. On deck, the Princess pitched her tent or rather two tents for, as Majocchi explained, there were two tents—one within the other. A sofa and travelling-bed were placed in the inner tent. He explained that the Princess slept every night in this tent. 'Did anybody sleep under the same tent?' 'Bartolommeo Pergami.' 'Were the sides of the tent drawn in, so as to shut them entirely in?' 'When they went to sleep the whole was enclosed, shut up.' He also said that he had prepared a hot bath for the Princess in her cabin, and that Pergami felt the temperature of the water and then handed down the Princess and closed the cabin door. They remained alone in the cabin. Majocchi went on to explain that he had slept immediately below the deck where the two tents were placed. 'Did you ever hear any motion over you?' 'I have heard a noise.'

[1] This was the scene of the horrible experience of seven Christian youths who were entombed by order of the Emperor Decius. They fell asleep and after 187 years they were roused by a peasant moving the stones from the entrance to the grotto. After shopping in Ephesus they peaceably expired. Gibbon distinguishes this curious tale from what he calls 'the insipid legends of ecclesiastical history' because it could be traced back almost to the time it was supposed to have happened and because it was believed far beyond the confines of the Christian world.

'What did it appear to you to be?' 'The creaking of a bench.' After getting back to Italy and after spending some weeks at the Villa D'Este the Princess and Pergami moved to the Barona or the Villa Pergami. Here they stayed for six weeks and according to Majocchi this villa was only 'a species of rough house where they make cheese for the farmer.' He then described their journeys through Germany and recalled that at the Golden Stag at Munich the Princess and Pergami had insisted on changing the rooms because those arranged were too distant from one another.

At this point the Lords showed some impatience because, as Lord Camden—a pillar of conservatism—objected—'it is past 4 o'clock, the hour fixed for closing'. Lord Grey thought that 'rather than sit for a whole year they had far better sit for a quarter of an hour more'. But the vote was taken, and it was settled to adjourn at four and not to exceed the time.

The fifth day started with particulars about the contents of the carriage in which, it will be remembered, the Princess and Pergami travelled alone.

'Was it your business to prepare the carriages, and the things that were put into them?' 'It was my duty.'

'Do you remember at any time in examining the carriage finding any bottle in it?' 'I found one bottle.'

'Was that usually in the carriage on the journey, when the Princess and Pergami travelled together?' 'It was.'

'Will you explain the construction of the bottle, as far as relates to the opening, or mouth of it, was it large or small?' 'About three or four inches in diameter.'

'Do you know from what you found from time to time in that bottle, for what purpose it was used?' Here the more respectable reports printed asterisks but the answer in fact given was 'For Pergami to make water in'.

Majocchi explained that he had been in the service of the Princess for three years, and he concluded his evidence with an account of Mahomet the exhibitionist, who joined the Princess in the holy land. He was asked about certain displays of dancing given by Mahomet though warned that he should only refer to these if the Princess had been a spectator. He said that Mahomet had exhibited a *giuoco* before the Princess. This was correctly translated as a game, play or trick. But it became clear that Majocchi had in mind a fandango with casta-nets, enlivened by the repeated cry of *Vima dima*. This the interpreter said he could not translate: presumably the words were eastern.

'Was anything done by Mahomet upon that occasion with any part of his dress?' 'He made use of the linen of his *brachese*, or large pantaloons.'

'Describe what use he made of the linen of his large pantaloons, and what he did with it?' 'He made the pantaloons go backwards and forwards (moving his person backwards and forwards).' He said that the *giuoco* was practised more than once in the presence of the Princess.

Brougham started his cross-examination of Majocchi innocently.

'Did you leave General Pino's service on account of killing a horse?' 'No.'

'You never killed a horse then at all?' 'Never.'

Some of the lords evidently whispered together and made it clear that they disapproved of these questions. Without showing annoy-ance Brougham turned to them and said: 'Your lordships must be aware that any symptoms of admonition must have great weight with me and are certainly calculated to withdraw my attention from the serious duty I have to perform'.

He concentrated on what Majocchi had said about the sleeping arrangements at Naples, when, it will be remembered, he had slept in the cabinet when Pergami was suffering from the effects of the kick from the horse. He was pressed by Brougham to say whether there was not a way between the Princess's room and Pergami's in addition to going through the cabinet and past the bed where he was sleeping which, as came out in questioning, was a mattress without curtains. Majocchi replied that 'I speak of one passage', i.e. through the cabinet. 'I have only seen that one, that I remember.' Lord Longford, a Tory and brother-in-law to the Duke of Wellington, asked: 'Will you swear that there was no other way in which a person wishing to go from the Princess's room to Pergami's room could go, except by passing through the cabinet?' 'There was, I think another passage going to the room of Pergami.' Question and answer were damaging to Majocchi's original evidence.

To much of Brougham's cross examination the replies of Majocchi were uniform '*Non mi ricordo*'—words easily spoken by an English tongue. They were to pass into the language as a phrase for expressing something which it was not convenient to remember. Brougham asked the interpreter for an exact translation of the words and was told that they meant 'I do not remember' or 'I do not know' and that they corresponded to the French '*je ne sais pas*'. Brougham said that he dissented from this translation, that the point was of consequence and that the phrase should be put to her Majesty's interpreter. 'How do you translate the words "*non mi ricordo*"?' ' "I do not recollect".' 'How do you render "I don't know"?' ' "*No so.*" ' Brougham admitted that it was strange for him—only a Tramontane, i.e. one who came from north of the Alps—to offer an opinion on this but he questioned whether the same words could sometimes mean 'I don't recollect' and at others 'I don't know'. An old, well-educated lord, who had been long resident at Turin, Lord Hampden, asked: 'How would the interpreter translate "This I don't recollect"?' The interpreter replied '*Non mi ricordo questo*'.

Sir William Gell then caused an interruption in the proceedings. Lord Mansfield, a reactionary lord, asked whether Sir William was to be one of the witnesses and was he present? Lord Mansfield had doubtless observed Gell below the bar, as he was one of the gentlemen attending the Queen. It was decided that no person could be examined as a witness who was present during the examination of other witnesses except with the leave of the house. Sir William withdrew.

Some details of the Princess's travelling habits in the Holy Land were brought out in cross-examination. She travelled on horseback by night, resting by day. She mounted at sunset and travelled all night till the rising of the sun. She became extremely fatigued and for the last hour or two of the ride she had to be supported in the saddle. Majocchi admitted that, when on the polacca, he and another servant had slept in the space between the inner and outer tents. Some time was spent on the nature of the Princess's travelling-bed. Majocchi explained that it was not 'a matrimonial bed', rather it was a mattress on which cushions were placed. 'Will you swear you ever saw, either on the land journey in Palestine, or on

1 Queen Caroline
From an engraving after the portrait by A. Wivell, 1820

2 Bartolommeo Pergami
From an engraving of the original portrait published, 1820, in Paris

3   Countess Oldi
(Lady of the Bedchamber to the Queen)
From an engraving by R. Page, 1820

4   Lt. Flynn R.N.
*From an engraving by T. Wright after
a sketch by A. Wivell, 1820*

5   Theodore Majocchi
From a contemporary engraving

6   Louise Demont
*From an engraving by T. Wright after
a sketch by A. Wivell, 1820*

board the ship during the voyage, one stitch of common bed-clothes, sheet, blankets or coverlids upon that bed?' 'This I do not recollect.'

Majocchi was next asked about sea-sickness. He answered that on board ship 'I am more unwell than well.' Brougham objected to this translation, and asked if any lord, who understood the Italian language, would agree with his objection. The Duke of Hamilton, who had married William Beckford's daughter, and was thought to be the proudest man in the British Isles, rose and stated that the meaning of the words was 'always, or almost always, sick while on board ship'. (The word used was '*sempre*'—in the same breath the witness added '*le piu parti*'.) Brougham naturally made play with this, and he pressed Majocchi to say that he had been incapacitated for more than 24 hours at a stretch. Objection was taken to the turn of these questions into Italian, and the interpreter said that it would be easy enough to put the question clearly to a man of literary education but 'with such a stupid fellow it is impossible'. The interpreter had already said, according to one of the reports, 'the witness is frightened out of his wits'. Brougham now took full advantage of the simplicity of this peasant-witness.

'Were there no sailors on board this ship?' 'There were.'

'Did they never come on deck?' 'I don't remember.'

'Did they always remain below in the hold with you?' 'I don't remember. I believe they did at night.'

'Do you mean to represent that the ship was left to go alone during the whole of the night, without sailors on deck?'

An effort was made to upset what Majocchi had said about preparing the bath-water, on board the polacca coming back from Jaffa. He held his ground, still asserting that Pergami had put his hand into the water to test the temperature, and had told him (Majocchi) to bring more hot and cold water in case they were needed. He was then pressed to say whether he had not made many approaches to members of the Princess's household asking to be taken back in her service after leaving it. He admitted that he had once made this request but denied that he had made it in writing 'for my misfortune I know very little to write'. He was closely questioned about his evidence concerning the dances or tricks of Mahomet—'the black

performer' as Brougham called him: these questions largely concerned the angle from which he and the Princess watched 'the
dance'. The Princess had a private theatre at the Villa, and he gave
some account of the acting. He said that the Princess and Pergami
were acting a comedy and 'I saw Pergami dressed as a sailor, performing the part of a buffoon, with a bladder, striking like a
fiddler . . .'.

Although, from the characteristic indifference of the Englishman
for the correct rendering of foreign names it is difficult to say for
certain, it seems that Majocchi, on leaving the Princess was employed
by the distinguished princely family of Odescalchi-Erba belonging
to the 'black' or papal aristocracy of Rome.[1] He was for nearly a
year with Marquess Odescalchi—probably his title would have
been more correctly translated as prince—serving him in Italy and
Vienna. He was particularly examined by Brougham on the question
of wages, no doubt to prove that the Princess was a generous
employer.

Then followed some significant questions which drew out that
Majocchi had been employed by the British ambassador at Vienna,
Lord Stewart, after leaving the Odescalchi family. The point of this
was that Lord Stewart was much involved in the Milan Commission,
and presumably secured Majocchi pending further developments in
the case.

'Did you go as a postilion and courier, or a lackey to the English
Ambassador?' 'The Lord Stewart gave me only my subsistence.'

'Do you mean that you became attached to his embassy as a sort
of private secretary or what?' 'I was always at the ambassador's, and
the ambassador gave me something to live upon.'

'Do you mean that you were in his house on the footing of a
private friend?' 'No, not as a friend.'

'When did you first see his Excellency the English ambassador
at Vienna?' 'I do not remember when I saw him; I saw the secretary.'

---

[1] In one version of the trial the name is spelt Onischalti, but it is almost
certain that the correct form was Odescalchi because Majocchi went with his
employer to Hungary where the Odescalchi family had estates. The point is not
without importance because it shows that Majocchi was in a good place when
approached to give evidence against the Queen.

'What was the secretary's name?' 'Colonel Dureno.' (Actually it was Durring.)

'Do you know a certain Colonel Browne?' 'I do.'

'What countryman is he?' 'I do not know of what country he may be.'

This was of course the member of the Milan Commission, and Majocchi admitted that he travelled from Vienna, with his father, to see Colonel Browne at Milan.

At four o'clock one of the peers pointed out that it was time to adjourn. Brougham said: 'May I implore your lordships to allow me to proceed . . . acting as a court of justice I entreat your lordships to beware how you stop short in the middle of a cross-examination . . . one unexpected answer (as had actually been the case to-day) might lead to half an hour's digression.' Brougham was allowed to proceed.

Majocchi said that he travelled from Vienna with his father who was 'a carter, a carrier, carrying merchandise with horses'.

'How does he happen to come to Vienna, your respectable father?' 'My father came to Vienna to take me.'

'What induced you to leave the service of the Marchese Odescalchi, whom you liked so well, as to accompany him to Vienna, and to go back with this respectable old carter to Milan?' 'My father told me to go to Milan together with him. . . . He told me that at Milan there was Colonel Browne who wanted to speak to me.'

'Do you go everywhere whenever anybody comes to say to you "Colonel Browne wants to speak to you": do you immediately leave your place to go to him?'

Loud cries of 'order' prevented the witness from answering. Brougham turned on the interrupters: 'Noble lords and judges are now present whom I have seen save the lives of their fellow subjects by such questions, and so put, and who could not have done it, if they had been disturbed by cries of "order".'

Majocchi then answered 'When my father told me so, I went to Colonel Browne directly.'

'If your father were to go and ask you to speak to Colonel Black, would you go there also?' The Solicitor-General objected to this question.

Brougham then asked if Majocchi's father had made a fortune by what he described as 'the lucrative trade of a carrier'. He asked how they had travelled and whether they lived pretty comfortably on the road. 'We wanted for nothing.' After returning to Vienna from the excursion to Milan to see Colonel Browne, Majocchi was re-employed by the Odescalchi family and went with them to Hungary as cook. Brougham then hinted that Majocchi had really been given leave of absence to meet Browne, and that the British Ambassador in Vienna had paid his wages. The questions then switched to his accommodation in London, and extracted the information that his wife and father were with him.

'How did you come here to-day? Did you walk or come in a carriage?' 'On foot.'

'About how far was it? Your shoes are quite clean; how many streets did you pass through?' 'I cannot tell the distance.'

'Do your father and wife live in the same hotel with you?' 'Yes.'

'Are there any other Italians but yourself, your venerable[1] parent, and your amiable wife?' At this question the House showed signs of disapproval, and Brougham was told that 'the question was irregular: that it was slanderous'.

Majocchi said that he had no idea of the name of the inn, and that he had no idea if he was to pay for his own keep. 'Were you ever in such a place before in your life, where you did not know whether you were to pay for your keep or not?'

Lord Falmouth, speaking from the gallery, said that he had a private engagement and that the House, having fixed four o'clock for the adjournment should adhere to it. He was met by cries 'Go on, go on'. Lord Donoughmore, a representative Irish peer, thought that the witness deserved protection, and that some part of the cross-examination might have been spared. The House adjourned with the understanding that on subsequent days they would sit till five o'clock.

When the House met on the following day (23 August) Lord Darlington, who was a powerful, sporting, northern lord and a life-long friend of Brougham, urged that the lords should have before

---

[1] Some authorities say valuable, which sarcastically would make better sense.

them printed copies of the evidence from day to day. He showed perhaps a certain naïvety by adding: 'The evidence given by the witness in support of the bill, on the first day, had made, he confessed, a very strong impression on his mind: but the cross examination which took place yesterday had, on the contrary, tended very much to diminish that impression.' A loud cry of 'Order, Order'. The Lord Chancellor pointed out that it was a rule that anything printed for the use of the house must be certified to be correct on the responsibility of the clerks. It was totally different for the newspapers, to which Lord Darlington had referred, because they could use a succession of reporters, retiring each quarter or half hour and had no responsibility to the house for literal accuracy. The short-hand notes of the reporters would have to be compared with the notes taken by the clerk of the house, and he doubted if any utility would be obtained by departing from their existing procedure. As is true of most Lord Chancellors Eldon was quick to discourage any variant from existing procedure.

Continuing his cross-examination, Brougham asked a number of questions about the Hanoverian baron who was believed to have spied on the Princess's habits on behalf of her husband.

'Do you recollect a German baron visiting the Princess of Wales at Naples?' '*Non mi ricordo.*'

'Did any German baron visit the Princess of Wales at the Villa Villani,[1] during her residence there?' 'There was a baron whom I think to be Russian, who twice paid his visits, but I do not know what name he had, and this is the same which was mentioned to me also yesterday.'

'Was the name of that person Ompteda or Omteda, or any name sounding like that?'[2] 'Precisely I cannot recollect the name by which he was called, for it was an extraordinary name.'

'Are you sure it was not Baron Pampdor?' '*Non mi ricordo.*'

[1] On Lake Como; here the Princess lived before she acquired the Villa d'Este.

[2] Baron Ompteda was the Hanoverian Minister at the Vatican. Being in Italy he was one of the original sources of the reports about the Princess which came back to England. Brougham's reference to Pampdor or Rampdor—as it was variously given—is not familiar to the editor.

'Do you recollect that baron, whatever his name was, at the Villa Villani more than once?' 'Once I remember, more I do not remember.'

'Was there not a room in the house of her royal highness, at the Villa Villani, which was called the baron's room, giving it the extravagant name whatever he had?' '*Questo non mi ricordo.*'

'Do you recollect a thunder-storm upon the lake, in which her royal highness's party of pleasure was exceedingly wet?' '*Questo non mi ricordo.*'

Particular attention was paid by Brougham to something which Majocchi had given in evidence. Referring to the sleeping arrangements at Naples where, it will be remembered, he had occupied a small cabinet between Pergami's room and the Princess's room, when Pergami was suffering from the effect of a kick by a horse, and in answer to the question where the rest of the Princess's attendants had slept he said 'they were separated'. Cross-examined by Brougham on that answer he replied: 'I said they were separated, but I meant that they were so situated that they could not communicate together.'

'Did you mean by that, that there was no passage, no way by which a person could go from the room of her royal highness to the rooms of those others of the suite?' Here the solicitor-general said that Majocchi in evidence had stated 'they were separated'. Brougham said: 'my learned friend seems to triumph in a mare's nest which he thinks he has found'. The Lord Chancellor intervened to say that the proper way was to tell the witness what answer had been given 'but to put a question on it'. Brougham then said that he had five or six witnesses to prove that Majocchi had not said *separato* but *lontano* meaning 'at a distance'.

'I have seen no other passage except the one leading to Pergami's room.'

On the question of what payment had been made to him before, during and after the journey from Vienna to Milan the difficulty of language became conspicuous. 'I remember to have received no money when I arrived at Milan; *ricordo di no*; *mi ricordo che no*, I remember I did not; *non so*; I do not know; *più no che si*; more no than yes; *non mi ricordo.*' Lord Rosebery interrupted to say that it was essential that they should know what the witness meant by '*ricordo di no*'. It seems fairly clear that what Majocchi meant was 'I recollect—not', i.e. I recollect that I was not paid. The Lord Chancellor explained that after the witness had been re-examined the peers would have the opportunity to put questions to him.

Brougham then said: 'My lords, I have done with the witness. I have no further questions to ask of him. In a common case I should certainly be satisfied with this examination. In this case I have certainly no reason to ask him a single question further.'

Re-examining the witness, the Solicitor-General on the question of payment for the journey to Milan from Vienna asked 'What do you mean by "*Non mi ricordo*"?' 'When I say "*non mi ricordo*" I mean that I have not in my head to have received the money, for if I had received the money I would say yes: but I do not remember it now, but I do not recollect the contrary.'

At the end of the re-examination the right of questioning the witness was thrown open to the Lords, and attention was particularly directed to the arrangements of the rooms at the Villa d'Este. The Marquis of Buckingham, the head of the illustrious house of Grenville and shortly to win the ultimate distinction of the ducal strawberry leaves, said that it would be impossible for them to master the evidence unless they were provided with a plan of the rooms. Brougham strongly objected to this because publication of the plan would give information to subsequent witnesses. 'Any man, whether he understood English or not, if he had eyes, must understand a plan . . . . A plan at once put them [the witnesses] in possession of all. There was an end at once then to *non mi ricordo* (a laugh); that vanished at once, and the tutelary saint of the plan settled everything.' The Lord Chancellor thought that a plan should be produced, and that it would be best if counsel could settle on one which was agreed by both sides.

Majocchi was able to produce a certificate of character—'I had it not in the hand-writing of her royal highness, but there is her seal; Scavani[1] wrote the paper'. He drew it from his pocket, held it at arm's length and exhibited it to the whole house. Brougham insisted that the document must be proved to be 'the act of her royal

[1] Count Schiavini, who accompanied the Queen to England.

highness'. Majocchi described Scavini as 'Equerry marshallo' in the household.

'Can you say whether Scavini had the general management and superintendence of the servants of the household?' 'I do not know who commanded, for Pergami commanded, Scavini commanded, both commanded; it was impossible for me to know which of the two commanded, who was the superior commander; Pergami came and commanded, Scavini came and commanded; all commanded.'

Questions were then thrown open to the House. Lord Ellenborough, who was to have personal experience of an intractable wife, asked: 'How was her royal highness dressed when she passed through the cabinet to Pergami's room at Naples?' '*Non mi ricordo.*'

Lord Grey asked 'Did you see her royal highness distinctly on that occasion?' 'Yes.'

'But you do not know how she was dressed?' 'I do not remember what dress she had.'

'Did you pretend to be asleep at that time?' 'As I am now asleep.' Interpreter—'He means that he was awake.'

The peers showed the greatest interest in the bath on the polacca. Lord Duncan, son of the great victor of Camperdown, asked if Majocchi could swear that none of the Princess's female attendants were with her in the bath-room. He answered 'Yes, I can swear to having seen nobody go into the bath-room of her royal highness'.

'Were you actually in the room, or merely at the outside of the door of the cabinet or the door of the inner room?' 'I was at the door when Pergami went upstairs to tell her royal highness that the bath was ready; when they came down Pergami told me "Be at the door, for if there be any need of water you shall give it me".'

'At which door was it, at the outer door or the inner door that the two pails of water were given?' 'At the door of the bathroom itself.' He explained later that a sailor brought the pails to the outer door.

In answer to Lord Grey who asked whether there was anyone else in the inner or bath room: 'I can swear and I do swear, that there was no other when Pergami and her royal highness came into the room, because I put myself at the door.'

Lord Auckland, an unmarried peer, asked: 'Did you remain in

the outer room during the whole time that the Princess and Pergami were in the inner room?' 'At the door with the two pails of water.'

The Lord Chancellor recalled how Majocchi had filled the bath in the *cabinetto* and he wished him to be asked whether anyone entered the *cabinetto* while Pergami went upstairs to bring her royal highness down. The answer was firmly 'no'.

Lord Auckland asked whether he saw the princess and Pergami 'quit the bathroom'. 'No, but I have seen Pergami come out of the room to go on deck, to call the maid to come down and dress her royal highness, and I have heard, with my own ears, when he said "Mademoiselle Dumont, [Demont] come down to dress her royal highness".'

'Could you at that time see into the bath-room?' 'When Pergami went out, he went out sideways, and immediately shut to the door.'

'How long had Pergami and the Princess been in the room before Pergami went to call the maid?' 'About half an hour.'

The Marquess of Huntly, who was in his late seventies, asked: 'Was Pergami on retiring from the bath-room dressed in the same way as when he handed the Princess in?' 'He was.'

Lord Darnley asked about the tent on the polacca. 'Was it that commonly called tent or merely an awning?' 'It was a tent which was spread on the deck by the means of a rope, and then in the evening it was closed as a partition, as a closed tent, it was closed all round; in the evening this tent was let down and was closed all round; and they said "Stop it well, stop it all round: see that there be no hole, no opening".'

Lord de Dunstanville recalled the occasions when Majocchi had slept on deck between the outer and inner tent and asked whether he had heard anything from inside. 'I heard two voices speak by whispering . . . .'

Finally Brougham put some questions about the efforts of Majocchi to get back to the Princess's service. He was allowed to put these questions through the Lord Chancellor. Brougham's last question in his rightly celebrated cross-examination was this. 'Did you or not also make application five or six times to Camera [an upper servant of the Princess's and more correctly Camara] to be taken back into her royal highness's service?' 'Softly on this point.

The first or second time that Camera arrived at Milan, Camera sent his son for me, and Camera told me, and I remember it as well as if it was now,—"Theodore Majocchi, do not enter into any service [i.e. with anybody else] because her royal highness wishes to take you back, and I shall pay you." This conversation must be put down, such as it is, and I beg to be allowed to speak. Camera told me— "Theodore, give me back the certificate of your good service, give me back such paper, and I will tell to her royal highness that you have not taken a further engagement—that you have not been in any further service, and she will pay you for the whole time you have been out of service—all the time you have been out of service, and all the damages or losses you have suffered: and I told Camera, "Camera, give me back my paper (because I had already given him my paper) because rather than go to serve her royal highness, on account of the persons that are about her, I will go and eat grass".' This conversation took place before he went to Vienna. Majocchi was then directed to withdraw. His ordeal was over.

4

Seen through the Key-hole

The next witness was Gaetano Paturzo, about thirty and 'of rather shabby appearance'. He was a Neapolitan, and was now the captain of a merchant ship. In April 1816 he was mate on the vessel on board which the Princess made her journey to Africa and the Holy Land. Before he took the oath, Denman, the Queen's solicitor-general, made a curious intervention. He asked Paturzo if he was a Roman Catholic, and then 'when did you last take the sacrament of the Lord's supper?' Denman explained these questions on the ground that for catholics an oath was not binding unless taken soon after confession and the Lord's supper. Despite this show of Protestant prejudice, the witness was sworn in the usual way. The acoustics were none too good, and the Lord Chancellor had to say: 'Have the goodness to keep up your voice, Mr. Attorney-General, and let the witness keep up his.'

Paturzo was largely examined on the sleeping arrangements on board *Il Vero Fidele*—the polacca. When he was questioned by the peers after examination and cross-examination he put in a plan, and the reproduction of that overleaf may make his examination easier to follow. The cabin of the ship, in the stern, he explained, was divided into two. On the right hand was the Princess's bed and on the left Countess Oldi's. Immediately beyond this was the dining-room with the dining-table in the middle, and next to this, on the right-hand side was Pergami's room and bed. The dining-room extended the whole breadth of the ship. After the travellers left Tunis and were sailing for Malta Pergami's bed 'was removed into the dining-room, and most especially, or properly, or particularly on the right hand of the dining-room'. (The interpreter was in difficulties here and explained that he could not give the meaning in one word. He suggested as the best translation 'to speak more correctly, on the right hand'.) The Princess's cabin was divided from Countess Oldi's cabin by a

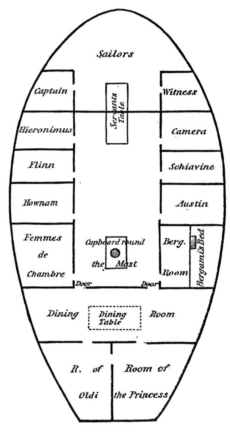

Plan of the *Il Vero Fidele*
From Nightingale, 'The Trial of Queen Caroline', 1820

painted canvas in which there was a door. There was also a door from the Princess's cabin into the dining-room.

'If the door you have mentioned was open [i.e. the door into the dining-room] could a person in the princess's bed see Pergami's bed?' 'Why not . . . in whatever situation a person was in this bed of Pergami's he could not help seeing the bed of the Princess when the door was open, the situation of the bed was such that they could not help seeing both together: but a person might stand up in the bed in such a position that he might not see the bed of the princess . . . .'

Of the return journey from Jaffa he described how he had helped in closing the tent, on board, at night. He affirmed that in the tent were a sofa and small bed.

'Have you ever seen the tent raised in the morning?' 'Yes.' He described how he saw the Princess either lying or sitting on the sofa, and Pergami on the bed, wearing 'his usual lower dress; and above he had a species of Grecian cloak or toga—a species of morning-gown with large sleeves'. He also said that the tent was sometimes closed by day. 'For how long a time?' 'A little time, half an hour or an hour.'

He continued that he had seen Pergami and the Princess walking arm in arm on deck. He also explained that when they were not walking he had seen them 'in different situations'.

'Describe some of them.' 'Sometimes sitting on a gun, with the arm of one behind the back of the other, because the gun was small, supporting each other with the arm: sometimes Pergami lying on his back upon his small bed, and the Princess standing near to the bed of Pergami leaning forward: but whenever this happened, the captain, now with one excuse, now with another, sent me away, because we are distant relations . . . . Sometimes I have seen Pergami sitting on the bench near to the main-mast, and the princess sitting on his lap or thigh, with an arm round his neck over his shoulder . . . . Pergami's arm was behind the back of the princess, and the arm of the princess was round the neck of Pergami.'

'Do you remember in the course of your voyage Saint Bartholomew's Day, the 24th August?' 'I do . . . During that day there was general mirth through the whole of the equipage, or the whole of the crew, which could hardly be kept in during the evening; afterwards dishes were set with lights to make an illumination all over the ship, and to all the sailors was given to drink; by the order of Pergami they had a dollar each: and all the crew danced, and they cried "Long live St. Bartolommeo! Long live the Princess. Long live the Chevalier." '

His examination ended by his saying that at Jaffa, where the party had embarked for Italy, Pergami was wearing an order with a yellow, or straw-coloured ribbon.

'What was that order called?' 'Saint Caroline.'

Paturzo stood up to cross-examination better than Majocchi had done. He was asked whether the little gun he spoke of was upon the deck. He replied 'On the deck—we could not carry it in our pocket'. He was closely examined about the arrangements for his journey to England and he replied: 'Those questions it is useless to put to me, because I know nothing at all about it.'

Denman also examined him about his accommodation in London and the arrangements for his fellow-witnesses.

'Where have you been since your arrival in London?' 'There; where all the rest were, where there is communication with this room . . . .' When he was asked how many were with him he said: 'I have not reckoned them; I think of my own business.'

'Do you mean to say that you do not know whether there are ten persons only or ten times ten?' 'Ten and ten times ten make a hundred; if I do know arithmetic that will do.'

When the turn of the lords came they examined him closely about the arrangements on the polacca. Lord Grey asked whether there were always ten or eleven sailors on deck at night. The witness agreed, only qualifying the statement to the extent that a few would be below 'helping to dress the horses'. Lord Grey then wanted to know whether there was a passage past the tent and whether the sailors did not pass it during the night. There was a passage on one side only and the sailors used it if they had to perform some service at the poop. 'When not, as is the custom of all sailors, they remained in the forecastle.'

Lord Ellenborough asked whether Pergami had any other known sleeping-place except the bed within the tent. 'Whether the Princess and Pergami slept under the tent I have not seen: but what I know morally is, that the Princess and Pergami slept in the tent, because there were horses on board, which made a great deal of noise, and they said they could not bear to sleep below.'

Lord Darnley asked him if he knew whether the Princess took off her clothes during the night. Paturzo replied: 'We must distinguish betwixt knowing and seeing; what I know and what I have seen: I have seen sometimes in the morning the princess open a little of the tent, and I saw her having a white gown on, a dressing-gown, or some gown or other, and she opened the tent just to take a morsel of air before the sun rose.'

At the end of that day's proceedings, which also closed Paturzo's evidence and cross-examination, the Lord Chancellor told the house that he had applied 'to the highest sources of information' (the judges) to find how far prosecutions against the witnesses (presumably for perjury) would affect the privileges of the House of Lords. He considered that the House should suspend those privileges if a question of a prosecution arose.

The next day, St. Bartholomew's Day, opened with a discussion over the legality of the oath sworn by the Italian witnesses. Nicholas Tindal, the fourth of the Queen's advocates, a barrister of singular learning and modesty, elaborated the point which, it will be remembered, had been rather bluntly made by Denman on the previous day. He quoted from an earlier authority that 'Every man of every religion should be bound by that form, which he thinks will bind his conscience most.' He argued that when people of eastern religions were sworn as witnesses in English courts they were sworn according to their own religions. The Lord Chancellor said: 'There can be no doubt as to the point of law. If a witness believed in no God, and had no belief in a future state, he could be no witness.'[1] Tindal stuck to his point: 'It surely would never be thought sufficient to swear a Gentos [Hindu] upon the Gospel.' He implied that the Italian witnesses should be sworn according to the method prevailing in their own country. Brougham characteristically supported Tindal's point: he recalled a case at the Old Bailey where a Chinaman, in the witness-box, was given a porcelain saucer which he held up, repeated some words and then broke the saucer. Brougham asked if a British sailor giving evidence in a Chinese court could be expected to regard an oath, so reinforced, as 'solemn'. The case was put to the judges. They were absent for 20 minutes and apologised to the House for the delay which was explained by their having to consult some books. The judges were agreed that if a witness took the oath in the

[1] This was changed by the Oaths Act of 1888.

usual form he might be asked if he thought it binding. If he said 'yes' he could not be asked if he thought any other mode of administering it would be more binding.

The next witness was Vincenzo Gargiulo, the master of the polacca which he named as *La Industria*—though he explained that it had since been turned into a Brigantine, and renamed the *Abramo*. From the plan given by the previous witness the vessel seems—at the time of the Princess's voyage—to have been called *Il Vero Fidele*.

The Master explained that the Princess had come, with Pergami, to inspect the polacca before actually embarking. There were originally two doors into the dining room from the bow end of the ship. The Princess gave orders that one of these doors was to be closed. It was nailed up. The door leading to the cabins on the right side of the ship (Pergami occupied the first of these) was the one which was left open.

The Master described the Princess's bed on board (that is in the cabin—not under the tent) as 'two sofas joined together' making together 'six palms and a half'. He said that this was the equivalent of six foot and a half, though a palm (roughly the length of the hand) is generally reckoned at some nine inches. He confirmed that the Princess and Pergami could see one another from their respective beds which were ten or twelve feet apart. The Master's description of the sleeping arrangements under the tent gave rise to great difficulties in translation. '*Sotto la tenda unito alla principessa.*' The interpreter explained that he translated this 'under the tent together with the Princess'. He also asked Gargiulo to confirm that he meant in two beds. The translator on behalf of the Princess pointed out that he objected to the word '*unito*' which would mean joined. He explained that the tent was generally opened up at eight in the morning: that the Princess was generally sitting on the bed and that Pergami 'entirely dressed' was seen coming out from under the tent. He described how he had seen Pergami, by day, lying on his back on the bed with the Princess leaning over him and that instructions were given for the tent to be closed. 'This happened many times.' He described how Pergami accompanied her when she went below to take the bath.

7 The Queen, in mourning for
the Duchess of York, arrives at
the House of Lords
*From an engraving by J. Chapman
after a drawing by G. Cruikshank,
1820*

8   William Austin
(The Queen's protégé)
*From an engraving by Robert
Cooper, 1820*

9   The Queen and Pergami entering Jerusalem
From a contemporary engraving

'Were there other occasions then, besides the bath, that rendered it necessary for the princess to go below?' 'The greatest reason was that for going to the water-closet: for the water-closet was down below.'

He was asked if he had seen Pergami do anything jocular. 'I have seen him once, under the Grecian robe that he had, put some cushions and pillows, and make some motions to make her royal highness laugh.' The Master was asked what was meant to be represented by the trick. He replied that it was an apish trick to make her royal highness laugh. 'That is no answer', said the Solicitor-General. One of the Queen's counsel drily remarked: 'It is not the answer, I suppose, which my learned friend wants.'

The cross-examination of Gargiulo was entrusted to Mr. John Williams—short, fierce and extremely able. He was subsequently a judge of the high court. Gargiulo was closely questioned about the financial arrangements made for his visit to London. He explained that he had seen Sir William A'Court, the British Ambassador in Naples, when he was 'endeavouring not to come to England' and that he was paid 1,000 dollars a month. He went on to say that if he had been able to carry on with his business, and discharge the cargo of grain on his ship he would have made a great deal more. 'I have already lost four thousand [dollars].' The captain, whom he had appointed in temporary charge of his ship had sold the cargo at five carlini less per bushel than was the proper price. (A carlini was worth about 5d.) When Mr. Williams said: 'Perhaps you have made a more profitable voyage here' he was greeted by cries of *Order* from the peers.

'Explain, if you can, how your coming to England makes any difference as to the profit or loss of that voyage?' 'Yes. I had ordered the captain to sell the cargo at not less than 24 carlini per bushel; the captain having arrived at Reggio, and hearing that I had gone away, has taken upon himself to sell at 21 carlini, and since my arrival here, I have heard that the price of corn was raised to 26 carlini, and now I am told that it has reached nearly 30.'

'Do you mean to state that your being here affects the price of corn in Italy?' *A murmur through the House.*

Mr. Williams observed, after the Lord Chancellor had said that there was no objection to the question, 'that it was usual for silence to be observed in those courts with which he was familiar—in those courts where the judges presided: their lordships would therefore excuse him if he did not quite understand the interruption.' The Marquis of Downshire, a popular Irish landlord, thought that every indulgence should be extended to the members of the bar, and that the House should act with the utmost impartiality. Lord Liverpool supported this and urged that their lordships ought to have a proper command over themselves, and that any reason for an interruption should be clearly stated. But for all this, the peers evidently felt that in this matter counsel was taking advantage of a rather simple foreign witness.

The questions from the peers to Gargiulo were once again principally directed to the tent on board the polacca, and developed the points which had already been made. Lord Lansdowne asked whether he had ever desired the mate to withdraw from that part of the deck where the Princess and Pergami were. 'No I do not remember, I do not know this business.' The answer seemed to excite some surprise, and the reason was that Paturzo had, it will be remembered, made a point of his being asked to withdraw by Gargiulo.

Lord Lansdowne: 'If you had for any particular reason been in the habit of directing Paturzo to withdraw, is it not probable you would have remembered it?' 'Now I understand it; once I remember to have seen her royal highness sitting and stooping on the bed of Pergami, and to have desired Gaetano Paturzo to go away, for it was not decent for him, who was a young man, to be present; because when I saw her royal highness stooping on the bed in that way, I sent away Gaetano Paturzo, who was a young man, not to see the thing which I thought indecent.'

The witness withdrew. There was then an interruption when Brougham asked if Majocchi could be recalled to be questioned by him. After discussion the Lord Chancellor advised the House that the questions might be put. It transpired that Alderman Wood had had a letter from a correspondent in Gloucester saying 'I have every reason to believe [that Majocchi] is a man who lived with Mr. Adam

Hyatt,[1] who brought him over from Italy'. He told people that 'he had been offered a considerable sum of money, and a place for life, if he would appear against her.'

At the bar Majocchi applied through the interpreter to be allowed as a favour to assure their lordships that he was ready to lay down his life in that place if his former testimony was not correct. 'Did you ever declare that the conduct of the Princess of Wales was highly becoming?' 'Of her conduct I always said that she was a good woman, but she was surrounded by bad people.' Brougham then pressed him to say what he had said to a clerk in a bank at Gloucester and during a journey on a stage-coach from that city, implying that in both instances he had spoken highly of the Princess and her conduct.

'Did you ever say to any person in England that you had been asked to give an account on oath respecting the conduct of the Princess of Wales?' This was followed by a vigorous exchange between Brougham and the Solicitor-General, Copley—friends but always rivals in politics and the courts. Copley said that, in framing such questions as this, it was always customary in the courts below to state the name of the person with whom the conversation was supposed to have been held. Brougham denied that this rule was general. Copley replied: 'I find my learned friend is totally unacquainted with the rules of the courts below.' Brougham answered: 'The Solicitor-General appears to me unacquainted with these rules, as well as with the first rule of all judicial proceedings, which is not to interrupt an adversary before he has concluded his observations. ... I shall therefore consider the rule, which the Solicitor-General attempts to establish, as a mere *dictum* of his own. ... I confidently appeal to your lordships, notwithstanding the monopoly of legal learning claimed by the Solicitor-General. ...'

Politely the Lord Chancellor said that he thought it would generally be thought 'fair and reasonable' to state the name first before asking the question.

[1] This is most probably Mr. William Henry Adams of Painswick House who took the name of Hyett: he swam the Hellespont in one hour 50 minutes. It is perhaps hardly necessary to explain that the phrase 'live with' meant as a domestic servant. In his original appearance Majocchi had not made it plain that he had lived, for a time, in England.

'Did you ever say to Mr. Johnson or to any other person in a stage coach in England "I have had considerable advantages offered to me, if I would be a witness against the Princess of Wales" or to that effect?' 'I lay my head or my life there, this offer has never been made to me by anyone.'

'The question is not whether an offer was ever made to you, but whether you have said that an offer was made to you?' 'I lay my life if I have ever said so.' The interpreter quoted the Italian. '*Eo netto la mea testa què se io no tatto questo discorso di giaramento.*' And he added 'I lay down my life if this be true, I will answer no more, because you ask me things I have never dreamt about: things that have never entered my head.'

Lord Ellenborough asked him whether, when he called the Princess *buona donna* he was referring to her conduct as a woman or to her conduct to him. 'I always said she was *buona donna*: for if I had said she was *cattiva donna* [a naughty woman], they would have fixed a quarrel upon me.'

Francisco Birollo was then called. He was in the service of a Piedmontese marquis, and had been in the Princess's household as cook. He was engaged by Pergami, whom he had known in the household of General Pino. He told the house that Pergami was employed by Countess Pino before she became the General's wife. He himself had been cook to the Princess on board the polacca and afterwards at the Villa d'Este and at the Barona. (This, it will be remembered, was the original name of the Villa Pergami near the Villa d'Este.) He explained that he left the Princess's household 'because it was too much labour'. He was then examined by one of the junior counsel for the Crown, James Parke who was to become a highly distinguished judge and to be created Lord Wensleydale. Parke examined the witness about the tent on the polacca.

'Did you ever see Pergami in the morning coming out of the tent?' 'Sometimes, but not in the morning early: about a certain hour he came out of the tent, and came there, on the forecastle, to make water. . . . Sometimes I saw him in the morning early, sometimes a little later, when I was already at the kitchen boiling potatoes for breakfast for the crew.' He was asked about Pergami's dress—

'He had on a gown, which he had made in the parts of Greece, which was of silk.'

On the eighth day, 25 August, the proceedings began by some complaints from the peers about comments in the press. Lord Ellenborough pointed out that Lord Stewart, the British Ambassador in Vienna, had to his certain knowledge been in England from July in 1817 for a year. Therefore there was nothing inconsistent in Majocchi's statement that he had been in the service of the Ambassador but that he did not remember seeing him. He described the conclusion drawn from this point by the newspapers to be 'as false as it was base'. Brougham complained of something said about his informants in Gloucestershire over Majocchi and Mr. Hyett, but the Attorney-General said that he had much more reason to complain than Brougham had: 'I do not know if your lordships ever see the newspapers: but there was, in one of them, *The Times*, a most unjustifiable attack on the law-officers of the Crown: and highly improper comments on the evidence.'[1] Lord Lauderdale, once ardently on the left and known among his circle of friends as Citizen Maitland, complained of a pamphlet called 'Peeps at The Peers' in which it was said that he received £36,000 of Government money. Tersely he said that he did not receive a farthing. When the roll was called Lord Sondes, a young peer still in his twenties, asked to be excused from attending because of illness.

Continuing his evidence, Birollo said that the Princess and Pergami used to come into the kitchen at the Villa d'Este and that they used to ask for something to be prepared for them to eat. The Princess would cut some pieces of what had been prepared, stick a fork into it and eat; then taking another piece she would say to Pergami: 'Here it is, you eat also.' He was closely questioned about Mahomet's trick or dance.

'Describe what Mahomet did in the presence of the Princess?'
'He did so (making a dancing motion) saying "*Deura*": "*Deura*"'
—or as another report had it '*Dami, Dimi; Dami, Dimi*'.

'Did he do anything with his trousers in the course of these

[1] In addition the more lurid particulars of the case were much quoted. A pious lady, Mrs. Inchbald, refused during the case to allow the newspapers to be read aloud 'in any mixed society of ladies and gentlemen'.

gesticulations?' 'He made a kind of roll to represent something—
I do not know how to call it decently. . . . He took it in his hand, and
made gesticulations: I cannot say what he meant to represent.' He
explained that by 'I cannot say' he meant that he did not know—
not that he was restrained by decency from saying what it was. He
ended his evidence by saying that he remembered the Princess
entertaining at Barona. At her balls were no gentlemen—only 'people
of the low or middle rank'.

Attention was paid by the peers to an occasion at Turin when the
Princess was going to court, to pay her respects to the sovereigns of
Savoy. Birollo had gone to the dame d'honneur's room, which
opened out of Pergami's room, with a ruff and a pair of gloves. He
noticed that Pergami's bed had not been slept in and that he was
coming out of the Princess's bedroom in a striped, silk morning-
gown, wearing his drawers, stockings and slippers. 'He scolded me.'
Examined by the Lords he was asked by Lord Lauderdale if he
could state what Pergami said on that occasion. He answered that
Pergami said: '"You scoundrel, what are you doing here? Who has
opened the door?" I said I had found it open and he said "Go away".'
He was then asked by Lord Lansdowne how he knew that it was the
Princess's room from which he saw Pergami emerging: 'Because I
saw her royal highness come out from the same room all combed
and dressed'. The Princess was to receive a visit from the King and
Queen of Savoy (Victor Emmanuel I); when they came to the inn
Birollo said that the Princess took the King's arm, and that Pergami
walked behind. Lord Morton, a respectable, middle-aged Scottish
peer asked whether beds in Italy were made up in a different form
for the day or night. The witness replied that 'in my house the bed
is made in the morning, but I never made a bed'.

The next witness was Samuel George Pechell, a post-captain in
the Royal Navy and a member of a distinguished service family. He
was in command of the frigate *Clorinde* on which the Princess sailed
from Civita Vecchia to Genoa in March 1815, and in January 1816
from Messina to Syracuse. On the first occasion the Princess dined
at the Captain's table, and Pergami waited. 'Did he wait at dinner
as the other servants, as a menial servant?' 'He did.' Before the
Princess embarked on the second occasion the Captain sent her a

message to say that he was 'ready to do everything in my power to make her royal highness comfortable while on board the *Clorinde*, provided her royal highness would be pleased to make a sacrifice which my duty as an officer compelled me to exact, by not insisting on the admission to my table of a person of the name of Pergami. ... The Princess said that she would like to think it over, but later sent a message that the request would not be acceded to and that she would accordingly provide for her own table'. Brougham, perhaps wisely, did not cross-examine the captain but Lord Oxford, not perhaps a very astute member of the Whig Party, asked; 'Supposing a lad who waited at my table should have the good fortune to be made a midshipman in his majesty's service ... would you afterwards refuse to sit down with that person?' The Lord Chancellor refused to allow this question.

The next witness was another post-captain, Thomas Briggs afterwards commander-in-chief at Portsmouth. He was in command of the *Leviathan* and he was ordered to Genoa in November 1815 to convey the Princess to Sicily. She was accompanied by Pergami who always dined with the Princess at the Captain's table. There were two cabins in 'the after apartments' of the *Leviathan* and he intended one as a bedroom for the Princess and the other as a drawing-room. He intended to put the Countess Oldi and the maid-servants in two adjoining cabins, and the men were to go anywhere, 'some in the ward-room and some in my cabin, reserving one part to myself'. This plan was altered by the Princess. Pergami was placed in Countess Oldi's cabin in which the doors were altered. Captain Briggs said that it was he who had conveyed the message from Captain Pechell to the Princess about Pergami. He explained to the Princess that if Pergami had ever acted as a servant on his ship it would have been quite out of the question for him to dine at the Captain's table.

Lord Ellenborough, who perhaps had rather rudimentary ideas of the dignity of a captain, asked whether his sleeping-room was closed at night or 'did he hang in a cot (hammock)?' Captain Briggs explained that he slept in a room which was closed at night and that he would probably (though not certainly) have heard anyone passing his room. The peers asked a great number of questions about the cots in the dining-room in which members of the Princess's staff slept, about the doors to the cabins, whether they were hinged and about the screens round the cots. Lord Lauderdale asked for some amplification of the conversation between the Princess and the witness about Pergami dining at the captain's table. She told Captain Briggs that Pergami was as good company for Pechell as he was for Briggs and she added: 'Well, I do not care, it is only to prevent the trouble of your keeping two tables that he dines with me at all: I do not care then.' Lord Derby, by this time an elderly peer with some experience of life's pleasures, asked one question.

'When the alteration that you refer to took place in the cabins, was that by desire of her royal highness or any other persons?' 'It was by command of her royal highness, the princess, to me.'

The next witness was Pietro Cuchi, who described himself as agent at the great inn at Trieste. He was examined by the Solicitor-General. The Prime Minister asked what he meant by 'agent': this he described as acting instead of the owner, 'Madame, of the Albergo Grande'. He described how the Princess had come to the Albergo in 1816: she arrived in an open carriage with Pergami, the rest of her household arriving about an hour later. The rooms allotted to the Princess and Pergami adjoined the inn dining-room, though Pergami's room only opened into the dining-room through the bedroom where his sister, the Countess Oldi, was sleeping. Cuchi explained that there were two beds in the Princess's room, and one bed in Pergami's room. In the morning he had seen Pergami emerge from the Princess's bed-room, and he was asked how he was dressed. 'He had a surtout made according to the Polish fashion, which had some gold lace behind, that reached from the waist down.' Asked if Pergami was wearing stockings he said 'Sometimes stockings and sometimes pantaloons, which are stockings and pantaloons together: but this I cannot precisely say for I was looking out from the key-hole of my room.' The reason for this clandestine view of the proceedings was that Cuchi was waiting to take in the breakfast service. He said that when the vice-governor of the city came to take the Princess to the theatre she gave him her right hand and gave her left to Pergami.

'Did you make any observation on the beds in the bedroom of the princess, whether they had both been slept in?' 'They were both tumbled.'

'After Pergami went away, did you make any observation upon the sheets of the bed in the bed-room assigned to Pergami?' 'The sheets had been put on the bed clean, and they were taken away clean.'

'How many chamber-pots were there in the bed-room of the Princess?' 'Two.'

'Was either of the two empty?' 'There was a good deal in each.'

He was also examined about the two hand-basins, but he did not remember whether they had been used; 'there are many travellers who wish to have two basins, and yet they are alone'. He was asked about their departure. 'They set out together without servants in the same open carriage.'

After Cuchi's cross-examination the Solicitor-General concentrated questions on the key-hole. Under cross-examination Cuchi said that the door behind which he stood was entirely covered with canvas, so that only members of the family (meaning the servants at the Albergo) would have known that there was a door there. The Solicitor-General asked how he could see into the dining-room if the door was entirely covered with canvas. 'I could see because there is a key-hole that looks into the dining-room.' In answer to questions from the peers he explained that when he was obliged to serve something at stated hours for any guest at the Albergo he always looked through the key-hole so that he was ready to serve.

The next witness was Meidge Barbara Kress, a married woman living at Carlsruhe who, before her marriage, had been employed at the Post Inn at Carlsruhe. She was examined by the Attorney-General. Her examination revealed the arrangement of the bed-rooms in the hotel: as seemed the invariable custom they led out of the dining-room. The Princess was in Room 10, the dining-room was Room 11 and Pergami was in Room 12. Kress was instructed to put 'a broad bed' in Room 12 before the Princess arrived. One evening during the Princess's visit Kress was asked to carry up some water to Room 12. Pergami was in bed and the Princess 'had sat on the bed'. 'Could you see whether Pergami had his clothes on or off?' 'I could not see that: but I had seen as much in the moment I entered as that the arm was white.' She went on to say that this white arm was round the neck of the Princess, but she could not say for certain whether the whiteness was his shirt or any other dress he was wearing. She was asked what the Princess did, and answered 'The Princess had jumped up, and was alarmed at the moment.'

'Did she jump up on your coming into the room and discovering them in that situation?' 'Yes, she had then jumped up.' The answer is of course capable of meaning that she had by then jumped up or that her next action, after the interruption, was to jump up, and there was considerable criticism of the interpreter. The Attorney-General asked the interpreter what the witness had really intended to say. Here Brougham genially observed that the Attorney-General was putting the question to the interpreter again because he had not got the answer which suited him. This led to what Lord Grey called 'bickering' between the two. The Marquis of Buckingham suggested that counsel ought to be instructed not to make such personal insinuations. Grey again intervened to express the hope that counsel would preserve a becoming sense of temper and not interrupt the coolness and decorum which ought to mark their proceedings. But when the questions were repeated the ambiguity remained. The interpreter said that the words used were *in der Hohe* 'in a state of being high'. The Bishop of Peterborough, who had lived for many years at Leipzig and had written a widely-read book in German against Napoleon, here interrupted to say that he did not think the interpreter gave the translation 'with the faithful meaning which the idiom of both languages required'. The Prime Minister said that no man was more competent than the right reverend prelate to judge of the fitness of the interpreter, and it was agreed that the Queen's counsel should be ready with their interpreter for the next day.

Examined on the following day the witness said: 'I saw that the princess jumped up, I withdrew, I was frightened.' Continuing, Meidge Kress said that she made the bed in Pergami's room, and that once she found a cloak in his bed. 'It was of silk, the colour grey.' Asked if she had ever seen anyone wearing the cloak she answered: 'I have seen a cloak the next day upon the Princess, but I cannot say it was the same ... it was of the same colour ... it was likewise silk.' She was then asked if, when making the bed, she had observed anything on the sheets. She used the word *wüste* in reply, meaning confused or in disorder. She was asked if she had made the beds of married persons, and she told the House that she had, and added that there were stains on the sheets on Pergami's bed.

Meidge Kress's evidence was, if true, crucial and it gave rise to a complete interruption of the proceedings and a highly involved wrangle over the technicalities of cross-examination. The point was raised on the ninth day of the trial, Saturday 26 August, and continued to be debated on the Monday and Tuesday. Counsel for the Queen asked to be permitted to cross-examine witnesses after the examination-in-chief but to be allowed to reserve till later the main part of their cross-examination. They complained that they were handicapped by a lack of knowledge about the witnesses, and that what they wished to do in this immediate cross-examination was to find out full particulars of those giving evidence against the Princess. The Lord Chancellor pointed out that this was inconsistent with the practice in the lower courts. However, after long discussion the House agreed that Brougham should be allowed to put the questions as he himself said 'within the narrow limits chalked out to me'. This meant that the questions were to be limited to particulars about the witnesses. After Brougham had cross-examined Meidge Kress for some time Lord Lauderdale, a warm partisan of the King in all these proceedings, interrupted to point out that the House had agreed to a cross-examination at this stage simply to deal with 'the situations in life' and 'places of residence' of the witnesses, but that Brougham was going far beyond this and was cross-examining Kress with the object of impeaching her credit as a witness. Brougham started to ask: 'Where do you live now?' He was stopped by general cries of 'No! No!', and the Lord Chancellor pointed out that such a question went 'directly to impeach her credit'. Presumably the reason was that Brougham was trying to show that she was in receipt of money from the supporters of the bill, who had brought her over and were housing her in London. After some debate the Lord Chancellor asked that those objecting to the question should say 'Non content'. The Non-Contents had it by a great majority.

But after a whole day's debate on the Monday, the Prime Minister on Tuesday advised the House to allow the Queen's counsel to cross-examine as they had asked. The principal reason for this change-about seems to have been that as Brougham had already been allowed to give Majocchi a second cross-examination and to give a preliminary cross-examination to Kress the House would have become inextricably entangled if they had now attempted to go back on their permission. It was moved by the Prime Minister—the motion subsequently standing in the name of Lord Harrowby, the Lord President of the Council—that 'under the special circumstances of the case' counsel should be allowed 'to proceed in the cross-examination in the way in which they had proposed'. The Lord Chancellor opposed it saying (as he must often have said when trying and delaying a cause in chancery) 'the only safe way is to adhere to established rules . . . I have tormented my mind with considering this subject in every light'. Counsel were permitted to argue the matter and Brougham was at his most masterly. He was light-hearted. 'Did their lordships believe that there was so much magic in the dress of a counsel at the bar, or such charm in his education and legal acquirements, as that he could at sight of a witness whom he never saw, nor ever heard of before, strike upon all those points of character and conduct which it were necessary to sift to ascertain moral credibility . . . he had as it were to eviscerate the truth from the witness.' And he could be serious. 'Oh my lords, monstrous indeed will be the disadvantage to which we shall here be exposed, in comparison with the situation in which the courts of common law would place us, if your lordships will now tell us that the course of your proceeding, and the only course will be, first to hear the examination-in-chief, then the cross-examination, then the re-examination, and after that nothing but what shall be previously submitted to the opinion of your lordships: no question to be asked a witness except through your lordships: no series of uninterrupted questions to be allowed us in the situation in which we are placed . . . monstrous will be the disadvantages which must environ us in the performance of our duty; and still more monstrous is it to tell me, that this is done in conformity with the ordinary rules of law.'

Lord Erskine, a former Lord Chancellor, a close friend of the Regent and now a septuagenarian, fought throughout the tangled debate for the Queen's counsel to be given a list of the witnesses to be called against her. Erskine also urged that the House should no longer meet *die in diem* but that they should forthwith adjourn to give the Queen time to prepare her defence. His efforts drew forth a notable tribute to him from his fellow Whig Lord Holland—'The attachment which he felt towards such a man, acting still, in the decline of life, upon the same noble principles which rendered his name illustrious at its outset, even degraded as the House stood in this disgusting business, compensated him, in some degree, by the gratification and delight which it elicited by the display of so much personal worth. . . .' But in the result Erskine's motion was heavily defeated and Harrowby's motion was carried by the narrow majority of 15.

In his cross-examination Brougham brought out the early life story of Kress. She had been chambermaid at the Post Inn at Carlsruhe for a year and three-quarters, until she married. She had been in service with various families in Germany ever since she left school. 'How old are you now?' 'Past 25.' Latterly she had been cellar-maid in various inns. 'Is *Kellermädchen*, which you have described yourself to have been, a woman who attends upon the man-keller?' 'She has nothing to attend to, but to clean the rooms of the inn.' She explained that she had been originally asked to come over and give evidence by 'our minister'—meaning Baron Berstett the Baden foreign secretary. She had also been approached by the ambassador from Württemberg[1] and by the Hanoverian ambassador, de Reden. She explained that she had been examined about her evidence in Hanover, and that she had also been interviewed in Frankfort where she had made it plain that she was reluctant to go to England. She was given a ducat for her trouble; she said that she would not go to England, but she was told that she might 'be obliged to go'. When Brougham asked 'Where do you live at present in England?' there were cries of 'withdraw, order, go on' and this set off the long discussion on cross-examination which has been described in the preceding pages.

[1] Baron Grimm. Some of the information about the Princess's behaviour was reported by minor German diplomats such as Grimm. The Queen Dowager of Württemberg was the Regent's sister.

The eleventh day, 29 August, started with Brougham's main examination of Meidge Kress. He began by asking where she lived in London, but as she could only say that she came, from where she was staying, by coach over a bridge, little progress was made. She gave some rather pitiful particulars of her family's background; her brother was a potter, a master-potter, her father was a serjeant in the army, and her father-in-law was a retired master-weaver. She denied that she had been paid anything for giving evidence except a '*dedommagement*', which was interpreted as 'compensation for the time lost'. She had begged not to be made to come over 'for I am a married woman, and I have other business to attend to'. She had used the words '*Entschädigung*' and '*Belohnung*' and once again the learned Bishop of Peterborough rose to point out that the former meant reward, the latter atonement for loss. In the course of her cross-examination she had admitted to being given some ducats to cover the cost of her journey to Hanover and she added that she had also been given one ducat by a gentleman in Frankfort for her trouble in calling on him. Brougham enjoyed himself asking if the 'ducat gentleman of Frankfort' gave her the ducat as an *Entschädigung* or *Belohnung*. She replied 'it may be an *Entschädigung* for my lost time'. Brougham asked her if when she was in Frankfort she had seen a gentleman called Mandeville and, sinking rather low, or Man Devil (laughter). 'I cannot recollect the name.'[1]

Brougham then questioned her about people coming to see the inn when the Princess was there. It was suggested that the Duke of Baden's minister (Berstett), a diplomat, came and Herr von Grimm —'As much as I could hear he is the ambassador of Württemberg.' Grimm had formerly lodged in the rooms occupied by the Princess, and moved into other rooms when she came. 'Did he not return after the princess left, and go into No 12 to look at what was there?' 'Yes, he ran about just when the rooms were left open, and he took again the room afterward.' She was asked about the Glashuit—a place near the gate of the city in which glass was made and the surroundings of which made an attractive pleasure-garden. She ex-

[1] This was presumably J. H. Mandeville, the secretary to the British Embassy at Frankfort. He lived till the 1860's, with a fund of anecdotes and reminiscences about old diplomatic life.

plained that she had been there only with her husband or with other servants and maids, and that before she married she went there by day—never at night. In the middle of her evidence Lord Hardwicke became suddenly indisposed and had to be immediately taken out of the House. It was evidently extremely hot and, following the interruption, Meidge Kress was overcome, and had to be revived with libations of cold water.

Examined by the peers she was asked whether, when the courier arrived, before the princess, and ordered a broader bed, he had given any reason. Brougham at once objected that what the courier said could not be received in evidence. Lord Mansfield, a strong Tory, asked whether the bed, when she made it, had the appearance of having been slept in by two people. Her reply was somewhat curious 'No, the cushions or pillows lay one upon the other—so far I recollect.' Lord Hood, the son of the Princess's old admirer from Greenwich days and himself one of her most ardent partisans, asked whether she had spoken to anybody else about the princess and Pergami. She denied doing this, but said that Monsieur Grimm had asked her about it. Lord Hood then asked 'How could Monsieur Grimm know anything about it, unless you had communicated it to someone?' There were murmurs of disapproval from the Lords, and Lord Hood was made to withdraw the question. He extracted from the witness that, pressed by Monsieur Grimm, she 'said it'. 'What were you asked?' 'He asked me have you never seen anything.' Lord Lauderdale, evidently with Lord Hood's questions in mind, said that these were not calculated to elicit or explain facts, or to lead to 'a just knowledge of the affair'—meaning presumably that they were aimed at the reliability of the witness. He thought it his duty to say this because their proceedings went out to the public in a manner that excited such a feeling as he had never before witnessed in the whole course of his life.

On the twelfth day, which was 30 August, the first witness was Paolo Raggazoni. He said that he was a master-mason, with 20, 25 or 30 men under him, and that he had been employed at the Villa d'Este. He said that while working there he had seen the Princess and Pergami walking in the garden arm-in-arm, and that he had seen them on the Lake alone in a canoe 'more than once, more than twice'.

He had also seen them in the garden 'the princess sitting in a chair with wheels or castors, and the baron behind pushing her to make her go'. Afterwards the baron got in the chair and was pushed by the princess. On one occasion Raggazoni was in a grotto in the garden, making a cornice to a round room. He heard someone come in to the adjoining room 'and I put myself under the scaffold to see who it was, and I saw Pergami and the Princess come: there were two figures, the figure of Adam on the right and the figure of Eve on the left, and Adam had the leaf of a fig below the navel, then they looked at those figures of Adam and Eve, and they laughed together.'

'You have told us that Adam had a fig-leaf. Was there any fig-leaf to Eve?' 'Yes.'

'Can you state how they were fastened on?' 'They were fastened with a little bough: they put aside this fig-leaf to see what was underneath.'

'When they removed the leaf in the manner you have described, what did they do?' 'They talked together, and looked sometimes at one sometimes at another, between themselves, laughing.'

One point in Raggazoni's evidence gave some difficulty. He referred to seeing the Princess and Pergami alone in the garden after an entertainment on S. Bartholomew's Day at the Villa D'Este. This was at one or half-past one at night. But in most parts of Italy the 24 hour clock was used, which was based on the principle that the 24 hours ended half an hour after the sinking of the sun, 'the immersion of the disk'. In winter, for example, noon in Italy was just after 7 p.m. Half past one in this case was consequently thought to be about half-past nine.

Raggazoni was cross-examined by Stephen Lushington, a fellow of All Souls and member of Lincoln's Inn, who was an ardent social reformer and was later to become judge of the Admiralty Court for many years. Raggazoni informed the House that he had been told by Rastelli, who is to appear later in this narrative as a witness, that 'I must go to Milan by order of the Government. . . . He told me "You must go because you have been living with the Princess at Como, and therefore you must go, and tell what you know." ' He explained how he had gone to Milan, been examined by Vimercati—

he was an Italian advocate, and the agent in Italy for the Milan Commission—and he was asked by Lushington in what manner he had been sworn before giving this evidence—'I took the oath upon the cross; I took the cross which I carry about with me, and I kissed it myself before Vimercati.' Lushington pressed him about his payment for the journey to Milan 'I have received nothing, not even this, which means not even a pin, not even a drop of water. I took my horse, I mounted my horse and I went.' Reverting at the end of his cross-examination to his reluctance to come to England he said that he had told 'the curate of my country [i.e. his priest], that I did not wish to come, and he told me that I must go'. Otherwise he denied that he had mentioned to anyone (except Vimercati) the facts which he gave in evidence. Re-examining him the Solicitor-General, in reference to his denial in the previous sentence said: 'Look at this gentleman (Mr. Bourchier); were any questions asked you in the place near this court, as to the circumstances to which you have now deposed?' Presumably the Italian witnesses were prepared before they gave evidence (as is customary in all English courts) about what they should say, what they should avoid saying and what they might expect in cross-examination. This was done, no doubt, in the part of the House of Lords prepared for the witnesses: Mr. Bourchier was Charles Bourchier, one of the partners with George Maule in the firm of solicitors conducting the King's case. Brougham strongly objected to the question not only because it was a leading question, but because it was quite irregular for counsel to set up his own witness to contradict himself. The Lord Chancellor and judges allowed the question, and the Lord Chancellor asked that the question and answer in cross-examination should be read. The shorthand writer was W. B. Gurney, who is referred to in Byron's 'Don Juan'.[1] His office was in Essex Street off the Strand and as he finished his sheets they were taken quickly for transcription to his office in Essex Street. Consequently there was some delay before the sheets could be retrieved, but finally Raggazoni made it clear that he thought the question—'From the time that you signed your deposition at Milan, have you had any conversation as to these facts, till to-day,

---

[1] He has been described by a distinguished lawyer, Lord Abinger, as 'an artist in stenography'.

with any person whatever?' referred to any conversation in Italy before he came to England.

The next witness was Paolo Oggioni, the under-cook at the Villa d'Este. He said that he first knew Pergami at Lodi between 1805 and 1809—'I have seen him about Lodi and I have seen him in prison.' Denman objected to this answer. The Attorney-General said: 'I thought I was justified in asking where the witness had seen Pergami in prison ... the question is not very important.' He was then asked about the balls given at the Barona and said that they were attended by 'country people of low rank in life'. The Princess did not dance with them: she either danced by herself or 'sometimes with Pergami'. Among the guests were the wife of the innkeeper and the daughters of the tenant who farmed the land of the Barona. He gave much the same evidence as had been given by the previous witnesses about Mahomet's dance. When he was asked what Mahomet did with his trousers he made certain motions which, as he was facing the peers, could not be exactly seen by those reporting below the bar.

He was cross-examined by Thomas Wilde, afterwards Lord Truro and Lord Chancellor. Wilde was plain, rather undistinguished in appearance with a stammering, monotonous voice and was not welcomed with open arms by Brougham and Denman, though he quickly established his pre-eminence in cross-examination. He began, with the amiable suggestion that Oggioni had been dismissed for drunkenness by the princess. This the witness denied. On leaving the service of the Princess he had been employed by a priest —the minister of the great hospital at Milan. He was particularly pressed whether the person examining him in England, 'held in his hand any paper to examine you from'. 'He did write, but I do not know what paper he had: he wrote down what I said.' Wilde then asked: 'The question is whether the person who examined you read a paper?' 'He did.' He was re-examined by the Attorney-General on this point who asked 'did he read it aloud to you, or was he reading it to himself?' 'He read it to himself.'

The examination by the Lords turned on the dances by Mahomet. Oggioni was asked to state whether her Royal Highness sent for Mahomet to perform the dance before her. 'Her Royal Highness never sent for Mahomet, her royal highness altogether did not send for Mahomet.' This was a baffling answer and the Prime Minister asked that it should be read over again. 'Her Royal Highness did not send for him—not altogether.' He was then asked whether he meant that he was not sent to fetch Mahomet or that she did not send for him at all. 'I don't know that any person was sent. When she came I saw her, but how long she stayed I paid no attention to, for I attended to my duty.' He added that she appeared to receive 'very great' gratification on these occasions. Lord Lansdowne asked him if he knew what the roll of Mahomet's breeches was intended to represent. 'It seems as if it was the *membrum virile*.' Lord Darnley wished to know if women were present during this exhibition as well as men. 'There were no women.' Lord Falmouth, a Tory, wanted to know who invited the company to the balls. 'They came; but I don't know who invited them, because I attended to my own business.' 'Then I understand they were not servants' balls?' 'They were not.'

5

Demont—La Chienne

≥o⊆≥

Oggioni was followed by the most important and most notorious of the witnesses—Louisa Demont, the Princess's *femme de chambre* or, as Creevey employing the same language, preferred to call her *la chienne Demont*. She was thought to be about 36, and was described as a brunette with an eye which was more remarkable for cunning than for intellect. Her dress was noticed. She wore a handsome, black satin hat ornamented with feathers, with a black veil falling down from one side. At the neck she wore a white muslin ruff 'highly plaited'. Her dress was black satin, 'vandyked at the top' and profusely decorated with flounces at the bottom. As an observer remarked 'she is the smartest-dressed of *femmes-de-chambre* but neither the youngest nor the prettiest'.

She was examined by the Solicitor-General. She said that she was a protestant, a Swiss and that she lived at Colombier just north of Lake Geneva. She was engaged as *femme-de-chambre* in 1814 when the Princess was travelling from north Germany through Switzerland to Italy. Much of the early part of her evidence—the engagement of Pergami as courtier, the sleeping arrangements at Naples, corroborated in detail what had already been said by Majocchi. When the royal party arrived in Naples she said that she did not remember the sleeping arrangements for the first night, but that on the second they were as described in Majocchi's evidence—Pergami's bedroom was near her Royal Highness's room and they were connected by the small cabinet, with the fire-place, and a passage. On the night in question the Princess had been to the opera and she told Demont, on getting back, that she did not wish William

00

Austin to enter her room 'because she wished to sleep quietly'. She had previously told Demont that Austin had become 'too big a boy' to sleep in her own room. She explained that in the princess's room were two beds—a large one and her Royal Highness's small travelling-bed. There were no sheets on the big bed. That evening the Princess was 'extremely agitated'. On the next morning she noticed that the little travelling-bed had not been occupied but that the larger bed had.

'Do you remember ever seeing Pergami at night in the passage of which you have made mention?' 'I do.'

'Where was her Royal Highness at that time?' 'In her bed-room.'

'Was she dressed or undressed or in what state?' 'She was un-dressed...I saw Pergami come out of his room and into the passage...he was going towards the bedroom of her Royal High-ness.'

'What was the state of Pergami's dress...?' 'He was not dressed.'

'...What had he on?' 'He was not dressed at all.'

'Do you remember what he had on his feet?' 'Slippers.'

'Do you remember whether he had any stockings on?' 'I saw no stockings.'

'Had he on any thing more than his shirt?' 'Nothing else.'

'When you saw Pergami coming along the passage...what did you do?' 'I escaped by the little door which was near me out of the apartment of the Princess.'

She was then asked about the appearance of 'the great bed' on subsequent nights. 'I have always seen the same thing—more than one person.'

She filled in the details of the fancy-dress ball at Murat's, the King of Naples, where it will be remembered from Majocchi's evidence that the Princess made three changes of costume, starting with the not particularly original idea of a Neapolitan peasant. Thus attired she stayed at the ball for about an hour, and then came back to change: Demont stayed in the ante-room but Pergami went with the Princess into her dressing-room.

'What dress did she assume the second time, what character?'

'The Genius of History. . . . She had her arms bare, and her breast bare, and the drapery in the same way as people represent the muses, or the Genius of History.'

'When you describe the arms bare, up to what part do you mean; the entire arm, or how?' 'I did not observe whether they were completely bare.'

She went on to say that the Princess stayed for about three-quarters of an hour as the Genius of History, and then returned again to change into a dress 'something like a Turkish peasant: something that had the appearance of it'. On this occasion Pergami stayed in the ante-room and emerged 'dressed like a Turk'. Together they went back to the ball, 'the Princess was under the arm of Pergami'.

She was then asked about an occasion when the Princess went to the San Carlo opera-house at Naples accompanied by her (Demont) and Pergami. 'Her Royal Highness was dressed in a red cloak; a very large cloak.' Pergami was dressed in a red domino with a large hat. When they got to the opera-house they went down to the pit and 'many ugly masks surrounded us, and began to make a great noise and hissed us'.

'Was there anything particular in the dress which her Royal Highness wore?' 'Her dress was very ugly, monstrous.' Lord Hampden, who had been in the diplomatic service in Turin, here interjected 'Very ugly—monstrously ugly dress'. Brougham strongly objected here—'One of the judges in this case enlarges the expression given in evidence by a construction which the words do not bear . . . a noble lord thinks himself called on . . .'. The Lord Chancellor interrupted him to say that 'if a noble lord did not think the answer correct, he had a right to have it corrected'.

Demont went on to describe the time when the Princess was at Genoa, the arrangements of the rooms, and the occasions when the Princess and Pergami breakfasted together. When they were there the Princess went to see a house in the country with a view to taking it because it was distant from Genoa 'where there were many English'. When Lady Charlotte Campbell left the Princess's service the Countess Oldi took her place. The Princess told Demont that the Countess wished to come as a *dame d'honneur* and that she was 'a noble lady'. Two months later Demont learned that she was Pergami's sister. She did not speak French at all, and Demont observed that 'she spoke very vulgar Italian'.

'Did you ever see any of her writing in Italian?' Brougham here objected, adding with sarcasm that 'it was the first time a woman has been asked to criticize the style of another woman in a language which is not her own . . . we beg that the opinion of this Swiss chambermaid on the manners of ladies of distinction may be put down and registered.' Demont was then asked: 'Did you make any observation upon the manners of the Countess Oldi; whether they were the manners, in your judgment of a gentlewoman or not?' Before she could answer the interpreter who, it will be remembered, was an Italian and had been rather floundering among the French idioms, said that he was in a difficulty because there was not such a word as 'gentlewoman' in the French language. This remark occasioned much laughter.

Demont then gave evidence about the sleeping arrangements at the Villa d'Este and on the Princess's travels in Italy. These were directed to the same points—Pergami invariably slept in a room near the Princess: Demont helped the Princess to undress and left the bedroom; the Princess invariably locked the door behind her. 'I have heard several times her Royal Highness lock it with a key after I was gone out.' (On all occasions there seems to have been another door giving access to the room in which Pergami slept.) When the Princess was in Sicily at Augusta her portrait was painted —once as a Turkish woman, and once as a penitent Magdalen. The latter picture was a three-quarter length.

'How was the upper part of the person, covered or uncovered, in the picture?' 'Uncovered.'

'How was the breast, was that covered or uncovered?' 'Uncovered. . . . As far as here (Passing her hand across her breast) . . . It was uncovered as far as here, about the middle of it.'

'Did you ever see that portrait in the possession of any person?' 'Pergami showed it me one day at Augusta.'

'Pergami's portrait was also painted at this time 'as a Turk'. According to the Turkish custom 'his dress was open as far as here' (the upper part of the chest). Demont added that she had seen one of the portraits of Pergami in a little box belonging to the Princess, and it was the one 'in the Turkish character'.

She gave some rather curious evidence about ear-rings. She was asked whether Pergami—when he first came into the service of her Royal Highness—had worn any ear-rings. She said that he had worn them and had later changed them for others. Later she saw the ear-rings which he had first worn 'in the ears of her Royal Highness'. Similarly the Princess wore the ear-rings of Victorine, sometimes wearing both the child's and Pergami's. 'She had two upon each ear, but separate: one of each pair upon each ear.... They were both in the same opening or hole.' The Princess did not confine her adoption of Pergami's effects to adornments. As a courier he had been accustomed to wear a red, silk cap. 'I saw a cap of red silk, of the same make on the head of the Princess.' She had also remembered seeing 'several times' in the Princess's room a black silk cravat which Pergami often wore in the morning. She was asked whether she knew what the French mean by *tutoyé*?' She said that she did, and that the Princess, addressing Pergami, often said 'thou' and that Pergami, when addressing her, merely said 'Princess'.

Demont had added some strange though incomplete facts about the ball at the Barona. She was asked whether she had ever heard Pergami say anything to the Princess about the behaviour of the guests on this occasion. She replied that Pergami had told a story to the Princess of something which had happened in the house then. 'The story was so indelicate I dare not repeat it.' She agreed that she was present when Pergami told the story to the Princess. The peers now grew rather restive—whether through feelings of modesty or anticipation history does not relate. Copley, for a lawyer, made a somewhat odd suggestion to the witness—'Without particularly mentioning the story, can you tell us generally what it was?' 'I have told you that I cannot repeat it.' At this the peers cried 'Strike it out', but there were a few cries of 'No'. Copley then said as though he had been a member of a masculine party over the port: 'Tell us what the story was.' 'It was a fullsome story relating to a gentleman and one of the young women.'

'What did Pergami tell of what passed between this person and the young woman?' 'He said all that had passed upon the bed....

Pergami related all that had passed.' The House was much dissatisfied with this piece of evidence, and the Lord Chancellor directed that it should be struck out.

Demont described an occasion when the Princess was staying at Scharnitz about 20 miles north of Innsbrück. Pergami had gone to Innsbrück to deal with passports, and Demont went to bed in the bedroom with the Princess. They went to bed at ten, Demont sleeping in a small bed on the floor. After she had been asleep, Pergami returned from Innsbrück and 'the Princess told me that I might take my bed and go'. She said that when this order was given Pergami was in the bed-room.

Later the Solicitor-General asked 'Did you ever see her Royal Highness in pantaloons?' Demont said that she had, and that Pergami also was present. 'Pergami turned round her Royal Highness, looking at her, and said "How pretty you are, I like you much better so."'

'At the time when you describe her Royal Highness as being in pantaloons, what was the state of her neck and her breast?' 'Uncovered; she was at her toilet, and was dressing herself.' Demont had been examined for a long time: she had asked to have a chair once and she had also asked permission to retire for a short time. The House adjourned at twenty to four on 31 August. Her ordeal was really to begin on the next day.

Her cross-examination by Williams started at 10 o'clock on 1 September: it lasted till well into the next day. Williams severely, suggesting that she knew sufficient English to understand the questions which had been put to her on the previous day by the Solicitor-General: 'Did you understand most of them, aye or no?' 'I understood some of them.'

'Did you understand the greater number or not?' 'I understood some of those which were the shortest, some of them.' She was then asked whether she had always been known in England as Louisa Demont. 'I took the name of the place where I was born, Colombier.' It was then suggested that when she was living in London, in Frith Street, she had passed herself off as Countess Colombiera. To all such suggestions her replies were uniform: 'I will not swear it, but I do not recollect it.' 'Was it a matter of no singularity to you being called the Countess?' But the peers made it clear that they were not going to allow bullying, and from some of them came loud cries of 'Order'.

Among a multiplicity of questions about the beds at Naples Williams paid some attention to Demont's own sleeping habits.

'Where did you sleep yourself at Naples?' 'In a little apartment above, above her Royal Highness's.'

'Did you sleep alone in that room?' 'We had two rooms, in the one of them I slept.'

'Did you sleep alone in that room?' 'I slept alone in that room.'

'Every night?' 'Every night.'

'That you will now swear?' 'That I slept in my room alone? Yes, I slept every night in my room alone.'

'The whole night?' 'The whole night in my room.'

'Alone?' 'Alone.'

'Every night and the whole of the night alone?' 'I slept all alone in my room.'

It was suggested to Demont that when the Princess wore the costume of Genius of History she went straight into the room where the Neapolitan gentry and nobility were assembled. It was also suggested that when she wore the Turkish dress other members of her suite also wore Turkish clothes so that they all formed a group. Later in the cross-examination, a small point arose which illustrated the interruptions to which counsel were liable and at which they complained. When the peers had cried 'Order, Order' at one of Williams's questions he said before reframing the question: 'After such an interruption I must have a little time to consider.' Asking about the land journey to Jerusalem, Williams said:

'Was not your sister, during that journey, constantly near the Princess?' 'When we stopped I sometimes was *auprès de* (near) her Royal Highness.'

Some difference here arose as to the proper translation of the word *auprès*.

A Peer said the word meant 'with'.

The Solicitor-General repeated the word 'with' to the interpreter.

Mr. Denman desired the interpreter would not take the meaning of the witness from the Solicitor-General.

The Solicitor-General.—'The suggestion was not mine, it came from a noble lord.'

Mr. Denman—'I object equally, although the suggestion did come from a noble lord. The interpreter was sworn, and such interference was most irregular.'

The Lord Chancellor.—'The English and French words must be both put down.'

Evidently the Queen's counsel had some grounds for thinking that Demont had not always been scrupulous about her own sleeping habits, especially at sea. 'Do you remember taking on board at Tunis a harper?' 'Yes.'

'A Jew?' 'Yes.'

She said that the harper slept in a cabin at the end of the vessel.

'Do you mean to swear that the Jew harper slept there every night on the voyage from Tunis until you landed?' 'I do not know where he slept every night.'

'Will you swear that you do not know where he slept any one night?' 'I recollect having heard that he slept there, but I never saw him: I do not remember precisely.'

'Then you do not know, do you, where he slept any one night, of your own knowledge?' 'No, I said that I did not know myself where he slept, but that I was told.'

'Nor any part of any night of your own knowledge?' 'Nor by my own knowledge.'

Demont admitted that she had been discharged from the Princess's service 'for saying something which I afterwards admitted to be false'.

Much of Demont's cross-examination was taken up with the contents of two letters—one to her half-sister, who was employed by the Princess, and the other to the Princess. These letters were in possession of the defence. Translations of the letters were put in by Brougham at the end of the cross-examination. They were written in 1817 shortly after Demont was dismissed by the Princess.

In the letter to her sister she describes innocent Swiss gaieties—'you know how fond I am of going on a sledge', but admits that she could not get rid of deep sadness at having been misunderstood by her Royal Highness. She said that in a numerous circle of friends she had expatiated on the many virtues of the Princess. She had kept a journal when she was with the Princess and this, which described the traits of sensibility and generosity which the Princess had shown on her travels, was handed round among Demont's friends in Lausanne. She went on to say that she had been asked to go to London 'under the false pretence of being a governess. . . . You see, my dear, with what promptitude the enemies of our generous benefactress always act.' The letter trails off with domestic details about clothes and furniture and the asthma and bowel pains of 'our good mother'. She referred to Monsieur ———— who wished to marry her, and ended by begging her sister to persuade her Royal Highness that 'my life shall be for ever consecrated to her'.

The second letter, which was written to the Princess, implored forgiveness 'which alone can restore me to life'.

For a long time Williams cross-examined Demont on various passages in these letters before they had been given in evidence; the point of this being that he was trying to shake the credit of the witness—to make her deny having written certain sentiments. Williams, for example, quoted a passage from the letter: 'You know that when this august princess is my subject I am inexhaustible. . . .'

'Will you swear you did not use the expressions which have just been put to you?' 'I will not swear because I am not sure of it.'

'Will you swear that you did not use them?' 'I will not swear because I am not sure of it.'

'Have you any doubt whether you did use them?' 'I do not recollect whether I have made use of them; I wrote frequently to my sister, and I do not recollect the expressions.'

The mode of cross-examination gave rise to a close, legal argument which was referred to the judges. They stated that in the lower courts a party could only be cross-examined on the contents of a letter if the witness were first shown the letter, and asked if he or she wrote it.

On the following day, 2 September, after some preliminary questions about the expense of her journey, her examination before Mr. Powell and the method by which she was sworn, Williams read the two letters. In the re-examination which followed the cross-examination by Williams on the same day, she set out the circumstances of her dismissal from the Princess's household.

'You stated yesterday, that you were dismissed for saying something which was not true; that in effect it was not true; explain the circumstances of your dismissal, and for what cause it was you were dismissed from the service.' 'I was dismissed from the service of her Royal Highness, because she had been told that Mr. Sacchi[1] had given out that her Royal Highness was in love with him, and that it was I that had told him from the Princess. I wrote a letter to Mr. Sacchi; this letter was taken up at the post; and because I said at the end of the letter, that the Princess loved and esteemed Mr. Sacchi as before—"*aimoit*" has two senses—as in the former time; I explained to her Royal Highness that I did not mean at all that it was love, but that her Royal Highness liked Mr. Sacchi in the same manner as other persons in her household. After this letter I was dismissed, because her Royal Highness thought that it meant love; and yet it was not love at all that I intended.'

'What were the expressions which were canvassed by her Royal Highness, the particular expressions which you allude to?' 'As far as I can remember, I said in the letter that her Royal Highness loved in the sense I have explained, and esteemed Mr. Sacchi as in former time; the words that I used were "*aimoit y estimoit comme dans le tems passé*", loved and esteemed as in the time past.'

'Where was that letter written?' 'At Pesaro.'

'That letter in which those words were used, "*aimoit y estimoit comme dans le tems passé*"?' 'Yes.'

'While you were writing that letter, did any person come into the room?' 'Mr. Pergami.'

'Did he see you writing?' 'Yes.'

'Did you put the letter into the post-office yourself?' 'Myself.'

'With your own hand?' 'With my hand.'

'Did you, on the following morning, see that letter in the possession of any person?' 'Yes.'

'In whose hands?' 'In the Princess's hands.'

[1] He was the Princess's courier, and a subsequent witness against her.

'Did you afterwards write a second letter?' 'Yes.'

'Was that letter also intercepted?'

Mr. Brougham objected to the question, stating that there was no proof of the former letter having been intercepted.

'Did you afterwards see that second letter?' 'I saw it a long time afterwards.'

'When you were writing that second letter, did you communicate the contents of it to any person?' 'To nobody.'

'To whom was that second letter addressed?' 'It was not addressed to Mr. Sacchi, there was another name; I do not recollect whether it was Penchaud[1] or not.'

'You have stated, that you did not communicate the contents of that second letter to any person; did her Royal Highness afterwards say anything to you about the contents of that second letter?' 'It was after this second letter that I was dismissed.'

'Did her Royal Highness mention any part of the contents of the second letter to you?' 'I do not recollect that she mentioned about the second.'

'Did you ever, on any occasion, state that her Royal Highness was in love with Sacchi?' 'No.'

'You have stated that Mr. Pergami was present at the time that her Royal Highness produced the letter, which you had put into the post-office?' 'Yes.'

'Can you state what he said in the presence of her Royal Highness at that interview, when they were talking about your dismissal?' 'Respecting the letter he said, that it was true I had said the Princess was in love with Mr. Sacchi. I made a proposal to the Princess, to write to Mr. Sacchi in order to have the truth from him, and Mr. Pergami opposed it.'

'What else did he do?' 'Mr. Pergami accused me of having passed a night in the corridor with Mr. Sacchi. I said that my sister was present, and might declare that I had slept with her.'

'Was your sister present?' 'My sister was there.'

'Had you slept with your sister?' 'I had slept with my sister.'

'Was that charge which was made by Pergami true?' 'It was not true.'

[1] A servant of the Princess.

The examination by the Lords opened with some questions about the large bed at Naples.

'State distinctly what was the state of that bed?' 'The bed-cover was extremely pressed down in the middle, and there were things upon the bed which I had never seen before.'

'What were those things?' 'Large stains.'

'Were those on the outside cover of the bed, or on the inside?' 'Upon the cover.' She later explained that the cover was white.

Moving to a different topic she said that, at the ball at La Barona, 'the women who were at the ball went out with the servants all about the house, and I also saw them going into the upper rooms'.

The paragraph in the letter describing what happened when she was taking 'some refreshment at my Aunt Clara's' and the messenger arrived asking her to go to London inspired many questions particularly the allusions to the enemies and spies round 'our generous benefactress'. She explained that these and similar remarks were included as *doubles entendres* which would be understood by her sister. She also explained that she was afraid her letter would be intercepted, and a peer at once asked why—if she really thought that—did she expose Monsieur ———— . (When the letter was first read Demont made a point of asking that the mention of his name should be excluded.) The long examination ended with a series of questions about the famous bath on the polacca. She was asked if she remembered seeing any wet linen lying about, and she said that she did not remember seeing any. Lord Morton contributed the curious piece of information that 'in that part of the world' it was not necessarily usual for people to use linen on coming out of salt-water.

Luigi Galdini was then examined. He explained that he was a mason with 15 or more men working under him. He was responsible for building the house of the Princess's agent at the Villa d'Este who was called Guggiaro. Galdini was making a cornice and Guggiaro told him on a certain evening to collect all the materials he wanted—plaster of Paris, marble and sand 'for I was working by contract'. As these materials had not come by nine o'clock on the following morning Galdini went up to the Villa d'Este to find

Guggiaro. He went into a room and saw Pergami and the Princess sitting together, he with his arm around her neck.

'How was the Princess dressed as to her bosom?' 'She was uncovered so' (passing his hand across his breast). He was then asked what the Baron did. 'He took away his arm from the neck of the Princess, got up and told me, what do you want from here, you dog?' The interpreter interjected that the words used were rather stronger than he had said, '*Razza di cane*' meaning 'Son of a dog'. He was cross-examined along the usual lines about payment and mixing in London with the other witnesses. The Prime Minister, recalling what Galdini had said in evidence asked 'do you mean that the breasts were bare?' 'I saw it so, and, as far as I saw, I saw it uncovered.' The Lord Chancellor then said 'how far did you see the breasts uncovered?' 'I did not stay to look; I saw it, and made my escape; I saw it in the twinkling of an eye, and it was uncovered as far as here; I saw the breasts (*ho veduto le mammelle*); I saw the breasts.'

The Duke of Hamilton, who was a partisan of the Princess, then asked exactly how the Baron's arm was placed. 'I am the Baron, and you (the interpreter) are the Princess (putting his arm round the neck of the interpreter).' He was then asked if the Baron's arm was on the Princess's breast. 'I have repeated it many times. I have even shewn it; must I repeat the same thing over again; I cannot say more.' A peer drew attention to the indecency of the witness's conduct in making such motions and then laughing. The Lord Chancellor thought it inexcusable. A few other witnesses followed in rapid succession and testified to seeing Pergami and the Princess together, seeing them kissing and walking 'arm in arm as man and wife'. One of these witnesses described how the Princess kept a nightingale and it was his duty to carry meat (presumably food) to the nightingale. Once when doing this he saw Pergami and the Princess kissing, and heard the Princess say 'Do not remain so long out, mon cœur.'

Giuseppe Rastelli gave evidence on Monday, 4 September. He had been the head superintendent of the Princess's stables and had served her for rather more than a year from the autumn of 1816. He used to accompany the Princess on horseback when she was out driving, and it was his duty to come to the carriage to receive instructions about the road they should take. On one occasion he rode up to the carriage for this purpose, and noticed that the Princess's hand was 'in the small clothes of Mr. Pergami'. 'Did you see that distinctly?' 'I saw it distinctly: I was ashamed at the moment when I came to the door.' In conclusion he was asked if he had ever seen the wife of Pergami. He said that he had seen her at the Barona 'but always when the Princess was not there'.

His cross-examination started with the suggestion that he had been dismissed from the service of the Princess for stealing corn. This he denied. He admitted that after leaving her service he had acted as a courier for the Milan Commission and was busy in collecting witnesses from North Italy and from Germany. He explained that he was in receipt of a pension of 260 livres a year on account of his services to Prince Eugene when he was Viceroy. Neither the peers nor the Queen's counsel could disturb his account of what he had seen when he rode up for orders to the open carriage.

The last important witness in support of the bill was Giuseppe Sacchi who had served the Princess as courier and equerry for a year. It was of these concluding witnesses that Creevey wrote 'much *dirt* and some *damage*'. Apart from confirming much that had been said about the arrangement of the rooms and the evidence about Pergami's access to the Princess's bedroom Sacchi contributed three salient points. He described a conversation which he had had with the Princess after the celebrated ball, with its undistinguished company, at the Barona. 'One day whilst I was in the court, and her Royal Highness and Pergami were there, the Princess told me these precise words—she said that she wished to make a present to some of these girls [i.e. those who had been at the ball] and then she asked me "How can we dress these young virgins (*virginelle*) Mr. Sacchi?" Then she asked me "Do you believe they are such?" I answered that as far as I was concerned, I believed them to be *oneste* (modest) girls, and I had nothing to say against them; her Royal Highness said to me: "I know, you rogue, that you have gone to bed with three of them, and how many times you have had intercourse with them." I being surprised at this compliment, endeavoured to persuade her Royal Highness that she was deceived; and Pergami, who was present, began to laugh and to cry aloud: "It is true, it is true, it is true." He also said that on a different occasion the Princess had remarked on seeing one of these "maidens"— "how much the population of Barona must increase." '

He described an occasion when the Princess was travelling from Milan to Rome, and stopped at Sarignano—not far from Rimini— where 'she was overtaken by violent pain'. Pergami and Countess Oldi had then prepared some hot cloths; as these were made warm Pergami and the Countess carried them into the Princess's bedroom.

On another occasion the Princess travelled from Rome to Senigallia—a bathing resort just to the north of Ancona—in July when the weather was hot. She travelled by night. As dawn broke Sacchi went to the carriage to draw the curtains. Two or three times he found them asleep, 'having their respective hands one upon another'. 'Her Royal Highness held her hand upon the private part of Mr. Pergami, and Pergami held his own upon that of her Royal Highness. . . . once I saw that Pergami had his breeches loosened from the braces, that he had the front part of his breeches, the flap, half-unbuttoned.'

The cross-examination followed lines which were tolerably familiar, the payment as an inducement to come, the details of the examination by the Italian lawyers in Milan and the opportunities for meeting the various witnesses in England. Sacchi admitted that he had been in England for some time and that he had lived with the Reverend Philip Godfrey at Aston near Stevenage. To the question whether he had been in easy circumstances when he entered her Royal Highness's employment he replied: 'I have always been, thank God, in easy circumstances.' And when he was asked if he had been as well dressed comparing the two occasions he replied: 'I have been always dressed equally.'

Much of Brougham's questioning turned on Sacchi's relations with the family of Marietti, who were the Princess's bankers in Milan. To one of the family he was supposed to have said that he had a lawsuit with the Princess and it was suggested that he said this as a *double entendre*—really meaning that he was to be a witness in this case. Brougham then asked: 'Did you ever represent to any person, after you left her Royal Highness's service, that you taxed yourself with ingratitude towards a generous mistress?' It was fairly obvious that the Queen's advisers were in possession of a letter from Sacchi to this effect. Before he could answer the Attorney-General objected to the question and this gave rise to some show of temper among the lawyers—a reminder that the case was in its fifteenth day. The Attorney-General was starting to develop his argument when the Lord Chancellor tersely interrupted: 'Sir, I cannot hear what you say: speak out.' The Attorney-General's point was that a suggestion of this kind, which was really designed to shake the credibility of the witness, should be broadened to include both speech and writing. Brougham held his ground but Denman gave a more spirited defence: 'In all the books of practice which I have ever read, in all the reports of trials which I have ever looked at, and in all my practice in the courts below, I have never known or heard of such an interruption as this before. . . . No power on earth—not even this court—but least of all those persons who were charged with having produced this perjured witness—had a right to object to that question or offer that interruption.' Mild as the Attorney-General was he 'warmly complained' of the use of the words perjured witness and Denman, owning that it was improper, begged leave to withdraw it. Brougham interrupting: 'It was used purely hypothetically—merely hypothetically.' Replying to the arguments of the Queen's counsel the Attorney-General said that the other side had admitted that their object was to get the witness to declare as to the contents of some written document . . . . Brougham rose: 'I never said any such thing (Order, Order). My lords, we have a right, when what we state is misrepresented to contradict (Order, Order). My lords (with vehemence) I have a right to do so.' (Cries of Order, Order.) Amidst which Mr. Brougham, raising his voice still higher, repeated, 'I have a right to do so.' (Renewed calls of order and increasing confusion.) 'My lords, I say that I have a right.' (Order, Order, withdraw) Lord Redesdale, a former Attorney-General and former Speaker of the House of Commons, rose to say that such interruptions must not be allowed. The Lord Chancellor then told counsel that he had it in command from the House that counsel must not interrupt each other while speaking. The case was submitted to the judges who said that they found it difficult to give an answer because there was no clearly established practice in the courts below, but they were all of the opinion that the counsel should ask whether the statement was made by parole or in writing.

The Attorney-General argued—and he was no doubt correct—that on re-examination he was entitled to re-examine on something said in cross-examination. He therefore went on to ask Sacchi whether any conversation had passed between him and Marietti, relative to his being a witness on the subject of the Queen. 'Marietti came to me in the morning, and told me that Mr. Brougham, the brother of the counsel of her Majesty, had called upon him, and as Marietti had received some favours from these two brothers...' Brougham at once interrupted: 'See, my lords to what your permission lends. (Order) Do any of the judges refuse to allow me to speak (some confusion).' The cry of Order! came from Lord Exmouth—the famous sailor. Lord Holland said that if Lord Exmouth felt so competent to instruct counsel in their duty as advocates, it might perhaps be as well if he went a little further and gave their lordships some light on their duty as judges.' The Admiral angrily replied: 'I am not to be set down on every occasion when the noble baron thinks fit to rise up.' The Lord Chancellor said that in the circumstances it was consistent with a counsel's duty to interrupt the witness. It was however agreed, once again, to submit the question of how far the Attorney-General might go along this line of re-examination, to the judges. The judges, though not unanimously, decided that counsel on re-examination had no right to go further than to draw forth an explanation of the sense and meaning of expressions used in cross-examination and that he had no right to introduce matter 'new in itself'.

When the examination was thrown open to the lords, Lord Grosvenor asked whether it was customary for persons in the situation 'you held under the Princess, to withdraw the curtains of the carriage without her permission'.

'As every morning I had a custom to go to the carriage of her Royal Highness, to see whether she had any orders to give me, so sometimes I found the carriage open, sometimes I found that the curtains were drawn, and having done so sometime, I was never reprimanded or even admonished by her Royal Highness that I had done any thing which was wrong.'

At the end of the sixteenth day the Attorney-General asked permission to be allowed to produce a further batch of witnesses. It transpired that when these unhappy persons had got as far as Beauvais, they heard of the rough handling by the English mob which had been given to some of the previous witnesses at Dover. Sacchi had alluded to this as the '*tumulto*'. Terrified, these additional witnesses had turned tail, and had gone back to Leghorn, rather than face the Dover mob. However on the next day the Attorney-General explained that he had heard from Milan that a longer interval must elapse before the Italians could come, and he therefore withdrew his request, and this virtually closed the examination of witnesses for the bill.

6

Brougham to the Rescue

The Solicitor-General then summed up the case for the bill. There were one or two points in the evidence which he developed. Pergami had been paid three livres (lira presumably) a day when he was in General Pino's service where he lived in a menial situation. When first employed by the Princess he waited behind her chair at table. He emphasised the extraordinary nature of her behaviour on the evening she went to the theatre at Naples—the famous San Carlo theatre. (It will be remembered that inside the theatre she was insulted by the audience.)

Copley painted the scene. 'The wife of the Heir-Apparent to the throne of Great Britain, at that time holding the supreme government of the country, having about her a suite of ladies and gentlemen, was desirous of going in private. Surely she might have selected some respectable person of her suite, some respectable inhabitant of Naples, some proper and decent companion, without materially infringing upon the privacy of the transaction; but she chose her chambermaid and her courier. It was a rainy night; dark, gloomy and tempestuous; a hired carriage was drawn up at a private door at the bottom of the garden; they traversed the terrace, the garden, got into the hired carriage at the private door, proceeded to the theatre, and there met with such a reception as obliged them to retreat and return home. Now great part of the evidence had been called, by the other side, invention; could this be invention? And, if it were not invention, to what conclusion did it lead the mind of every man acquainted with transactions of such a description?'

He also emphasised the exchange of pictures between Pergami and the Princess.

'While they were at Catania, a picture of her Royal Highness was painted, in the character of a "Penitent Magdalen". He need not describe to their lordships what a "Penitent Magdalen" was; nor was it necessary to state that, in such pictures, the person was always considerably exposed. That picture was afterwards found in the possession of Pergami. For whom could they suppose it to be painted? Would they not conclude that it was painted for Pergami, the more particularly, when the picture of Pergami, which was also painted at this time, was seen in her Royal Highness's possession? Her Royal Highness was present when that portrait was painted. She settled Pergami's dress, she fixed his turban, she arranged the neck of his shirt, observing, "*Je l'aime mieux comme ça.*" All the circumstances led to the same conclusion.' He traversed all the charges brought by the various witnesses and brought out the cumulative weight of their evidence.

Copley's speech kept strictly to the facts without passion. He allowed himself a reference to '*non mi ricordo*'—'the changes which had been rung upon that circumstance might produce an impression upon low minds, although it could produce none on the minds of their lordships'. He was content to state the evidence and to argue that in any court of law it would amount to a proof of adultery.

'Upon the sort of proof required in cases of adultery he should merely observe, that he did not recollect a single instance, in cases of adultery, where the actual fact was fully proved in evidence. The crime was always to be inferred from accompanying circumstances, which left no doubt of the fact upon the mind of a rational and intelligent man. On this point of proof he would beg leave to quote the opinion of one of the most enlightened judges that ever sat in this country. He had received this opinion from one of his learned friends who had taken notes of it at the time it was pronounced by the learned judge. It was in the case of Loveden *v.* Loveden, before Sir William Scott,[1] in the Consistory Court, in the year 1809. The learned judge there stated, that there was no

[1] Lord Eldon's brother, afterwards Lord Stowell.

necessity, in a case of that nature, to prove the actual fact of the adultery, for that could not be proved in 99 cases out of 100, where there was still no doubt of its having taken place. The uniform rule was, that where the facts were proved which directly led to the conclusion that the act of adultery had been committed, such proof must be taken as sufficient.'

'In cases like the present every thing was to be inferred from the general conduct of the parties; and it had been clearly shown that the Princess and Pergami were constantly conducting themselves like lovers, or like man and wife during the day, while every preparation was made to prevent the interruption of their intercourse during the night. The familiarities at the Villa d'Este were not spoken of by one, two, or three witnesses, but by a body of testimony as set doubt at defiance. Walking arm in arm in the gardens, alone in a canoe upon the lake; embracing and kissing each other, where such intimacies were proved, even between persons in an equal rank of life, accompanied by a constant anxiety for access to the bed-chamber of each other, no court could refuse to draw the inference that adultery had been committed. To go through the whole series of evidence would only be to fatigue the House: but what would be said to the testimony of Raggazoni with respect to the statues, to the figures of Adam and Eve? He remembered that in the very case upon which he had already stated to the House the judgment of Sir William Scott, in that very case a letter had been produced written by the lady to her lover, in which she related some circumstances of an indecent nature. To that letter as evidence the learned judge had most particularly adverted; saying that no woman would have so written to a man unless adulterous intercourse had taken place between them. That observation applied most fully to the case in point.'

In ordinary circumstances the case against the Queen would have been regarded not only as overwhelmingly strong but as proved beyond reasonable doubt. The difficulty was that the evidence, for all its picturesque details, was in danger of foundering against the rocks of popular prejudice. Those rocks were not so much the belief in the innocence of the Queen or even the unpopularity of the King as a revulsion against authority. This was noted by a shrewd

observer—though a Conservative—J. W. Croker. He said that the
mob adopted her 'because she was in opposition to the King and
Government'.

In an attempt to rally opinion the Prime Minister said that
he and the Government were ready to withdraw the clause
which made it possible for the King to divorce the Queen;—
'the object of the bill was to uphold the honour of the country,
and not to relieve the illustrious individual at the head of the
state'.

On the twenty-first day of the proceedings, September 9, the
Lords decided to adjourn for three weeks, in order to give plenty of
time for the defence to collect the evidence for their case.

The defence opened on Tuesday, 3 October with a speech
by Brougham. Although Creevey at intervals went out of the
House of Lords during this remarkable oration because the
atmosphere was 'damned hot', and the speech 'damned dull'
he used the word 'perfection' at the finish. The diarist Charles
Greville said that Brougham's speech 'was the most magnificent display of argument and oratory that had been heard for
years'.

He started in a very low tone of voice which was heard with
difficulty by the reporters. He quickly moved into a threat of recrimination against the King. 'He would now remind their lordships
that his illustrious client, then Caroline of Brunswick, arrived in
this country in the year 1795; she was the niece of the Sovereign,
and the intended consort of the heir-apparent, and was herself not
far removed from the succession to the crown. But he now went back
to that period solely for the purpose of passing over all that had
elapsed from her arrival until her departure in 1814; and he rejoiced
that the most faithful discharge of his duty permitted him to take
this course. But he could not do this without pausing for a moment
to vindicate himself against an imputation to which he might
not unnaturally be exposed in consequence of the course which
he pursued, and to assure their lordships that the cause of the
Queen, as it appeared in evidence, did not require recrimination at present. The evidence against her Majesty, he felt, did not
now call upon him to utter one whisper against the conduct of

her illustrious consort, and he solemnly assured their lordships that but for that conviction his lips would not at that time be closed.

He amusingly admitted that the Queen left England for Italy, and that she moved in society 'inferior probably to that which, under happier circumstances, she had known'. But he added that learned counsel would have to make the most of this admission 'for it was the only one that would be made to them'. With characteristic ingenuity he threw the blame for the Queen's association with inferior companions on to members of the House of Lords. 'He admitted that when the Queen was here, and happy, not, indeed, in the protection of her own family, but in the friendship of their lordships and their families, that she moved in more choice and dignified society than any in which she has since had the good fortune to be placed. The charge against her was—that she went to Italy, and that, instead of associating with the peers and peeresses of England, she took to her society only foreigners. He fully admitted that her Majesty had been under the necessity of associating with Italian nobility, and sometimes with the commonalty of that country. But who are they that bring this charge? Others might blame her Majesty for going abroad—others might say that she had experienced the consequences of leaving this country and associating with foreigners; but it was not for their lordships to make this charge. They were the very last persons who should fling this at the Queen; for they who now presumed to sit as her judges were the very witnesses she must call to acquit her of this charge. They were, in fact, not only the witnesses to acquit, but had been the cause of this single admitted fact. While her Majesty resided in this country she courteously threw open her doors to the peers of England and their families. She graciously condescended to court their society, and, as long as it suited certain purposes which were not hers—as long as it served the interests in which she had no concern—as long as she could be made subservient to the ambitious views of others—she did not court in vain. But when a change took place—when those interests were to be retained which she had been made the instrument of grasping, when that lust of power and place to which she was doomed to fall a victim had been satisfied—then in vain did she open her doors to their lordships and their families; then it was that those whom she had hitherto condescended to court—and it was no humiliation to court the first society in the world—abandoned her.[1] Her Majesty was then reduced to the alternative of begging society in this country as a favour, or of leaving it. She could not, by humbling herself, have obtained the society of British peeresses, and must have sought that of other classes, or gone abroad. Such, then, being the circumstances, it was not in the presence of their lordships that he expected to hear the Queen reproached for going abroad. It was not here that he had thought any one would have dared to lift up his voice, and make it a topic of censure that the Princess of Wales had associated with foreigners—with some of whom, perhaps, she might say she would not, and ought not to have chosen under other and happier circumstances. Up to this period her Majesty had still one pleasure left. She enjoyed, not indeed the society, but the affection and grateful respect of her beloved daughter. An event, of all things most grateful to a mother's feelings, soon after took place—the marriage of her beloved daughter. Of this event her Majesty received no announcement. Though all England was looking towards the approaching event with the deep interest it was so well calculated to excite—though all Europe was looking at it with the liveliest feelings, and with all the knowledge of the interesting event which was about to take place—still there was one person, and one only, left in ignorance of the whole proceeding, and that solitary individual was the mother of the bride. All that she had done up to that time to deserve this treatment was, that she had been charged, and afterwards acquitted, of an alleged crime, and her perjured persecutors rendered infamous; and this treatment she received from his Majesty's servants, some of whom had risen in power by having made her a tool to promote their own interests. The Queen heard of the event of the approaching marriage of her only child accidentally; she heard it from a courier, who was going from this country charged with a notification of it to his Holiness the Pope—that ancient,

---

[1] This presumably means that when her husband became Regent, with virtually unrestricted powers, those who had formerly sought her company began to shun it.

intimate, and much valued ally of the Protestant Crown of England.'[1]

When he was 26 Brougham had travelled extensively in Italy, and could certainly claim to know the country and its customs. He could not resist twitting his opponents with their more insular outlook. 'When either the Attorney-General or his colleague, the Solicitor-General, spoke of the passing occurrences in Italy, they evidently spoke from their instructions, and not from any personal knowledge of their own upon the manners of the country; for symptoms of having ever been in Italy, they showed none. They had clearly never been there, or else they could not have spoken of the manners of Italy as they had done. For instance, see that they had said about the masquerade: "Who ever", said the Solicitor-General, "was seen for any proper purpose going to a masquerade in this sort of disguise?" What a pity that her Majesty did not, to suit the view of his learned friends, go to the masquerade in a state coach, with coachmen in splendid liveries, with lacquies bedizened out from head to foot, with all the pomp and show of state ceremony. What a pity she did not, on such an occasion, adopt this suitable and becoming state paraphernalia, instead of quitting her house in a private coach, instead of going out through a back-door. Why had she not the eyes of the world upon her when she went forth, instead of quietly passing without pomp or show? It was a wonder that his learned friend did not go on and say, "Why did she go in a domino and disguised cap to a masquerade? Who ever before heard of this disguise on such an occasion?" How little did his learned friends know, when they talked in this manner, of the royal recreations of Murat's court! He would refer to another part of his learned friend's speech, where he said that "During her Majesty's residence at Naples another circumstance took place to which it was his duty to call

---

[1] This was an extremely amusing passage, though remote from truth. If it were true it would have meant that the Princess did not write to her mother. There is indeed a well-known forged letter, perhaps composed by Brougham himself, in which the Princess goes fully into her approaching pregnancy.* This was written for public consumption, but it is most improbable that the Princess and her mother did not correspond.

* See Aspinall, *Letters of George IV*, vol ii page 203.

their lordships' attention. A masquerade was held at a theatre called, he believed, the Theatre of St. Charles. To this entertainment her Majesty rose to go in a very extraordinary manner, accompanied, not by Lady Charlotte Lindsay or Lady Elizabeth Forbes, or even by any of the gentlemen of her suite, but by the courier Pergami and a *femme de chambre* of the name of Demont. The dresses chosen by her Majesty for herself and her companions to appear in on this occasion were, as he was instructed, of a description so indecent as to attract the attention of the whole company, and to call forth marks of general disapprobation. Indeed, so strong was the disapprobation, that her Majesty, finding she was recognised, was under the necessity of withdrawing with her companions from the entertainment, and returning home." Now, what did Madame Demont say, when called upon to describe this "most indecent and disgusting dress" of her Majesty? Why, all that the perseverance and ingenuity of his learned friend could extract from the witness (no very unwilling one) was, that the Princess, on that occasion, wore what she (Demont) called "ugly masks"; for, strange as it might appear to his learned friends, she went to the masquerade in a mask! Indeed, if she had not gone so, she would have had no business there.'

Although the Austrian Emperor may have cold-shouldered the Princess, Brougham was able to show, in an entertaining passage, that she had not lacked royal companions. 'She was constantly received [by illustrious company], and with suitable respect, after her return from the long voyage. She was courteously received by the legitimate Sovereign of Baden,[1] and the still more legitimate Bourbon of Palermo.[2] She was courteously treated by the legitimate Stuarts of Sardinia,[3] whose legitimacy stands contradistinguished from the illegitimacy of the family whose possession of the throne of these realms stands upon the basis of public liberty and public rights. She was received even by a Prince who ranks higher in point

[1] Grand-Duke Charles V who married Stephanie Beauharnais, Napoleon's adopted daughter.

[2] King Ferdinand of the Two Sicilies.

[3] King Charles Emmanuel of Savoy who was descended from Charles I and after the death of the Cardinal York was regarded by some as the legitimate sovereign of England.

of legitimacy—the Bey of Tunis.[1] (A laugh). She was also received
with the same respect by the representative of the King at Constantinople.[2] In fact, in all those countries she met with that reception
which was due to her rank and consideration.'

The character of the witnesses, and the general presentation of the
case was next attacked by Brougham.

'He trusted their lordships would suffer him now to dwell more
minutely upon the statement of the case as opened by the Attorney-
General, and the case as proved by his learned friend. The case, as
opened, it was of no little importance to dwell upon. Was it not
marvellous to have such a case, and to be capable of adducing in
support of it such witnesses? . . . In the ordinary cases of criminal
conversation, the two very witnesses who of all others were deemed
of the utmost importance were the female's woman in attendance, and
the man's body-servant or serving-man. These were the servants
who must know the fact, if the criminal conversation took place.
They had these witnesses here; they therefore had their case under
the most favourable auspices—they had the man's valet, and the
woman's maid. These, in an ordinary case, would be deemed conclusive witnesses. The man's servant was rarely to be had for the
prosecution, from the nature and manner of the action; but if counsel
could get the female servant, they generally deemed their case
proved. They had also, if their case were true, the very extraordinary,
unaccountable, and unprecedented advantage of having parties to
proceed against for the fact, who, from beginning to end, concealed
no part of their conduct under the slightest or even most flimsy
disguise. Throughout the whole of the proceedings these parties,
knowing they were watched, discarded all schemes of secrecy—
showed an utter carelessness of the persons who were watching
them—threw off all ordinary trammels—banished from their
practice every suggestion of decorum and prudence—and, in fact,
gave themselves up to the gratification and indulgence of their
passion, with that warmth which is only found in the hey-day of
young blood. . . . Thus it would be seen that they were sitting to-

[1] The laugh is difficult to explain—perhaps it was heard because the Bey's
family had seized the throne a century earlier.
[2] Sir Robert Liston.

gether in familiar proximity. The act is also seen with the addition of the lady's arm round the neck, or behind the back, of her paramour. When it is necessary to trace their conduct a step higher in the scale of criminality, and exhibit the parties in such an attitude as to leave no room for explanation or equivocation, the act is done, not in a corner, apart from any scrutinizing eye, but in a villa filled by servants, and where hundreds of workmen are at the very time employed; and all this too is done, all this saluting is performed, in open day, and exposed to the general gaze. Especial pains are taken that the slander shall not be secret, but, on the contrary, that it shall be liable to the most widely-diffused publicity. It would not do that Pergami, upon his departure on a journey from the Queen, while in Sicily, should salute her Majesty before the servant entered the room. No; the exhibition of that act was reserved for the presence of a servant to tell it. The same was the case in the story about Terracina.[1] All the parties were on deck; they could not take the salute in their own cabin; it must be delayed until Majocchi enters to witness it. Even the act of sitting on Pergami's knee upon the deck is adjusted in the presence of the crew and passengers. Care is taken that it shall be directly seen by at least eleven persons. The frequent and free saluting on the deck, which, when committed in a particular manner, must leave little doubt of the subsisting intercourse between the parties—even that must be done, not at night, nor in the dark and privacy of the cabin, but before every body, and in open day. But the case which their lordships were called upon to believe was not left there, for the parties were represented as having taken the indispensable precaution of granting even the last favours within the hearing of witnesses. They were described as habitually sleeping together in all their journeys by land and sea. She could not even retire to change her dress but Pergami must attend in the dressing-room—first, of course, the parties taking care to have a witness present to speak to the fact. He could not dwell with calmness upon the representation of these disgusting scenes, with the peculiar features of enormity which were attached to them, without repeating, that exactly in proportion as they partook of the most aggravated character, and denoted an utter contamination of the

[1] Where Pergami landed after the long voyage.

mind, precisely in that extent were increased pains taken that they should not be done in a corner. No hidden places or recesses were selected or chosen by the parties for the free and safe indulgence of their passion from the prying eyes of those about them. They sought no secluded chamber in those places of abomination so well known upon the Continent, and which are degraded under the dignified name of palaces. The parties took no opportunity of seeking those hidden haunts of lust which might have been so hastily found. They sought no island among those which were the seat of such scenes in the times of antiquity, when society was less scrupulous of the conduct of its members than now. They sought no haunts among the Capreae of old, to revive in them those lascivious acts of which they were the ancient scene. They acted, on the contrary, before witnesses —they conducted themselves in open day-light, in the face of couriers, servants, and passengers. Was such folly ever known before in the history of human acts? Was ever folly so extravagant disclosed in the most unthinking acts of that youthful period when the blood boils in the veins? Was ever, even then, in that proverbial period of thoughtless levity, a being so recklessly insane as to have acted in this manner? There never was, he believed, such an instance in the history of human passions.'

Next Brougham attacked the witnesses and especially the preparation of their evidence in interviews with the Milan Commission.

'Their leading man, the captain of this horde of witnesses, the great delineator of the plan of accusation, Majocchi, the renowned Majocchi, himself testified to what? To any positive act of criminality? Oh, no! What, then, did he testify to? Any thing which by a liberal or judicious mind could be admitted as indicative of criminality? Strange it was, but important to be observed, before he entered upon a closer examination of this person's declarations—of the statements of this true and faithful creature—well did it deserve to be noted, that even his testimony fell far short of the charges as set forth by Mr. Attorney-General. He conjured them also to bear in mind that there was not one of the witnesses who had appeared at their bar who had not previously been examined, and who had not made some deposition before the Milan tribunal. Let them now then well mark the distinction; let them contrast with these persons the rank, station, character, and conduct, of those individuals to whom, indeed, Mr. Attorney-General had alluded in his opening speech, but whom he did not choose to call in support of his allegations. Not one of the witnesses on the other side, not one of the persons employed to destroy the reputation of a Queen of England, not one was to be found who had not gone through the discipline and drilling of a Milan tribunal. At that great receipt of perjury—(and he meant nothing disrespectful to any particular member of the commission) —but at that storehouse of false-swearing, and all iniquity, was every witness against her Majesty the Queen regularly initiated. How could it be regarded as necessary, with a view of purifying evidence, that it should first undergo a drill at Milan? However cautious some persons might be inclined to appear, he doubted whether they would require a probation of this sort. But, indeed, it had turned out not only that witnesses had been long kept in England, but that many had been maintained on the opposite coasts of Holland and France. It appeared, too, that they had been maintained at an enormous rate, far beyond every rule of proportion that ought to have been observed. Sacchi, who had filled a post abroad, not above the office of a servant in his most prosperous days, lived in splendid idleness for a long time in England, enjoying for that period the luxury and attendance of a field marshal.' He followed this by a somewhat far-fetched attack on Italian evidence in general, instanced by the value attached to it by Englishmen in Tudor times.

He concluded an eloquent passage by reminding the peers that they were not compelled to condemn the Queen. 'He conjured their lordships to remember that they were not now sitting in their capacity as a court of judicature, they were not compelled to take the cognizance of this matter, or to bring it to any issue. They might, if they pleased, dismiss it; they might give it the go-by; and, gracious God! what was there in the case to induce the Peers of England to pursue a Queen to destruction! What was there in the testimony brought from out their *presidia* in Cotton Garden—what was there in that to induce them to run counter to a sentiment almost universal? O, let it not be said, that in that sacred temple, that sanctuary of justice, the Peers of England, with a rash hand, had made up their minds to bear down its most venerable symbols, upon grounds so weak and so fallacious, and to sink themselves in eternal condemnation at the tribunal of after-ages.'

Brougham here paused, and threw himself on the indulgence of the House for a short relaxation. This was readily granted.

After an absence of three-quarters of an hour, Brougham re-entered the House. 'He had, he observed, to crave their lordships' pardon for the delay which his absence had unavoidably occasioned. He would now submit to their lordships all that occurred to him on that part of the case which was connected with the evidence.'

The remainder of Brougham's speech was principally concerned with a detailed analysis of the evidence, and an effort to controvert it. What he had to say of Majocchi's evidence about the princess going through his room *en route* for Pergami's bed-room is a characteristic example of his method.

'He (Mr. Brougham) must also remind their lordships of the incredible story told by Majocchi, when he would have them believe that the Queen, having free access to Pergami's room, through rooms where no person slept, she chose rather to pass through an occupied room. The witness would at first have represented that there was no other access, but, after much equivocation and perjury, he admitted that there was another access; yet, having admitted that the Queen had easy, safe, and ready access to the place of guilt, he represented that she preferred passing through another room where Majocchi slept—where he slept in a bed without curtains; that she preferred passing through a room so small, that she must have touched the bed—through a room where a fire was burning; and, what was the most monstrous of all, they were to believe that, to make detection sure, she stopped in her passage through the room, and looked in the face of Majocchi, to ascertain whether he was asleep. The whole of this story defeated itself.'

Brougham's gifts of sarcasm were always well-developed, and he displayed them to advantage when he commented on the evidence of Gargiulo who, it will be remembered, had disliked the possibility of endearments between the Princess and Pergami being noticed by his youthful relative Paturzo.

'He (Mr. Brougham) thought that the Princess of Wales, stooping on a bed in a vessel with her arm round a gentleman, and from time to time kissing him, not a very ordinary sight even for nautical men, nor such a sight as they could forget. Yet the master and his mate forgot, or differed most materially in the history of this matter. The mate said he had seen the Queen sitting on Pergami's knee near to the mainmast. He (Mr. Brougham) stated this minutely, because the mate considered it important. The mate meant to say that his evidence was given with particular accuracy, if not correctness. Yet he said it was not on a gun that the Queen sat on Pergami's knee. Not one word did he say about kissing and similar facts, the most important of all. Their lordships would, therefore, conclude with him that they did not happen. The captain, on the other hand, stated that it was on a gun, and not at the mainmast, that the Queen sat on Pergami's knee. But did they speak to the same time? Yes, for the captain said the mate saw it at the same time. The mate, however, had not seen it; and his learned friends had not dared to ask him any questions respecting it, because the captain had not had time to be trained sufficiently. He (Mr. Brougham) merely mentioned these circumstances, to show that the story could not be true, because, if it were, such differences would be impossible. Yet those pure, fastidious, and good scrupulous witnesses, from places chaste and sacred as the garden of Eden before the fall—from Messina and Naples—displayed a nicety of moral caution that was exceedingly exemplary. The captain, because the Queen was seen leaning over Pergami without touching him, desired the mate to go away, because, on account of their relation as master and mate, he was bound to protect his morals, and also because the ties of blood imposed a responsibility upon his conscience. Therefore he would not let his mate be near that part of the ship. He never said that the Queen wished him to withdraw, or that there had been any order from Pergami; the guilty pair cared not who saw them: but the virtuous Gargiulo, reviving, in the modern Mediterranean, a nicer sense of purity than the ancient ocean there had ever seen, would not allow his relation to view such a pair; for when they were so near they might touch, and that in the presence of the mate Paturzo . . . .'

Over the evidence about the position of the Princess and Pergami in the travelling-carriage Brougham grew indignant. He described the evidence as of a nature so disgusting and offensive, that he felt it difficult even to make the slightest allusion to it. Did their lord-ships think it very likely that any woman—he might almost say the most miserable prostitute discharged from Bridewell—would commit, in the face of open day, what had been charged against the Queen by Rastelli? Would they believe, that with the knowledge that a courier was travelling by the side of the carriage, the blinds of which might be raised, the Queen would run the risk of blasting her character, even among the most abandoned of her sex, by going to sleep in the position described by Sacchi as that in which he had discovered the Princess and her chamberlain? But the credulity of the House must be stretched yet many degrees; for if it could persuade itself that this had happened once, it would be nothing to what Sacchi had sworn he had been in the constant habit of seeing, again and again. He (Mr. Brougham) appealed to their lordships, whether this story had the smallest appearance of probability; whether, unless the parties were absolutely insane, such conduct could be accounted for. He was now saying nothing of the physical impossibility of the thing, at a time when the carriage was travelling at the rate of nine or ten miles an hour, over such roads as are found in that part of Italy, with their hands placed across each other, while the parties were both fast asleep, and, of course, without any power over their limbs. To overcome this difficulty would require the evidence of philosophers, who had witnessed an experiment so new and so strange. The witness had not ventured upon any des-cription of the carriage, excepting that it had curtains: but what would their lordships say, if it should be proved to have been an English carriage, with glass and spring blinds? What if he (Mr. Brougham) showed, that the blinds could not be raised without opening the door to get at the springs upon the inside?'

Cuchi, the waiter from the hotel at Trieste, was treated with savagery. 'Did their lordships recollect the waiter from Trieste, Cuchi? But they could not forget his aspect, if they had his name. Did they not recollect that physiognomy—the never-to-be-forgot-ten expression of that face—those eyes—that nose—that lecherous mouth, with which the wretch stood there to repeat the falsehoods, the wicked suggestions of his own filthy imagination, to which he had sworn at Milan? Would they not for ever remember that hoary pander from Trieste?—the manner in which he told his story—the haggard look which gave him the appearance of an inhabitant of the infernal regions, and which must have reminded their lordships of the great Italian poet's description of a broad-faced tailor in Hell peeping and grinning through the eye of a needle? But the testimony of that wretch would be contradicted. He, at all events, should be punished.'

He reverted again to Demont's evidence and how she had testified to seeing—as Brougham expressed it—Pergami naked in the corridor. 'Without stockings or even a morning gown, there meeting the chambermaid, not retiring at her approach, nor she at his, but pursuing his course with a steadiness of pace, and a firmness of composure, with which few wedded men sought their legitimate and bridal couch.'

Inevitably he devoted time to the credibility of the Italian witnesses, admitting that 'if their evidence was to be believed then the Queen was worse than Messalina, or as bad as Marie Antoinette was represented to be when the Jacobins of Paris covered themselves, even themselves, with complete infamy, by the charges against their Queen. But if a witness swore not only what was not true and not correct, but had falsely sworn what could not be true—if a witness swore to his own invention—if he swore, to use plain language, a lie, in any particular, however unimportant—good God! what character was safe? What escape remained for the purest innocence from the toils of an enemy, or the fabrications of a conspirator, if they believed one word of such a witness's testimony, and separated the lie from the other part which rested on the credit of him who fabricated the lie? What person could be safe from mercenary and spiteful villains? One of their lordships might be charged with a crime that nature abhorred—a crime of the greatest horror to his mind, and the greater in proportion as his mind was alien from the very thought, and his feelings alive to the infamy of the bare supposition. The best and most distinguished of their lordships might to-morrow be placed in the situation of one so charged, and must be convicted if a perjured scoundrel was to be believed upon such a principle of selection and separation of evidence. If one of their lordships were so charged with a crime which in this country was held in such abhorrence, that even the charge, contrary to strict justice, destroyed reputation before trial, he must forfeit his reputation if the charge should be supported as it might be, and the principal part of the testimony were believed. No perjury could be detected in the principal circumstances. All the skill and experience of the ablest counsel might attempt such detection in vain. The accused had only to take care that only one person should speak to the chief part, to choose his time, and to select his place. Where contradiction could not be offered, by choosing the time and selecting the place where one of their lordships might have been, refutation would be rendered impossible, prevarication unlikely. But before any court the accused would be acquitted if the villain told a clear unimpeachable story of the principal circumstances, and yet told the least falsehood on the most unimportant particular. He asked, then, for the Queen, no other justice; he desired for her Majesty no other security but that which their lordships would require, and be entitled to, before any other court.'

His speech closed with these words. 'Their lordships would recollect... a great passage in the sacred volume. He called it a great passage, because it was full of instruction, because it was just, because it was eloquent. The two judges were prepared with evidence fitted to their object, and well arranged. They hardened their hearts, that the look of their innocent victim towards heaven could not divert them from doing the purposes of unjust judgment, or from giving a clear consistent story. But their falsehood was detected, and their victim was saved, by the little circumstance of a mastick-tree.[1] This was a case applicable to all conspiracies and plots. This little circumstance was of the unessential, but decisive kind, which the providence of Heaven made use of to detect perjury. Such were Demont's letters; such Majocchi's banker's clerk. Such, my lords, is the case now before you, and such is the evidence by which it is attempted to be upheld. It is evidence—inadequate, to prove any proposition; impotent, to deprive the lowest subject of any civil right; ridiculous, to establish the least offence; scandalous, to support a charge of the highest nature; monstrous, to ruin the honour of the Queen of England. What shall I say of it, then, as evidence to support a judicial act of legislature, an *ex-post facto* law? My lords, I call

[1] *Apocrypha*: History of Susanna.

upon you to pause. You stand on the brink of a precipice. If your judgment shall go out against your Queen, it will be the only act that ever went out without effecting its purpose; it will return to you upon your own heads. Save the country—save yourselves. Rescue the country; save the people, of whom you are the ornaments; but, severed from whom, you can no more live than the blossom that is severed from the root and tree on which it grows. Save the country, therefore, that you may continue to adorn it—save the crown, which is threatened with irreparable injury—save the aristocracy, which is surrounded with danger—save the altar, which is no longer safe when its kindred is shaken. You see that when the church and the throne would allow of no church solemnity in behalf of the Queen, the heart-felt prayers of the people rose to Heaven for her protection. I pray Heaven for her; and I here pour forth my fervent suppli-cations at the throne of mercy, that mercies may descend on the people of this country richer than their rulers have deserved, and that your hearts may be turned to justice.'

The official account tells us that the learned gentleman concluded his eloquent and powerful speech at half past twelve o'clock on Wednesday, 4 October, having occupied more than five hours on the previous day. It had evidently made a strong impression on the House, and for some time 'the noble lords were occupied in re-marking on its tendency'. Several peers withdrew, and were seen in consultation in the passages. Lord Erskine rushed from the House in tears.

7

The Queen's Friends

The Lords agreed to allow John Williams to make a second speech before any evidence was called. The Lord Chancellor said that such a proceeding was 'quite new', but he conceived that in this important case the peers would exercise 'a sound discretion' in permitting Williams to address them. Williams opened his speech with the weighty, though possibly unconvincing assertion, that the case against the Queen 'presented to the mind nothing but pure and un-mixed evil, without the slightest portion of benefit' to a greater extent than had any other case 'from the commencement of the world'. After eulogising Brougham and 'his honourable and glorious exertion', he said that his task was merely to collect the few scattered remnants which had been left behind. He made the point that the charges against the Queen extended geographically over three-quarters of the globe, without being pinned down to any particular date but as having occurred in the course of a period of six years. From that he went on to assert that the whole case was 'founded and bottomed on perjury'. He spoke scathingly of the German diplo-mats who had helped the case forward—'a brace of ambassadors' who represented states inferior to England and therefore 'in some degree under its control'.

He next dealt with the Solicitor-General's challenge—'I defy you to call Bartolommeo Pergami.' Perhaps not everyone was convinced by Williams's rejoinder to the challenge; 'suppose the person were produced at the bar, did not the experience in the world of every man show that, supposing the crime of Pergami more or less, his answers at the bar upon this subject must necessarily be of one description only?' He presumably meant that whether innocent or guilty Pergami would have replied to the charges with a stubborn denial.

He ended by pointing out to the House that the Queen had wished a chamberlain of the Grand-Duke of Baden, who had been with her at Carlsruhe, to come and give evidence on her behalf. Permission was refused by the Grand Duke. The defence had also wished to call General Pino, in whose service—it will be remembered—Pergami had been. However the Austrian government had said that he must not appear in uniform. Bereft of his appurtenances he declined to come. The Lords expressed concern on these two points, and James Leman, who was a young clerk in Mr. Vizard's office—Vizard being the Queen's solicitor—described his journey to Carlsruhe in September, to see the Baron d'Ende, who was the chamberlain in question. In an interview on the road between Carlsruhe and Baden the Baron agreed to come, but some days later stated: 'I have bad news for you, the grand duke will not let me go.'

The second witness was Mr. Anthony St. Leger, who had been the Queen's chamberlain from 1808, had gone with her to Brunswick in 1814 and had left her service only for reasons of health. His evidence was simply to show that his health had made it impossible to continue in the service of the Queen.

Lord Guilford was next examined. He was the youngest son of Lord North, the Prime Minister; he was an accomplished linguist, widely travelled, a philhellene who was received into the Greek church when he was 25 and remained a member of it till his death. As a peer he was examined in his place in the House of Lords and, by leave of the House and with his permission, counsel put their questions to him direct and not, as before, through the Lord Chancellor. He was the brother of Lady Charlotte Lindsay, and saw much of the Queen when she first arrived in Italy. At Civita Vecchia he was in the same house with the Queen, and described how she had entertained Mr. Falconet, a banker in Naples, and his English or American wife. 'Does your lordship know, whether she was a person who associated with the first ranks in that country?' His reply was rather baffling: 'As far as persons in her situation associated with the principal people, I believe she did.' At Civita

Vecchia, Pergami had waited at table: later in the year, when Lord Guilford visited the Queen at the Villa d'Este, Pergami 'was sitting at the table of her majesty'. He was asked about the Countess Oldi: 'From your conversation with her did she speak the patois or the pure Italian?' 'She spoke, to the best of my recollection, a very good intelligible Italian, with rather an accent of the Lombardy, but not very remarkable . . . .' Examined by his fellow peers he was asked by Lord Grey about the Countess Oldi's manners. 'Her manners were perfectly inoffensive: there was nothing remarkable about them, very modest, nor particularly vulgar.'

'Nothing you would denominate as vulgar?'—'Not as vulgar, certainly not; the exact shade of vulgarity I cannot now charge my memory with: I do not remember having considered her as vulgar in her conversation with me, not the least; I do not remember that the impression upon my mind was that of having conversed with a vulgar woman.'

'Did you observe any particular difference between the manners of the Countess Oldi and other Italian ladies?'—'I cannot say that I did; she did not strike me as being a woman of remarkably fascinating manners, remarkably refined, but I did not see any great difference between her and other Italian ladies.' Lord Ellenborough asked him about the manners of Pergami: ' . . . They were perfectly unobtrusive: he was not forward.' He added that it did not strike him that Pergami was superior to the station in which he had formerly lived. Questioned by Lord Belmore, an Irish representative peer, he admitted that he had recommended his sister, Lady Charlotte, to resign her situation in the Queen's household. Brougham objected to this question, on the ground that counsel had been restrained from putting it, and the shorthand-writer was asked to obliterate it from his notes.

The next witness was Lord Glenbervie who had married a daughter of the Prime Minister, Lord North. He was an elderly, gossiping raconteur who had been at the bar and a member of the House of Commons. He was an uninteresting man. He had been with the Princess at Genoa in 1815 and described how then Pergami had waited at table on the Queen, standing behind her chair—'he often helped her and me to wine and other things'. He was asked about the company which he met at a ball given by the Queen. He described them as 'all the society I was in the habit of meeting, the principal ladies and gentlemen of the place'. Nearly a century later Lord Glenbervie's diary was published. His only comment on the Princess at Genoa was this: 'She has no English attendant with her but Dr. Holland and a Mrs. Falconet, a banker's wife at Naples, and they are both dying to leave her and are determined to leave her.'[1]

The third member of Lord North's family to serve the Queen was the most constant and perhaps the wisest friend she had— Lady Charlotte, married to John Lindsay, a younger son of Lord Balcarres.

Lady Charlotte's true feelings about the Princess were confided to her journal and were not published till long afterwards.[2] 'I am too well aware that hers is not a character capable of real friendship. Of this I have had various proofs in her conduct to me, on occasions when both my comfort and my reputation might have been materially injured by her caprice; and by experience I know that, while appearing to consult and trust me, she would in fact be guided by the counsels of mischievous and foolish persons, as long as their counsels agreed with her own inclinations.'

Her evidence was, however, favourable—she had walked with the Princess in the garden at Naples known as La Favorita: Pergami had walked behind them. She had travelled in a carriage with the Princess: Pergami had come to the window and said '*à boire Madame*'. He had been given a bottle of wine from which he drank, returning it to the Princess.

Replying to questions from the peers Lady Charlotte emphasised the familiar treatment of servants which had ever characterised the Princess.

Lord Calthorpe, rather a humble lord, 'ridiculously egotistical' but a Whig, asked her more particularly about the Princess's treatment of servants: 'During your acquaintance with her Royal

[1] *The Diaries of Sylvester Douglas* (Lord Glenbervie). Edited by Francis Bickley. Constable, 1928.
[2] *Journals and Correspondence of Miss Berry*, edited by Lady Theresa Lewis, 1865.

Highness, had your ladyship observed in her a degree of familiarity towards her menial servants, both male and female, that is unusual in persons of such high distinction?'—'I certainly think that her Royal Highness was peculiarly affable and familiar in her manner to all her servants.'

'Does your ladyship think that that condescension greatly exceeded that which is usually shown among the higher classes in this country towards their inferiors?'—'I think the higher classes in this country are much more apt to be exceedingly kind and condescending to their servants than those perhaps of a rank beneath them, and I think that her Royal Highness's manners were very peculiarly so.'

'Does your ladyship think that those manners were peculiar even in a foreigner?'—'I am perhaps no very good judge in that case, but foreigners are I think more apt to converse with their servants than English people, they have less reserve; and I think that her Royal Highness had certainly that sort of familiarity that I have observed in foreigners in conversing with their servants.'

The Lords, in examination, also brought out that Lady Charlotte had spent 24 days only with the Princess, and that they were only at the beginning of her sojourn in Italy. More damaging was the admission that the salary, as lady of the bedchamber, was of particular service to her.

'Did not your ladyship say, upon quitting the service of her Royal Highness, that if it had not been for an anxious desire to assist a particular individual out of the savings in that service, you would have quitted the service long before?'—'I think it is very possible I might have made use of those words; I do not distinctly recollect that I did, but I think it is possible.'

This was brought out in cross-examination, though Copley was not successful in making her admit that she had said when she resigned from the Princess's service that it was 'a vast relief' and that 'no woman with any regard to her character could remain in the service of her Royal Highness'. She said afterwards that Copley treated her as if she had been a murderer at the Old Bailey. Her re-examination by Dr. Lushington took the following form:

'You have been asked as to communications which took place verbally, upon the subject of your ladyship's resignation; to whom was that communication made?'—'To my husband.'

'To any one else?'—'To no one else.'

'Is Mr. Lindsay a person in distressed circumstances?'—'He is.'

'Has he been so for a considerable period of time?'—'For some years.'

As Creevey says, 'Lady Charlotte burst out a crying.'[1] We can hardly be surprised at this, when we also learn from Creevey that her husband, 'the person in distressed circumstances', had sold her letters to the Treasury for use in the proceedings against the Queen.

This supposition had a curious sequel. Lushington, in his speech for the defence, severely attacked the Crown's lawyers for violating the confidence which ought to exist between husband and wife, and of Colonel Lindsay's supposed sale of the letters he said that 'such an act of gratuitous infamy, he would venture to affirm, was not surpassed by anything to be found in the records of any court of justice—no not even in the annals of the Old Bailey'. Subsequently in the proceedings, Lord Balcarres entirely denied the whole affair, and he said that Colonel Lindsay had put into his hands all the correspondence which had passed between himself and Lady Charlotte 'and, having read the correspondence, he could, on the honour of a peer and gentleman, assure the House that there was not in the letters one word which bore either directly or indirectly on the unfortunate case before their lordships'.

The next witness was Lord Landaff, an Irish peer married to an Irish wife, a great gambler and a personal enemy of the King. He had met the Princess in Naples in 1815, and later in the same year at Venice. He lodged at the Gran Brettagna—the Princess had one side of the hotel and he the other. The Princess's sitting-room was immediately opposite his sitting-room, and he occasionally went in though he could not remember if he had knocked beforehand. Later in examination by Brougham he was asked if he had been in Italy at additional times to those he had mentioned, enquiring whether

---

[1] The Creevey Papers, 1904, i, 323. In her journal Lady Charlotte says that she broke down in the questions immediately preceding this which concerned the deaths of her brother and sister in 1817.

he had had the chance really to know Italian customs. He replied: 'Two years.'

'Does your lordship know whether it is the practice in Italy for men as well as women to be in ladies' bed-chambers in the course of the morning?'—'I think it is a very common practice in Italy for men to attend ladies' rooms as much as women.'

'Is it an ordinary practice in Italy for men to see ladies in their bed in the morning when they call?'

The Attorney-General said he objected to the question.

The Lord Chancellor said that the witness must state whether it was from his own knowledge he spoke.

'Your lordship is requested to speak from your own knowledge, and your own practice and experience?'—'I have seen many ladies in bed in a morning.'

'Was that in the ordinary intercourse of society?'—'It was.'

'Were those ladies of unimpeachable conduct and character?'—'They were, as far as I know.'

'Did your lordship at the same time see other gentlemen enjoy their society in the same manner?'—'I have.'

'And at the same time with your lordship?'—'At the same time my brother and I were together; and we have frequently gone together into rooms where ladies were in bed.'

'To make a morning visit?'—'To make a morning visit.' The Attorney-General, in cross-examination, made a pertinent point.

'You have been asked whether you were in the habit of visiting her Royal Highness, and going into her chamber without notice; did your lordship mean her bed-chamber?'—'No, certainly not; her sitting-room.'

Mr. Keppel Craven then gave evidence. He was a son of Lord Craven and the Margravine of Anspach, and was a traveller of note, and the intimate friend of Sir William 'Topographical' Gell. He had lived since 1805 in a villa at Naples and was later and perhaps less appropriately to live in a converted convent at Salerno. He was one of the Princess's chamberlains, joining her in 1814 and staying with her till she was at Naples in March 1815. Craven's evidence was first directed to the original engagement of Pergami. When the Princess arrived in Italy, the Austrian governor of Lombardy,

General Bellegarde, had appointed the Marchese Ghisiliari to serve the Princess as Chamberlain while she was at Milan. The latter had recommended Pergami and had said that he had known him and his family for a long time.

Craven said that he accompanied the Princess to Naples, and that the King had met her outside the city. (This was an exceptional civility, though it came from Murat and not from a member of one of the established ruling houses.) Craven rather neatly parried any questions about the accommodation in Naples for the Princess by saying 'It was very inconvenient; for Sir William Gell and myself had two very bad rooms.'

On the subject of William Austin he said that he was responsible for advising the Princess that the boy was too developed to continue sleeping in her room. 'I said that the people in Italy might make some observations upon it.'

He was cross-examined by Copley about an occasion when he had seen the Princess and Pergami in the garden of the house where the Princess was staying in Naples.

'Did you ever, either to Lady Charlotte Lindsay, or to any other person, state that you had made a representation to her Royal Highness as to what had been observed with respect to her Royal Highness and Pergami on the terrace of the garden attached to the house at Naples?'—'I did so; I did not mention it to Lady Charlotte Lindsay, but I mentioned it to a person at Naples; I mentioned that I had spoken to her Royal Highness about it; it was with regard to what I had observed.'

'What you had seen?'—'Yes.'

'Have the goodness then to state what it was that you saw, and what you represented?'—'I saw her Royal Highness walking in the garden, and Pergami was near, he was walking also in the garden; I knew there was a spy at that time at Naples; I had had information of it from England; that being the case, I thought it necessary to caution her Royal Highness with regard to any outward appearances that might be misconstrued.'

'When you say you had information from England, was that by letter?'—'It was by letter.'

'Was there any other person in the garden except her Royal

Highness and Pergami at the time to which you allude?'—'She said there was.'

'Did you see any other person?'—'No, because she walked on a sort of terrace, which was much higher than the rest of the garden; there might have been other persons whom I did not see.'

When the peers had the chance to ask questions, Lord Combermere, the distinguished cavalry general in the Peninsula, asked: 'Was Pergami walking behind her Royal Highness on the terrace or how?'—'He was walking a little way behind her.'

'As servants usually do behind their mistresses?'—'Yes.'

'What impropriety did you conceive there could be in that?'—'I did not conceive there was any impropriety.'

'Why then did you give that advice to her Royal Highness, if you conceived, as you have now stated, there was no impropriety in Pergami walking behind her Royal Highness?'—'Because I understood there was a person sent as a spy upon the Princess, and he might put that down as an impropriety, though I did not think so myself.'

'Can you state who was the person so pointed out to you as a spy?'—'The letter did not contain the person's name, but I was told afterwards who it was by a gentleman at Naples.'

Craven was also pressed by the Lords about the impression which Pergami's manners had made on him. Craven left the Princess in March 1815, when Pergami was the courier; he did not see her again until 1819, when Pergami was the chamberlain. He drew a distinction as will be seen from the following examination, between Pergami the courier and Pergami the chamberlain. But he said in general that his manners were above the situation of a courier—'they were not so servile and fawning as those of the Italian servants in general'.

The Earl of Donoughmore.—'You have mentioned just now, in answer to a question put, as to the manners of Pergami, that you did not make any observation upon those manners till he became a gentleman, but that from his becoming a gentleman, you did not see any thing inconsistent in those manners; what was the period at which he ceased to be a servant, and begun to be a gentleman?'—'I do not know what the period was, for I was not with her Royal Highness.'

'To what period then was it you directed your answer when you said you did not make any observation upon his manners till a particular period, which was when he begun to be a gentleman; what was that period to which you referred?'—'It was the first time I saw him when he was raised to the situation of chamberlain.'

'When was that?'—'It was a year ago, rather more.'

'He had not begun to be a gentleman when he was walking on the terrace?'—'No.'

The next witness was Sir William Gell. A Derbyshire country gentleman, with a taste for travel and classical antiquities he is perhaps sufficiently described by certain changes in Byron's 'English Bards and Scotch Reviewers'. Originally the poet wrote: 'I leave topography to coxcomb Gell.' Having met Gell he changed 'coxcomb' to 'classic'. When Byron visited Troy he changed 'classic' to 'rapid', adding a foot-note—' "Rapid" indeed! He topographised and typographised King Priam's dominions in three days.' But Sir William was an entertaining, amusing man with a relish for the company of eminent persons.

His entry to the House of Lords to give evidence was distinguished by a solicitous attention to his gout from the Lord Chancellor. 'My lords, I understand Sir William Gell has got the gout; he is most certainly, therefore, I hope, entitled to a chair.'

Gell had accompanied the Queen when she left England in 1814, had been her chamberlain till 1815, and then, being resident in Rome, had attended her intermittently. In examination he added some picturesque details to what Keppel Craven had said about the engagement of Pergami by the Marchese Ghisiliari.

'Be pleased to state to their lordships in what manner the Marquis Ghisiliari conducted himself towards Pergami when he took leave of him?'—'Pergami was, I believe, about to mount his horse; the Marquis Ghisiliari being in his uniform as chamberlain of the Emperor of Austria, and with his key as chamberlain, denoting what was his employment at the moment, took Pergami round the neck in the street, and kissed him twice before all the people; which we observed, as it was a singular thing when people were just come out of England, though a common custom in that country.'

'When you say the common custom in that country, is it the

common custom between equals and gentlemen?'—'Between equals, and perhaps not otherwise.'

'Among the higher ranks is it not the custom?'—'It is the common custom among gentlemen.'

He said that Pergami always treated the Queen with the most marked attention—but nothing 'singular or particular'. Gell was always treated by him, when the Queen was not present, perfectly respectfully. 'I should say, on all occasions rather more respectful than was necessary: he generally required to be pressed to sit down; that sort of behaviour.' When he was examined by the Lords, he was pressed on this point by the redoubtable Lord Ellenborough—'Did you ever observe any thing in the conduct of the Princess of Wales towards Pergami, in her conduct, manners, conversation, or looks, to induce you to entertain an idea that there was an adulterous intercourse between them?'—'Upon my honour I never saw the Princess speak to Pergami but on matters of business, though I was in the house for three months at once with them.'

'Can you give a more distinct answer to that question?'—'I never did.'

'Was there any thing in the manners of Pergami which made it disagreeable to you as a gentleman to share with him the duties of chamberlain?'—'Quite on the contrary; he was remarkably attentive to me, and would have handed me down stairs with candles[1] if I would have let him; I was obliged to explain to him that it hurried me, being lame, and to request he would let it alone.'

'Do you consider that that conduct, on the part of Pergami, was the conduct of a gentleman?'—'Perfectly so to me.'

'Did Pergami, while you were in the service of her Royal Highness, take more than a fair share of the duties of chamberlain?'—'Certainly not.'

'Did you observe any thing in the conduct of Pergami towards the Princess, which would have been different from the conduct of any English chamberlain?'—'Nothing, but that he was more attentive.'

He repeated what Craven had said about the civility of the King Murat of Naples to the Princess. He described how the Princess

[1] A civility in Italy generally reserved for cardinals or royal persons.

went in state to the San Carlo Theatre as the guest of the King and
Queen. The opera *Medea*[1] was given, and a ballet. When he was
asked how long the Princess stayed, he replied: 'I remember very
well, because I was very lame, and had to stand behind her royal
highness the whole night, and it must have been at least 12 if not half
past 12.'

Sir William was full of information about Mahomet's dance.
He was asked whether he had seen a Moorish dance in the Eastern
countries and answered: 'Not only in the East but in Spain and
Portugal.' He was asked to describe the dance and the Lord
Chancellor playfully intervened to say: 'Recollect, Mr. Williams,
that Sir William Gell has the gout.' Williams then asked:

'Can you give any description, verbally, of the manner in which
it is usually performed?'—'I believe every body in London has seen
the Spanish Bolero dance on the theatre; it is something like that;
in one part of the exhibition the two performers run up together,
sometimes in an attitude of defiance, and sometimes in an amorous
attitude; the same dance prevails over all the South of Europe, and
every body sees it without making any remarks upon it, ladies and
gentlemen, from Madrid to, I believe, China; and people may see
it both in Rome and Naples.'

He was closely examined about the passport given to the Princess
when she was in Rome in 1820. This was an order for post-horses
signed by Cardinal Gonsalvi, the Papal Secretary of State, which
Gell said was the equivalent of a passport. He had seen this document
but whether he could be questioned on it, if it was not produced,
led to an involved argument. The reason why the Queen's counsel
were concerned with this was that it was made out in the name of
the Princess Caroline of Brunswick although she had in fact just
become Queen Caroline of England. Denman slipped in a popular
aside against the Roman church, when speaking on this legal point—
'the Pope's secretary of state waited not for any judgment of the
British legislature—he wished not for any act of Parliament to
dethrone and degrade a Queen.' But it was decided that the matter
could not be pursued further, without the production of the document.

[1] Presumably the melodrama by Benda.

Gell certainly placed the Princess's fancy-dresses, when she entertained the King of Naples, in a less unfavourable light. On the now famous appearance as the Genius of History he was asked: 'Do you remember the particular dress of the Princess of Wales upon that occasion?'—'I remember it perfectly well, it was a dress which I should say is best exemplified by the figure of the Towneley Curiatius[1] in the British Museum, or Mr. Hope's Minerva[2]; it was meant to imitate one of those statues.'

'Was there any thing indecent or indecorous in the style or nature of that dress?'—'The whole world is capable of judging; those statues are very much draped, completely covered.'

'In point of fact upon that occasion was the dress of the Princess of that description?'—'As nearly imitated as dress of that kind can be imitated, as it appeared to me.'

At the end of the questioning by the peers Copley asked, in reference to the same occasion—'When her Royal Highness appeared in a Turkish dress, did she or did she not wear trowsers?'— 'I happen to know what those trowsers were; she did wear trowsers, made in the form of Turkish trowsers; I beg to explain what they are, the trowsers that her Royal Highness wore are very much like a common petticoat sewed slightly together between the legs at the bottom, such as are commonly worn in the Levant.'

Gell was a highly entertaining and amusing man, and against his evidence would have to be set a series of letters, under such titles as Adonis or Gellius Aulus which he wrote to friends at home describing, in less decorous language than he used in evidence, the behaviour of his royal employer.

Sir William Gell's valet, William Carrington, was next examined. He had formerly served as a midshipman in the navy. His evidence concerned the sleeping arrangements at Naples. He said that Pergami had changed his apartment after the first night 'because the room was so low he could not stand up in it'. He said that Pergami had moved to a fresh room separated by a passage and three other rooms from the Princess's room. He was asked if he knew Majocchi

---

[1] Mr. Charles Towneley's collection of classical statuary had been in the Museum since 1805.

[2] Thomas Hope, the collector and virtuoso.

and whether he had ever heard him mention the Baron Ompteda.[1] Both the Attorney-General and the Solicitor-General objected strongly to the question, arguing that a conversation between the valet and Majocchi about a third person could not be taken as evidence. The Queen's counsel, Dr. Lushington, rounded on the government lawyers ' . . . Was it possible to contend that, to ascertain the fact whether Ompteda had not acted as a spy on her Majesty, had suborned her servants, that he had broken locks, forced doors, in order to steal papers, with the view of fabricating charges to affect the character, the honour, and even the life of the Queen— shall it be said that an explanation to prove that fact is not relevant to—'

Lord Redesdale interrupted, and moved that the learned counsel should withdraw. 'The learned counsel had no right to pursue the course of examination he proposed. He could not impugn the conduct of Baron Ompteda by conversations which had passed between the witness and another person.'

The Lord Chancellor observed, that certainly that could not be done.

When counsel came back, Lushington went on to explain that Ompteda's behaviour was really a direct point in issue because the plots against her which he engineered explained why the Princess took care that some of her male attendants should sleep near her. Brougham intervened to argue that it was perfectly open to the defence to try to show that Majocchi had said something in evidence about Ompteda, which he must have known to be incorrect. 'Whenever the name of Ompteda was mentioned, *per fas aut nefas*, an objection instantly came from the other side.' The point resolved itself to this, Majocchi had been asked if he remembered a quarrel taking place between Ompteda and Lieutenant Hownam. He said that he did not know the cause. The Attorney General said that the Queen's counsel should have asked Majocchi if he had ever told Carrington that he did know the cause, and not attempt, without having put that question, to extract the answer from Carrington.

[1] Ompteda was the Hanoverian *chargé d'affaires* at the Papal court. He ingratiated himself into the confidence of the Princess, and undoubtedly attempted to suborn the servants.

The point was then put to the judges. After retiring for some time the Lord Chief Justice gave the unanimous opinion of the judges that the courts below would not admit a witness A being questioned about a conversation with witness B on which witness B had not himself been cross-examined.

While the judges were absent Lord Lauderdale raised the point whether the House should continue to examine witnesses in the absence of the judges. Lord Holland thought on the contrary that the judges were present only to state points of law and the construction of Acts of Parliament. The House agreed that the examination of witnesses should continue until any point of law or construction arose.

John Whitcombe was next called; he was examined by Tindal, and explained that he had been valet to Mr. Craven for nearly seven years. He corroborated what Gell's valet had said about the arrangement of the rooms at Naples. When he was asked whether he knew where Mademoiselle Demont slept he said that he did, and this admission gave rise to the following examination—

'Have you ever been in that room?'—'Yes, frequently.'

'Have you been in that room by night as well as by day?'—'Late as well as early.'

'At the time you have been in that room, has Mademoiselle Demont been there also?'—'Yes; she invited me, generally, to go there.'

'When you have been in the room, has there been any other person there besides yourself and Mademoiselle Demont?'—'There has been sometimes Preising (Annette we called her generally), but it was seldom she stayed long when I was there.'

'Have you then been alone in the room with Demont?'—'Very frequently.'

'At the time you have been so alone with her, has the door been locked or not?'—'Locked and bolted.'

The Solicitor-General objected to the last part of the examination. It was impossible not to see the object for which the learned gentleman had put the last question; and that, he apprehended, was not an object which could be legally pursued by him. He supposed that it was unnecessary for him to argue the point.

Mr. Tindal.—We will not, then, push this matter any further, my lords.

The Lord-Chancellor.—Really you have pushed it already as far as you possibly could.

Mr. Denman said, if it were only the last question that was objected to, he had no reluctance to withdraw it.

The Solicitor-General observed, that the rest of the answers might stand, as they were immaterial.

Whitcombe gave a rather different account of the masked ball from that described by Majocchi and the earlier witnesses: he said that Pergami and two of the other servants were dressed 'something after the Turkish costume', but that later in the evening Pergami was in 'plain clothes' handing round lemonade.

After counsel had finished examining Whitcombe, who had withdrawn from the bar, Lord Erskine rose and read to the house Madame Demont's evidence—he promoted her from mademoiselle —to the effect that she had always slept alone, 'all alone' for the whole night. He was then challenged by the Prime Minister, who asked him what question he planned to put. He replied: 'I mean to ask him whether he spent any part of any night, or the whole of any night, in the room of Madame Demont, when she was there and in bed.'

Copley, speaking with the greatest deference and respect of the views of Erskine as a former Lord Chancellor, said that the question could not be put. It was, he thought, a clear and undeniable point of law, that a witness could not be asked if she had committed an immoral act, or, if asked such a question, compelled to give an answer, if she objected to it. It was equally clear and incontrovertible, he thought, as a point of law, that if the witness thought proper to answer the question, and deny the fact attempted to be insinuated, that it would be incompetent for the party to negate her denial by proof. If he were right in that position of law, which he thought incontrovertible, then he submitted to their lordships that they could not suffer that to be obtained circuitously, or by a side-wind, which could not be attempted openly and plainly.

Lord Erskine then made a characteristically odd intervention. The Lord Ellenborough, to whom he refers, was the Lord Chief

Justice, who died in 1818, and the father of the peer who, it will be remembered, had asked questions of the witnesses in this case, revealing his sympathies with the King.

Lord Erskine said he remained unconvinced that his question ought not to be put; for he thought not only that the question he was putting to this witness might have been put to Madame Demont, but also that she might have been legally asked whether he had ever slept with her. He affirmed that that might have been done. 'It was a course which he had himself often pursued at the King's bar; he had repeatedly asked a witness questions which went to show his criminality. He was perfectly ready to admit that the witness was not bound to answer; but if he answered, what reason was there to take that answer as conclusive, and not to be shaken by other testimony? He remembered that once, before Lord Ellenborough, he had insisted upon sifting such a question: it was objected to, and he tendered a bill of exceptions, which bill he was not under the necessity of arguing; it went to all the reason of the judges, and received the assent of the most eminent men at the bar whom he had consulted on the occasion. He had over and over again put such questions. He should state what passed in conversation between himself and Lord Ellenborough at the time. For that noble lord's learning and abilities he had ever entertained the greatest deference and respect. Suppose, said he (Lord Erskine) to Lord Ellenborough, that you had been taking a walk among the new improvements in the neighbourhood of Bloomsbury Square, and that some fellow dared to charge you with the commission of a crime, which, if proved, would justly degrade you in the eyes of the world. I know that when the charge was made, the first thing you would do, perhaps, would be to send for me, to undertake your defence. Suppose that we had every reason to believe the fellow who made the charge to be a scoundrel false and wicked enough to make it with the view to extort money. The examination, we will suppose, commenced. I said to the fellow, "Who are you, Sir?"—"A captain of a ship." "Of what ship?"—"Of a ship that has sailed abroad." "Abroad! where?"— "She is gone to America". "Look nearer to me, Sir; let me see, do I not recollect you? are you not the very man that I unsuccessfully defended once, on a charge of returning from transportation?" He

10   The Attorney-General
(Sir Robert Gifford)

*From an engraving by T. Wright after
a sketch by A. Wivell, 1821*

11   Henry Brougham addressing the
House of Lords in defence of the Queen

*From an engraving by T. Wright after
a sketch by A. Wivell, 1821*

12   Thomas Denman (the Queen's
Solicitor-General)

From an engraving by R. Page, 1820

13   The Lord Chancellor (Lord Eldon)

*From an engraving by T. Wright after
a sketch by A. Wivell, 1820*

14 Sir George Hayter's painting of the House of Lords
during the progress of the Bill, 1820

Lord Grey is speaking and is examining Majocchi; the interpreter
   is on Majocchi's right
The counsel standing is Lushington
Gurney—the shorthand writer—is seated on the extreme right of
   the picture
The Press is on the extreme left, and the editor of *The Times* is
   the seated figure with his face turned to the left
The Duke of Clarence is standing in the left-hand gallery

15   Brougham announcing the abandonment of the Bill to the Queen

may, I know, object to answering this question and have all the credit of his refusal to answer it; but have I, or have I not, a right to put it? The judge may say, No, it can't be put; but, should your client be found guilty of the charge, you can then prove the witness to be the person you represent him, in a motion for a new trial.' This, said Lord Erskine in a continuation, was the way in which he put the point to the late Lord Ellenborough: and he added at the time, what he felt still, that to deny him the course for which he contended, and point him out in the room of it such a remedy, was a mockery of justice, and most ruinous to the rights and liberties of the subject. 'Nothing, therefore, was so fatal to the public security, as the first position taken by the Solicitor-General. But, waiving that altogether in this case, and referring to the witness Demont's evidence—she is asked, and she answers over and over again that she slept alone, during the whole and every part of the night in her chamber: she made no objection to answer; no objection was taken elsewhere: he had a right, therefore, to try the validity of the answers she had recorded, and to ascertain whether she had lain with any body else at the time when upon her oath she declared she had re-mained alone in her chamber.' He concluded by asserting that he had a right to have the witness recalled, and asked if he was in Demont's room on any night when she was in bed there.

The Lord Chancellor said that the questions put to Demont were designed to ascertain whether, out of her own mouth, she had ad-mitted guilt of an immoral offence. She had denied that fact, and he added: 'in my opinion, speaking both judicially and as a peer, witnesses could not be called to contradict that denial.' Lord Erskine had therefore to be content with the questions and answers to John Whitcombe which follow.

Lord Erskine.—'Where did you sleep in the house at Naples during the time you were there?'—'In a small room next the Honourable Keppel Craven.'

'Did you sleep there every night?'—'Every night during the time I was in the house.'

'Did you sleep in your room during the whole of every night?' —'I slept there after I went to bed; I was not in bed till 12 or 1 o'clock.'

'And you never went from your own bed to any other bed during the night?'—'No.'

'You after those three nights went into lodgings?'—'Yes.'

'Did you during the time you were in your lodgings, ever sleep in the house you had left?'—'I never slept in the Princess's house afterwards.'

At the end of his evidence Lord Hood asked whether Whitcombe had been in Demont's bedroom after he went into lodgings. He replied: 'Yes, frequently.' He is presumably distinguishing between a little evening dalliance in Demont's bedroom and sleeping the night there.

Majocchi was then recalled and the familiar '*non mi ricordo questo*' was heard again. He entirely denied that he had ever discussed Ompteda with either of the valets, and still less that he had stolen the keys at the Villa d'Este to have false ones made. 'Never, never; I never spoke of this Baron.'

8

The Doctor and the Sailor

❧⊙❧

William Carrington's examination was then resumed. He said that when in 1817 the Princess was staying at the Villa Ruffinelli, at Frascati—it belonged at this time to Lucien Bonaparte—Majocchi, who was preparing the Princess's carriage for the journey to Rome, had told him that Ompteda had prepared the duplicate keys. There was also a reference to the same thing by Majocchi in the servants' hall at dinner with the rest of the servants. Majocchi dined with the livery servants: Carrington did not. He said that he was able to speak Italian, sufficiently 'to make my way in Italy'. He said that Majocchi had spoken in Italian, and was asked to repeat in Italian the exact words which Majocchi had used— '*Lui hanno detto a mi, vudres che lui lasciar me e fare il mio dovere, che lui vorrebbe bastonare e mazzare come un cane in mezzo alla strada.*'

On two minor points he was closely pressed by the peers. He had said that Frascati was four miles from Rome—four 'Roman or geographical miles'. It was, in fact, 15 miles. His service in the Navy attracted questions. He had said that he served on the *Poitiers* with Sir John Beresford but, not liking the sea, he had been given his discharge. He came from Essex, near Colchester, and had served as a boy in the merchant service. That renowned sailor, the Duke of Clarence, asked him if he went by the same name on the *Poitiers* as he did now.

The Duke of Clarence.—'Having stated that you had been in the merchant service previous to your going on board the *Poitiers*, are you to be understood to have joined that ship as a midshipman, capable of doing your immediate duty, or as a youngster?'—'I went with Sir John Beresford on board the *Poitiers*.'

'Do you mean that you entered as a youngster to learn your duty, or did you go upon the quarter-deck of that ship as a positively effective midshipman?'—'I was not a mere youngster; I did not go upon the quarter-deck for some time; but I understood I was to be a midshipman.'

'Are you positively sure that from the time you joined the *Poitiers*, you were rated midshipman?'—'I am not certain whether I was rated at the time or not; I was rated at the time I left it, which I saw upon my ticket.'

'You are perfectly clear in your own mind that you left His Majesty's service for no other reason than at your own request?' —'Nothing else.'

John Jacob Sicard was next examined. He was born in Anspach and came to England about 1790 as cook to the Marquis of Stafford. After 10 years he was engaged as cook to the Princess (in February 1800) subsequently becoming her *maître d'hôtel*. His evidence corroborated that of the other witnesses for the defence. He was examined by Brougham about the occasions when he might have walked with the Princess.

'Have you ever had occasion to walk near her Royal Highness, or with her Royal Highness?'—'Many times, by her command.'

'Have you ever walked so with her Royal Highness in a garden?' —'Yes, in the pleasure ground at Blackheath many times.'

'Upon those occasions, has her Royal Highness talked to you in walking?'—'Very condescendingly.'

'Has her Royal Highness ever had occasion to take your arm in those walks?'—'Except on steps or rising ground, and sometimes her Royal Highness, in the way of conversation, I have had the honour for her Royal Highness to put her hand upon my arm, by saying, "you understand what I mean", or, "do not you agree with me"; and I believe their lordships may have had an opportunity of that.'

'How long have you ever had the honour of walking with her Royal Highness upon those occasions?'—'Half an hour, or sometimes more.'

Cross-examined by Copley he was asked whether he had a pension; he explained that he was paid £400 a year, continuing at her Majesty's pleasure. He further explained that his salary was £300, and that he had been paid a further £100 when he came to England to act as the Queen's *homme d'affaires*. He had left Italy in the spring of 1815, had expected a summons to rejoin the Queen but this had never come, and he had not seen her again until he went out to announce what he called 'the melancholy news' of the death of George III. From a private letter to Brougham, which was written by his brother, James Brougham, we know that Sicard was believed to have plundered the Princess, and it is alleged that after coming back from Italy in 1815 and going back in 1820 with 'the melancholy news' he had received some £11,000 from her. But as a witness, regardless of his financial dealings, he gave some interesting sidelights on the domestic arrangements of the Princess's 'family'.

It will be remembered that a point had been made in the case against the Queen of her having had breakfast with Pergami. Sicard was asked by Copley: 'Who were the servants that breakfasted together at Naples?' 'In the steward's room, there were all the upper servants, Pergami, me, Hieronimus, Mademoiselle Demont, and Barber, Lady Elizabeth's servant.'

'Will you undertake to swear that Pergami breakfasted at Naples in that room regularly?'—'Mostly with us, for he was very fond of meat, and used to go into the coffee-room, what we called the office, and have some meat for his luncheon or breakfast. He did not like tea; they do not take breakfasts in Italy, not tea, not one out of a thousand.'

'When you say they do not take breakfast, do you mean they do not take tea for breakfast?'—'No. They take it later, and make a meal of it.'[1]

Examined by the peers he was asked by Lord Lansdowne:

'Can you state, from your knowledge, whether at Naples the Princess of Wales breakfasted alone with Pergami?'—'Never, never to my knowledge.'

'Is it probable that such a circumstance could have occurred without your having known it?'—'It might have been, but I do not believe it.'

[1] Rather confusing: he means by 'it' breakfast or déjeuner.

'Did Pergami eat and drink with other livery servants?'—'At the steward's room, the upper servants' room, there were two tables; the livery servants dined below.'

'Did you ever know any other person that ate and drank at the steward's room, permitted to dine at the Princess's table?'—'Not to my recollection.'

'At what hour did the Princess usually breakfast at Naples?'—'According—no regular hour; eleven, twelve, or one.'

He was asked by Lord Ellenborough about Pergami—

'Did it occur to you to make any observation upon his manner?'—'Not in an uncommon way.'

'In the common way?'—'I saw his behaviour always was proper.'

'Did he appear superior to the situation in which he was hired?'—'He was not quite so chatty as the Italians in general were; but I believe he behaved very properly, so far as I saw.'

'Is the single circumstance of his not being so chatty as common Italians were, the only circumstance that distinguished him from other couriers?'—'His behaviour in general; I was never acquainted with any couriers in general, but he behaved very well in my opinion.'

'Did he appear to be superior to persons in his situation?'—'Not particularly, he behaved very properly in his situation, civil, and obliging, and attentive to his duty.'

'Did you consider him too much of a gentleman to act in the situation of a courier?'—'Not exactly so, he never showed himself in that way, he never refused to do any thing that he was told.'

'Did you consider that his manners were rather those of a gentleman than of a courier?'—'He might have been rather more of a gentleman than of the lower sort.'

The most important part of Sicard's evidence turned on the sleeping arrangements at Naples. He explained that Pergami changed his bedroom after the first night or two because he (Sicard) wished that a man-servant should be made available to sleep near a certain glass door, which led into the garden, thinking that it might be unsafe and provide easy access for a marauder. He also seems to have made it clear that it was possible for a person to go from Pergami's room to the Princess either through the cabinet (in which Majocchi claimed to have slept) and along a passage or through the garden.

Perhaps the most straightforward witness on behalf of the Queen was Henry Holland, a young doctor, at this time in his early thirties, though as was true of many of the English witnesses he had left the Princess's service in 1815. Moreover he had not a great deal to add since his medical duties required him to be 'very little about the person of the Princess'.[1] He denied absolutely that the Princess had come into Pergami's room when he was dressing Pergami's damaged foot. Lord Calthorpe asked him about the Princess's treatment of Pergami—'Do you recollect at any time, or under any circumstances, her Royal Highness conducting herself towards Pergami in a manner that you could consider at all inconsistent with the relation in which a Princess of Wales ought to stand towards a menial servant?'—'I must remark, in answer to that question, that her Royal Highness's demeanour towards all her servants was extremely familiar. I should say at once, that I never observed any difference between her manners to Pergami and her manners to any other of her servants; I may be perhaps allowed to add to that, to her principal servants.'

Holland was pressed about remarks he was supposed to have made to 'a minister at York' which were derogatory to the Princess. Lord Rous, a Tory, asked if he had not originally intended to dedicate his book of travel[2] to the Princess: 'I have not the slightest recollection that I ever said so.' Lord Rous went on to ask whether Holland did not think it very extraordinary that the Princess should have introduced him to the Countess Oldi, without stating who she was. Brougham was quickly on his feet to point out that Rous was assuming 'a thing which was not to be found in the whole four corners of the globe—namely what was passing in the mind of an individual'.

The next witness was an interesting member of the Gell-Craven

[1] Holland has been accurately described in the *Dictionary of National Biography* as 'more fashionable than scientific'. In his memoirs he describes how he was summoned to attend three ladies who were made ill by apprehension at the prospect of having to give evidence in the House of Lords. He adds that in fact one only was examined—presumably Lady Charlotte Lindsay—'and that in a way to justify her fears'. He adds that the Queen was the person least excited or affected by the proceedings. (*Recollections of Past Life*, 1872.)

[2] *Travels in the Ionian Islands, Albania, Thessaly, Macedonia during 1812 and 1813*, which was published in 1815.

fraternity—Charles Mills of the Villa Mills on the Palatine Hill.[1]
He was pressed about the company entertained by the Princess at
Rome. After naming two or three Italians he said that the Abbé
Taylor was her constant guest, and that he remembered Lord Kil-
worth, Lord Mountcashell's heir then in his middle twenties,
being there and, that he had met Cardinal Gonsalvi coming down-
stairs but otherwise 'I never saw any of their eminences'. For the
rest he remarked nothing in the pronunciation of the Countess Oldi
and asserted that he had never seen Pergami behave towards the
Princess 'otherwise than with the utmost respect'. Long afterwards
the Duke of Buckingham, who saw him in Rome, said that he had
given evidence at the Queen's trial 'and perjured himself more than
most'.[2]

Joseph Teuillé next gave evidence: he had been on the staff of
Beauharnais, and his brother had been a general under Napoleon.
In 1800 Pergami was *maréchal-de-logis* (quartermaster) in an Italian
regiment of hussars of which General Teuillé was in command. In
1809 he was in the household of General Pino, who commanded a
division of the Italian army in Spain. The cross-examination by
Parke opened with this question: 'Did you know Pergami when he
was in prison at Lodi?' Teuillé replied: 'I never heard anything of
it.' He was cross-examined about Pergami's exact position with
General Pino which he described as '*particulier*', meaning a courier
particularly attached to the General.

The fifteenth witness was Carlo Forti. He was in the service of
the Princess and, rather unexpectedly, claimed to be a nephew of
the Duchess of Torlonia. His examination by Brougham was largely
concerned to disprove what Sacchi claimed to have seen when he
went up to the Princess's travelling carriage. He claimed that Sacchi,
on the occasion in question, had not ridden on horseback but had
travelled in a caratella or calash. He could not ride, because when he

[1] This is Charles Andrew Mills (1760–1846), who came from the West
Indies originally. In writing a history of Glyn Mills's bank I had mistakenly
identified him with Sir Charles Mills (1792–1872), though feeling that there was
some improbability in the connexion of Lombard Street and the Palatine Hill.
Mr. H. V. Morton, in his delightful book *A Traveller in Rome*, puts the matter
straight, and correctly identifies C. A. Mills.

[2] *Private Diary of Richard Duke of Buckingham*, Hurst and Blackett, 1862.

had run a post or two he was all chafed. He also claimed that the Princess had not travelled alone with Pergami but with Countess Oldi, who sat between them. In the middle of the journey Countess Oldi, feeling unwell, had changed places with Demont.

Cross-examined by Gifford he said that he was still in the service of the Queen, and that he had last seen Pergami at St. Omer, to which place he had travelled with the Queen on her journey to England. He also said that Pergami was now known as the Baron della Franchina. He listed all the members of Pergami's family employed by the Princess. Countess Oldi was *dame d'honneur*, Faustina (another sister) was in charge of all the linen, Louis the brother was an equerry, Bernardo the cousin was prefect of the palace and Francesco, another cousin, was accountant. The cross-examination of this witness ended merrily enough.

'Were you not, at that time when you were with her Royal Highness, confined in prison?'—'I was not.'

'Nor at any other time when you were there with her Royal Highness?'—'When I was with her Royal Highness, never.'

'Was it before that period then that you were in prison?'

Mr. Brougham objected to this question. His learned friend assumed that the witness had been in prison.

'Were you ever in prison at Rome?'—'How, in what way in prison?'

'Did you ever sleep in prison; were you ever confined in prison?'—'Once I was arrested at a watchhouse at Piazza Colonna for five days.'

'When was that?'—'It was when I went to fetch the money from the banker, the Duke of Torlonia; when I was at Storta, the postillions would not give me the horses, and the postillions began to ill-treat me, and I began to retaliate, to beat them; the postillions came seven against me with their stable forks; I drew out my pistol and fired, and at that time arrived the courier of Monsieur Calcagnini, and he held my arm at the time that I had pulled the trigger to kill one of the postilions, and he in this way got the fire himself; then the governor, Monsieur Calcagnini, saw that I was right, kept me five days under arrest, and then let me go.'

'Was not the postilion killed?'—'I did not kill the postilion.'

'Was not one of the postilions killed upon that occasion?'—'No postilion was killed upon that occasion.'

'Was the courier injured?'—'He was wounded; I made him a hole as large as that here, in the belly.'

'Did he not die in consequence of that wound?'—'He was 40 days ill; he was my friend; it was through an accident.'

Re-examined by Brougham he explained that he wounded the courier by accident. 'He was, he is still my friend.' He went on to say that he fired to kill one of the postilions. Brougham asked: 'Do you mean one of the seven postilions, who were attacking you with pitchforks?' 'Yes; and I might have killed perhaps three or four of them, for my pistol had two bullets in it.'

The two next witnesses were of the first importance. They were two officers in the British Navy, and the Prime Minister told the King that 'if these persons should deny the facts, whether truly or falsely (provided it was done with constancy), to which the witnesses have deposed, it is impossible to answer for the result.'[1]

The first of these was Lieutenant Flinn R.N., or perhaps more correctly spelled as Flynn and called, with a refreshing disregard for what was correct by the Queen—Captain Fling. He had served in the Royal Navy, was living in Sicily and had also served in the Neapolitan Navy and claimed to have received an order of merit and fidelity from the King of Naples. He was in command of the polacca in which the Princess sailed to the East; all orders from the Princess were transmitted to the 'working' captain of the vessel who, it will be remembered, was Gargiulo. He said, under examination, that he had arranged the cabins on board: at Tunis, they took a surgeon on board and in consequence Pergami's berth was changed. He denied the evidence of Gargiulo, about the tent on deck on the voyage back from Jaffa and said that if people had been talking inside the Princess's tent their conversation would have been heard either by him, who slept on deck, or by the steersman. He claimed that the light had been put out from under the tent on his instructions so as not to give warning to pirates, whom he claimed were about, and had been seen by him. It will be remembered that Majocchi and the other Crown witnesses had made a point of the bath taken by

[1] *Letters of George IV, op. cit.*

the Princess on the polacca, which she did in the cabin. Flynn asserted that 'the tub' was too big to go into the cabin.

During his evidence Flynn was allowed to consult a memorandum or log which he claimed to have kept during the voyage. In cross-examination he told Copley that this was written in Italian. He later became confused and said that it was written partly in Italian and partly in English.

'Did you not tell me that the log was written in Italian?' 'Yes.' 'Now you mean to say it was written partly in Italian partly in English?' 'Part of both, to my recollection.' The official report continues: 'Here the witness, who seemed for some time previous, to be labouring under indisposition fainted, and was removed from the bar. On coming to himself he requested leave to withdraw, and was led out of the house. The Lord Chancellor immediately ordered the windows to be thrown open. . . .'

'I knew that he was lying, and I looked hard at him. He fainted away and was taken out of court', Lord Lyndhurst used to say in later life.[1]

Flynn had also to face a severe cross-examination from Copley on the furnishings of the tent. He asserted that her Royal Highness slept on the sofa and that the bed was there 'for persons to sit there during the day'.

'Have you any doubt that during that voyage, and the whole of it, Pergami slept upon that bed under the tent?'—'I cannot say where he slept, it is impossible for me to say, I can only repeat that I never saw him in bed.'

'Have you any doubt that he slept on that bed every night on the voyage from Jaffa to Syracuse?'—'I cannot say.'

'Have you any doubt upon the subject?'—'I must certainly doubt whether he did sleep there every night, or whether he did sleep there at all I cannot say, for I never saw him there, nor do I know where he slept.'

'Do you mean to say you entertain doubts whether he did sleep there, and believe that he did not sleep there?'—'When I never saw him there, I have every reason to doubt that he did not sleep there.'

[1] Theodore Martin, *Life of Lord Lyndhurst*, London, 1884.

'Do you mean by that to say that you believe he did not sleep there?'—'I believe he did not sleep there.'

'Where did he sleep?'—'I do not know; I never went to look where he slept.'

'Did you ever see him sleep in the cabin in the voyage from Jaffa to Syracuse?'—'I never went into the cabin in the day-time, to see whether he was there or not.'

'Did you ever see him, during any part of that voyage, sleeping in the cabin?'—'I do not know; I never went into the cabin to see whether he slept there or not.'

'Did you ever, either by night or in the morning, see him, during any part of that voyage, sleeping in the cabin in his former place?'—'I do not recollect having seen him there.'

'Do you mean now to repeat, that you believe he did not sleep under the tent?'—'I must again repeat that I do not know where he slept.'

'Not knowing where he did sleep, you mean to have it believed that you do not believe he slept under the tent?'—'I believe he did not sleep under the tent.'

'What is your reason for believing that he did not sleep under the tent?'—'Because when I went to see her Royal Highness one night, I did not see any one there.'

'Was it light or dark?'—'It was dark.'

'Of what country are you a native?'—'I was born an Englishman, part of an Irishman.'

'It being dark, and not seeing him when it was dark, is that the only reason for your belief that he did not sleep under the tent?'—'The light of the binnacle was quite sufficient to give me an opportunity of seeing whether he was there or not; it was dark at night, but there was the light from the binnacle that reflected into the place when I opened it.'[1]

'Attend to the oath you have taken; upon the night when her Royal Highness called you, and when you say there was a light from the binnacle, will you take upon yourself to swear that Pergami was not on that bed?'—'I do swear to it.'

Shortly after these questions, the house adjourned. It was of course

[1] The binnacle was the lighted box in which the compass was.

incredible that on a voyage of several weeks the captain should not have known where the chevalier slept. The next morning, before counsel came to the bar, Lord Grosvenor asked the Lord Chancellor if it was still his opinion that witnesses might be prosecuted for perjury. The Lord Chancellor declined to give an answer to what he called 'the most extraordinary question he had ever heard'. Extraordinary it certainly was, but Lord Grosvenor was not alone in thinking that Flynn was being reckless in his answers.

Lord Kingston, once affectionately greeted by George IV as 'You blackwhiskered rascal',[1] treated Flynn to a searching examination. He began by asking the measurements of 'the Princess's bathing-tub' on the polacca. The answer was at least six foot long, and two and a half to three feet deep. The cabin was 10 or $10\frac{1}{2}$ feet long, and the lieutenant explained that the tub could not be put in the cabin because of the Princess's sofa which 'never was removed'. Lord Kingston followed this by close examination of the lights, the pirates and the binnacle.

'Did you not say that the lights on deck in the tent were put out for fear of pirates seeing you?'—'Yes, after our departure from Jaffa.'

'Where did the binnacle stand?'—'By the mizen-mast.'

'Just before the helmsman?'—'Yes, close to the helmsman.'

'Was the binnacle where the light was put in glass all round?'—'Glass the forepart and glass on the afterpart.'

'Did you keep the afterpart open; were you not afraid of the pirates?'—'The forepart was generally kept open; there was a hole on the afterside of it; also a very small hole, just sufficient to enable the helmsman to work at the compass.'

'On what side was the door into the Princess's tent?'—'There was no door.'

'Where was the entrance?'—'It hauled up, it was not confined to the deck, by putting your hand on the lower part, you could lift it up.'

'When you went to her Royal Highness on being called, where did you lift up the tent?'—'The afterpart, close to the mizen-mast.'

'When lifted, could you see all through the tent, all over it?'—'With the reflection of the light of the binnacle I could.'

[1] Creevey, vol ii 30.

'And you can take upon you to swear, there was nobody there but the Princess of Wales?'—'I can.'

'You slept on the tiller?'—'I did.'

His antecedents and how he came to be associated with the Princess were the subject of questions by Lord Donoughmore.

'How long have you been a lieutenant in his Majesty's navy?'—'I have been eleven years a lieutenant.'

'What was the origin of the acquaintance you had the honour of having with the illustrious person who is the subject of this bill?'—'After the siege of Gaeta, where I had served as a volunteer, I was sent to Rome with a general, who commanded Gaeta, from thence I returned to Naples, where I received private instructions from the Neapolitan government to proceed to Corsica on a secret excursion, to make inquiry respecting the situation of Murat, the Ex-King of Naples; then after having sacrificed myself four nights and four days in continuing in the woods among the Corsicans, to gain intelligence respecting Murat, I returned to Naples; having delivered those reports which I had gained to the Prince of Hesse, I returned to Messina. The gun-boat which I then was serving in had orders to proceed to Corfu; but before the wind permitted for her to sail, Captain Briggs came in in the *Leviathan*, and I was presented by Captain Briggs to her Royal Highness; from that moment her Royal Highness inquired what I was going to do, and as I had nothing particular to do, she invited me to proceed on the voyage with her, which I did.'[1]

Lord Donoughmore also put a shrewd question about the tent on the polacca. 'Do not you conceive that the crew would take particular care not to incommode her Royal Highness during the night by passing too near the tent?' Flynn agreed unless 'the occupation of the ship had necessitated their passing'. Lord Donoughmore also asked how it was that although Flynn could not say where

[1] The siege of Gaeta, when the city was defended by Prince Louis of Hesse-Philippsthall, was in 1808. There is presumably an interval of seven years between this and Flynn's secret expedition to Corsica where Murat went after Waterloo. This passage from Flynn's evidence perhaps explains Creevey's comment: 'This cursed Flynn is still going on. . . . He is evidently a crack-brained sailor . . .'. Creevey *op. cit.* i 323.

Pergami slept during the month's voyage he could yet feel competent to say so decisively that he did not sleep under the tent.

Here Brougham interrupted: 'Really, my lords, I cannot admit this question to be put.' The Duke of Clarence, after asking that counsel should withdraw, thought that Brougham's language was not suitable to the dignity of the House. The Lord Chancellor thought that the language was 'not exactly what it ought to be'.[1] On his return Brougham apologised, adding equivocally that he would use that language which was most congenial with his feelings and with the respect that was due to their lordships.

The rest of the examination by the peers was principally concerned with the binnacle. The Duke of Clarence showed that his experience as an officer in the Royal Navy had not been wasted. He pointed out that Flynn had been accustomed to the sea for 19 years—eight as a midshipman and eleven as a lieutenant—and suggested that he must have known how to keep the binnacle alight without throwing a beam towards the tent or towards the sea. The Marquis of Buckingham asked that as he knew pirates were 'hovering about' did he not take means to diminish the light. 'Sometimes a flag was thrown over it ... but you could see through the bunting.'

William Carrington who, it will be remembered, was Sir William Gell's servant, was then called and re-examined. His life story so far as it was revealed by the evidence gives an interesting glimpse of the kind of men serving in the Royal Navy. He had said in evidence that he had served as a midshipman on the *Poitiers* under Sir John Beresford, a fine sailor and subsequently admiral of the fleet. Examined by the first Lord of the Admiralty (Lord Melville) he admitted that he served on several other ships before this as quartermaster and that he had been pressed into the service. He explained that he had, as a boy, lived at St. Oswyth (near Colchester) and that he had been in the merchant service. When Sir John Beresford told him that he would be promoted 'I told him I did not wish to be on the quarter-deck, for I had no friends or money to support me on the quarter-deck.'

[1] Brougham throughout treated the peers as though they were a pack of jurymen on the northern circuit. On one occasion Lord Exmouth, the naval hero, asked for the protection of the House from Brougham's 'insulting gaze'.

'You never heard that Sir William Gell had asked your discharge?'
—'I saw Sir William Gell when he first came passenger on board the
Poitiers, going to Lisbon; he came home passenger in the same ship;
he saw me on the poop; he asked me many different questions respecting the ship, and also for a spy-glass to look at a ship in the
convoy; it was not a very good one; he sent me down to get his,
which I did; and another circumstance happened—I was standing
by the wheel at the gun, and he called me into his cabin, which was
under the break of the poop, to put on the half port to prevent the
water coming in: there were many other little things he asked me to
do in the cabin, as he had no servant: when we drew near the land,
he said, I am very much obliged to you for your attentions to me
during the voyage; I cannot give you any money, but if there is
any thing I can do to speak to Sir John Beresford, I shall be very
happy to do it; I said, there is nothing you can do for me with Sir
John Beresford but to ask him whether he can get my discharge, as
I am not capable of appearing as a gentleman on the quarter-deck,
which I understand I am to be, and I had rather leave it; he told me,
you ought to consider it well—what will you do when you get on
shore? I told him that I would prefer any thing rather than stopping
in the navy in that sort of way; that I had no means of supporting
myself as a gentleman. He said, consider you are now rated as an
officer; I said, I understand that, but I cannot support it, and therefore I had rather leave it: he said, are you sure that you had rather
leave the navy, and that is the thing you would wish to be asked; I
said yes, that is it: he said, I will ask you to-morrow morning, and
you will consider about it more, if you are sure you had rather leave
it than remain as a midshipman on board: the next morning he asked
me again, and I told him the same—that I had rather leave the navy;
he mentioned it to Sir John, and Sir John said yes, he certainly would
do it, there was no difficulty. When we came to Portsmouth, we lay
there some time, till at last Lieutenant Alcock, the commanding
officer of the ship, called me upon the quarter-deck, and said, here
is something concerning your wanting your discharge from the navy
—what is it you mean? I told him what I had said to Sir William Gell
concerning Sir John; he said you must be mad to go to leave the navy
now, now you have got what you have been looking for; I said, it is

true I have got it, but I have not the means of supporting it, and I had rather be discharged than remain as a midshipman without any support to appear like a gentleman as the others do: he said, you must be mad, it cannot be so; I shall write to Sir John to say you have altered your mind, or something to that purpose: I said, pray do not do that, for that is my mind and my wish, and I shall write to Sir William Gell to ask Sir John to remember his promise, which he did. After that Sir William and Sir John met, and they thought it was something very mysterious; Sir William said we will prevent it; we will send a man down: there was a man sent down to know whether it was my wish, as I had stated before, which it was: there was an acting captain sent, Captain Jones I think it was, on board the *Poitiers*, who gave me a ticket of leave of absence, told me I was to go to London to Sir John Beresford, and there to receive my orders, which I did. After I came to London, Sir John told me, you are in the same mind, that you wish to leave the navy, I said yes, it is my wish; very well, he says: he ordered me to stay for a few days, and then, when I went to him again, he said, you are to go down to the *Thisbe*, and ask for your papers, and then come to me again: I went to him: I believe he sent a letter, whether he sent the letter by me or by the post I am not certain, to the commanding officer. I went to the *Thisbe*; they told me there were no papers there for me, and they knew nothing of my name at the present: I went back to Sir John; he told me, it is of no consequence, you remain as you are, and go where you like; if you choose to go into service or any where, nobody will trouble you; if they do, you will apply to me, and I will give them an answer. After which he gave me a written certificate by his own hand. After I had been abroad two years or better with Sir William Gell, I saw Sir John Beresford again; I told him I had not received the last pay I had due from the *Poitiers*; he says, that is very odd, I will give you a letter to a gentleman in Somerset House, and you will go and receive your pay, which I did; and I have never been asked any questions about the navy since, till I came before your lordships.'

The Duke of Clarence was proceeding to ask him questions which he had already answered, and Brougham pointed this out. The Duke replied: 'I am very blind, and cannot see it without my glasses', and then in his inconsequential way he added: 'no man breathing can admire more than I do the abilities of the learned counsel.'

Some days later, Admiral Sir John Poo Beresford was examined. He said that there was no man who behaved better than Carrington, but that he had never been a midshipman and never had any reason to suppose that he would be one. If Carrington had ever stated that it was financially difficult for him to accept promotion 'I should have maintained him, as I did others in the Service, till he could pay me again . . . . After I knew he was to be Sir William Gell's servant it was very unlikely I should propose him to be an officer in the Service.'

9

I Believe He Did

On the seventh day of the defence (10 October) the most important witness for the Queen was examined. Though the best of all appearing—perhaps on either side—he was decisive in damaging the Queen's cause in the eyes of all unprejudiced observers. Joseph Robert Hownam was a lieutenant in the Royal Navy, having held the rank since 1809, and having been in the service some seventeen years. His father was a royal page, having been for most of his life with George IV or Princess Charlotte. He himself had served in the *Africaine* (Captain Manby—the officer who appeared in the Delicate Investigation) the *Lively* (Captain Hammond) the *Centaur* (Sir Samuel Hood), the *Barfleur* (Captain M'Cloud), the *Lavinia* (Lord W. Stewart), the *Resistance* (Captains Adam, Rosenhagen and Pellew), and the *Undaunted* (Captain Usher). At the time of the case he was settled at Rouen with his wife and family. In April 1815 he had been summoned to join the Princess at Genoa when she was planning her expedition to Southern Italy and Africa.

He amplified the story in some important particulars. It will be remembered that the Hanoverian, Baron Ompteda was believed to have spied on the Princess and to have suborned her servants. In his evidence, on examination, Hownam said 'I called him out.' He denied that he did this on the 'direction' of the Princess: he did it on her 'representation'. The challenge was written in English.[1]

He said that everywhere (except Vienna) the Princess was received

[1] Ompteda is believed to have named Switzerland as the place where the duel might be fought, which venue was virtually impossible for Hownam with his duties in attendance on the Princess. Sir Edward Parry, *Queen Caroline*, 1930.

with the greatest attention and respect by persons of the first distinction and by the foreign courts. For her part her conduct and demeanour were 'everything that was majesty and grace'.

He agreed that the Princess was in the habit of playing games with the servants, but 'more to amuse William Austin than anything else I believe'. They were *Petits Jeux* (forfeits) and *Colin Maillard* (Blind Man's Buff). He edged near trouble when he was asked about the theatre at the Villa d'Este and whether he had ever seen the Princess play Columbine to Pergami's Harlequin. (In Italian comedy Columbine was the mistress of Harlequin.) In examination by the peers he was asked by Lord Combermere—

'During the period of your residence in Italy, have you ever seen any entertainment, either at the house of her Royal Highness or at any other place, in which the characters of harlequin and columbine were sustained in the same manner that they usually are in this country, in what is called a Harlequin Farce?'—'All I have seen is, I have seen Louis Pergami [Pergami's brother] in a harlequin's dress, and more than once I have seen him.'

'Can you state whether you have ever seen the part of harlequin sustained in Italy in the same manner that it is in England?'—'I do not think I ever did.' Previously, in cross-examination, he had been closely questioned on this point—

'Have you not seen her perform the part of columbine when Louis Pergami was the harlequin?'—'I do not recollect that, but it was before more than 200 persons she performed; I do not recollect what parts she performed.'

'Do you recollect Louis Pergami performing with her Royal Highness?'—'Every body performed on the stage together, at least all the household; the piece, whatever it was, was composed of the persons of the house.'

'Was Louis Pergami one of them?'—'He was.'

'Will you swear that you do not recollect her Royal Highness performing the part of columbine?'—'Upon my word it is not marked on my memory that she performed the part of columbine.'

'Do you mean that the general conduct of her Royal Highness was such, that you have no recollection of her performing the part of the columbine with Louis Pergami?'—'I do not recollect whether she performed the part of columbine; there were two or three pieces that evening, she may or she may not; I do not positively remember that evening.'

'Or on any other evening?'—'No, that was the only time that was performed; there were rehearsals to that little piece that was performed.'

'I thought you said there were two or three pieces?'—'Yes, on the same evening; I do not recollect perfectly what they were; amongst the rest there was a dance I believe.'

'Did her Royal Highness dance?'—'Yes.'

'Do you mean to say you do not remember whether her Royal Highness danced with Louis Pergami on the stage that evening?'— 'I do mean positively to say, that I do not recollect having seen her Royal Highness dance with Louis Pergami; she may, or she may not.'

'Was not one of the pieces a harlequinade?'—'Yes, I think it was.'

'Who performed the part of harlequin?'—'I have seen Louis Pergami dressed as harlequin; he had the dress.'

'Having recollected who was the harlequin, do you not remember that her Royal Highness was the columbine?'—'No, I do not recollect the fact; if I was to say it, it would be only because you say it; I do not recollect that her Royal Highness performed the part of columbine, the thing is not sufficiently impressed upon my memory to declare that it was so.'

'You will not say that she did not perform the part of columbine?' —'I will say as much one way as the other; I do not recollect.'

'Do you remember any part that the Princess performed that evening upon the stage?'—'Yes, I think she performed the part of an automaton.'

'What do you mean by an automaton; in what way did she perform?'—'The history was—it is long ago that I do not recollect, but it was a man that wanted to sell an automaton, a woman in fact that you could wind up to any thing; I forget the history of the thing; it was a farce upon the person who bought it, to find his mistake; it is a long time ago, I do not recollect the whole of the story; it was a little story composed by the Princess herself, I believe.'

'Then her Royal Highness was the automaton?'—'Yes, I think she was; she was in fact.'

Lord Limerick, an extreme Tory, who 20 years later was narrowly to escape the indignity of having his corpse hurled into the Shannon by his Irish compatriots, asked: 'What did the automaton do; was she sitting, standing, lying, running, or what?'—'I think in a box standing up.'

'Do you conceive that these acts, so stated by you, are consonant to the high dignity of the royal personage about whom we have been speaking?'—'I do not consider it in the least derogatory to her Royal Highness's rank, knowing the pleasure she takes in that sort of entertainment.'

Hownam, in reply to Lord Auckland, described Pergami's dress when he was a courier: 'I think it was a bottle-green and gold, turned up with scarlet.... A very handsome dress.... It was not a hussar's dress: it was richly embroidered with Brandenburghs.'[1]

Hownam's examination lasted for part of the 7th day, the whole of the 8th day and a large part of the 9th day. The Prime Minister, at the close of Hownam's cross-examination, rose to say that the proceedings should be adjourned for a quarter of an hour so that the witness might have refreshment. This he declined, but he was accommodated with a chair. At the start of the proceedings on the eighth day the Lord Chancellor remarked that after he had ordered that the windows should be opened, *somebody* had shut them. He would take care that an officer of the House was stationed at the windows to see that 'the unknown *somebody*' did not shut them.

Hownam was closely questioned about any familiarities, which he might have witnessed between Pergami and the Princess.

'You have stated, that you saw her dining with him, when he was a courier, in his courier's dress, that he afterwards walked with her at the Villa d'Este arm in arm; they went out together in a canoe alone, and that he then began regularly to dine with her Royal Highness; do you think that degrading or not?'—'I never saw her Royal Highness walk arm and arm with him, until he began to dine regularly with her Royal Highness.'

'You must perceive that is no answer to the question, do you

[1] Ornamental facings to uniform.

consider that which you have stated as degrading to her Royal Highness or not?'—'I do not.'

'Have you never represented it to her as degrading to her that Pergami should dine with her?'—'I never did.'

Hownam's examination really turned on the tent on board the polacca on the way back to Italy from Jaffa. In his examination by Tindal he had explained certain further points about the tent:

'You re-embarked at Jaffa at your return?'—'We did.'

'Was the weather at that time hot, or otherwise?'—'Excessively hot, it was the month of July.'

'Had you any cattle on board the vessel of any kind?'—'We had.'

'What did they consist of?'—'Horses and asses.'

'Had you more on board on your return that you had on your voyage out?'—'We had none in going out.'

'In what part of the vessel were those animals kept?'—'In the hold.'

'Did they make any noise in the course of the night or the day?'—'The general noise of horses and such animals.'

'Was there any smell occasioned by the animals being put in the hold?'—'Yes there was, certainly.'

'Where did her Royal Highness sleep on the voyage from Jaffa homewards?'—'Under the tent, on deck.'

'By whose direction was the tent put up?'—'By direction of the Princess.'

'Did it remain permanently on the deck from the time of your quitting Jaffa to the end of the voyage?'—'It did.'

'Do you recollect, at any time, any complaint made by her Royal Highness as to the rate of the vessel's sailing?'—'Yes, I do.'

'What was the complaint?'—'It was on the return from the island of Rhodes to Syracuse; the voyage became excessively tedious, and the Princess, naturally anxious to get on shore, attributed it to the want of sailing of the vessel; I stated, that she could not be supposed to sail so well with a tent on deck; her Royal Highness said, as to the tent, I do not care at all about it, I would as soon sleep without it.'

'What was the occasion of her Royal Highness sleeping under the tent during the return voyage?'—'In consequence of the excessive heat, and the animals on board.'

After this came Gifford's question about the sleeping arrangements on the return voyage from Jaffa. 'You have said that you did not know where Pergami slept; upon your oath do you not believe he slept under the tent?' 'I have heard he did sleep under the tent.' 'I do not wish to know what you have heard.' 'And I believe he did sleep under the tent.'

Re-examined by Tindal he was asked to give the grounds for his belief.

'Because in the time of the squall on the coast of Karamania, which made her Royal Highness come down below, Pergami told me the sea came into the tent, consequently he must have been there, or he could not have known it.'

'Have you a distinct recollection as to the dress of Pergami on that occasion?'—'No, I have not.'

'The question is not how he was dressed, but whether he was dressed or not?'—'Oh, he was dressed.'

'Do you believe he was dressed every night when he was under the tent?'

The Solicitor-General was astonished to hear such a question from his learned friend. He was astonished to hear him say, 'Do you believe he was dressed?' to his own witness; and apprehended the question could not be put.

Mr. Brougham was no less astonished at the objection of the Solicitor-General.

The Lord-Chancellor thought that, under the circumstances of the case, the question could not be put.

Earlier in his evidence Hownam had spoken of the need for a man to sleep near her Royal Highness in case of an accident or a rough sea. Lord Limerick then asked a series of questions, beginning: 'What did you conceive the necessity to arise from?'

'I never represented the necessity myself; but upon the occasion of thinking of it, I must confess that I think it was necessary for some person to be near her Royal Highness; a woman alone upon a ship's deck at sea, I should think perfectly authorised in having some person near her.'

'Would not that necessity have been equally met by any of her numerous suite having either their hammock slung upon deck, or some person mounting guard outside the tent, instead of sleeping in a covered tent, in the dark?'—'The thing never suggested itself to me before; but the suite was not so numerous as to admit of one person being always on watch round her tent; there could have been only Captain Flynn and myself, as to the Count Schiavini, you could not expect from him, a man who had never put his foot on a ship's deck before, to keep such a watch upon deck.'

'Could not a hammock have been slung equally well for any such person, as it was slung for Lieutenant Flynn, who usually did sleep on the deck?'—'A hammock might have been slung there, but the act of Flynn's bringing his cot on deck was merely to have the cool air, to be more comfortable.'

'Would it not have equally answered the purpose to meet that necessity you have stated, if a female had been placed in that tent instead of a male person, or besides the male person, the tent being equal to the containing three persons?'—'I cannot say as to that, there might have been fifty other ways, as to that matter; we might have all of us slept round the tent outside as well as one.'

'Was there ever any order given to the officer of the watch to watch especially over the person of her Royal Highness?'—'No, I do not recollect it; the officer of the watch was the mate of the vessel.'

'Were any suspicions entertained by you of the crew, or any part of the crew?'—'None.'

'Then it was not from any apprehensions of the crew you conceived it necessary that a man, a male, should sleep under the tent upon the deck with the Princess of Wales?'—'When I saw the thing, I looked upon it in that way.'

'In what way?'—'That it was not at all improper that he should have slept there, her Royal Highness being on deck by herself.'

'Are you to be understood to say distinctly, that you do not conceive there is any impropriety in a male person sleeping in the same tent, the lights being out, with a female?'—'From the manner that the hatchway was open, and all the doors below, there was no mystery in it whatever.'

'As you are a married man, would you have any objection, or conceive it improper that Mrs. Hownam should so sleep in a tent in the dark with a male person?'—'I trust that every man looks upon his wife without making any comparison or exception; I never made the comparison.'

'You cannot form an opinion upon it?'—'I cannot form an opinion.'

Mr. Brougham objected to these comparisons. He observed, that if it was taken down in the minutes, it might give a meaning to the former answer of the witness, different from that which he certainly intended. The inference might be, that he wished no comparison to be made between Mrs. Hownam and the illustrious person, and such an inference would be untrue.

Lord Limerick said, he had made no comparison. He did not wish either to hurt the feelings of the witness, or to have any thing put in the minutes that ought not to appear.

'Do you say that you see no impropriety, situated as the tent was open towards the deck below, in a male and female sleeping so placed in such a tent?'—'I do not conceive there was any impropriety in the thing, because I must have felt it, and I did not feel it; I have seen so many situations that her Royal Highness has been placed in, in the course of her travels, that I do not look upon it as improper.'

'What do you mean by saying, you have seen so many situations, in the course of her Royal Highness's travels, that you do not think it improper?'—'At Ephesus the Princess of Wales lay under a sorry shed, that you would hardly put a cow into in this country, in the midst of horses, mules, Jews, Turks—all I can say is, that the idea did not strike me as improper.'

'In the early part of your cross-examination you said that you did not know where Pergami slept; after a considerable time, after many questions, you were induced to form a belief, and to state that Pergami slept in the tent. I beg to ask what is your reason for stating that early in your examination?'

Lord Liverpool submitted that this was not a proper question; it was a sort of inference to be collected from the testimony of the witness, a matter of reasoning by and by.

Lord Darnley, after asking some questions about Pergami, suddenly asked: 'Have the goodness to state the age of Mrs. Hownam?' 'About thirty.' He then went on: 'Have you always lived together as man and wife ought to do?' Amid cries of order and 'considerable confusion' the gallant sailor was heard to say 'we have'.

In his examination Hownam had said that he had gone up the ladder which, it will be remembered, linked the dining-room and the tent but, finding the tent in darkness he had returned to the dining-room. Lord de Dunstanville asked—'You have said that at night you sometimes went up the ladder from the dining-cabin to the tent, but that finding the Princess had retired for the night you withdrew; how do you reconcile this proceeding with your opinion that there was nothing indecent in Pergami passing the night in the tent with her Royal Highness?'—'I withdrew from the impossibility of getting on deck, as the tent came close round to the combings of the hatchway, all round on the side on which the ladder was placed.'

'You stated that there was no light in the dining-room?'—'I think not.'

'What was the occasion of your going into the dining-room, and from thence into the tent?'—'From the habit of going up there all day; I did not know that the tent was closed; it was not absolutely in the night; ten o'clock, I think I said—towards the evening.'

'At what period of the year was this?'—'We left Jaffa I think on the 17th July, and we arrived at Syracuse, I think, on the 20th of August.'

'Do you mean to say, that at that period of the year, it was not dark at 10 o'clock?'—'It was night-time, it was dark; it was as dark as it is at such an hour in such a climate.'

Lord Darlington asked some questions about the sleeping habits of the Princess in the tent, and about her dress—

'You have frequently mentioned her Royal Highness sleeping in the tent on board; the sleep, when you mentioned her sleeping in that tent, is it to be understood that you meant that she rather reposed upon the sofa, than slept, in the general acceptation of the word sleeping, going to bed, and pulling off her clothes, for the sake of rest; are you to be understood that she reposed with her clothes on, when you make use of the word sleeping?'—'I do not believe her Royal Highness ever took her clothes off on board the polacca, except to shift herself in the day, to change her dress; that is my firm belief.

I mean in the voyage back from Jaffa; on the first voyage she slept in her cabin.'

'You did not positively state that you knew that Pergami was under the tent?'—'I never saw him there.'

'If you state that it was your belief that he was under the tent, do you also believe that Pergami reclined in the same manner on the other bed with his clothes on?'—'I do not think Pergami ever took his clothes off either, while sleeping under the tent, for I never saw any bedclothes on that bed.'

In the examination by the peers Lord Lauderdale asked a question which set out the incongruity of the Princess's conduct—

'Recollecting that you have dined at her Royal Highness's table with Pergami, whom you have seen serve at her Royal Highness's table, with Louis Pergami, who has served you at her Royal Highness's table, with Pergami's sister, and with his mother; and when you recollect the circumstance further, that you have sworn to your belief that Pergami was under the tent with her Royal Highness at night, between Jaffa and Capo d'Anza; do you persevere in swearing upon your oath, that you have seen her Royal Highness do nothing improper or unbecoming of her station?'—'I speak for myself; I had no greater claim to sitting at her Royal Highness's table than either of those people; I have seen people sitting at her Royal Highness's table while their fathers have been waiting at table; and I never saw any thing in the conduct of her Royal Highness, knowing the way she treats everybody, to authorise such an opinion.'

'Did you ever wait at her Royal Highness's table?'—'Never.'

Mr. Brougham.—'A lieutenant in his Majesty's navy is asked if he ever waited at table!'

The Lord-Chancellor.—'Mr. Brougham, object to the question if you think it improper, but you are not to make such observations if a question offends you.'

The Earl of Lauderdale.—'I am the last that would have asked such a question, had not the witness said that Pergami and his relations had as great a claim as he to sit at her Royal Highness's table.'

'Have any of your relations sat at her Majesty's table?' 'I do not believe they ever did.'

After Hownam's evidence the diarist, Charles Greville, wrote:

'all unprejudiced men seem to think the adultery sufficiently proved.'[1]

Granville Sharp, no doubt a relative of the great philanthropist and emancipator, gave evidence—what would be called to-day expert evidence—about the Moorish dance. He was in the army in India and in reply to Denman said that he had seen the dance in Calcutta.

'In what places?'—'In the government house.'

'Who was governor at the time?'—'The Marquess of Hastings.'

'Was his excellency present while this dance was exhibited?'—'He was.'

'Was the marchioness there?'—'She was.'

'And other ladies?'—'Yes, other ladies.'

'Do you remember whether the Bishop of Calcutta[2] was present?'—'Yes, the Bishop of Calcutta was present.'

'Was his lady there?'—'Yes, she was.'

Some days later Sharp appeared again to admit that his memory was at fault in saying that the Bishop—and presumably his lady—had been present at the dance.

[1] *The Greville Memoirs* 1814–1860. Edited by Lytton Strachey and Roger Fulford. 8 vols, 1938.

[2] This was Bishop Middleton, the first Bishop of Calcutta. He once said that the 'fabric of idolatry' in the East would never be shaken merely by preaching.

'Who is the Party Against Me?'

❖❀❖

Santino Gugiari was the next witness; he was employed at the Villa d'Este as factor and he described his duties as being to keep a watch upon the working people, to mark their accounts and to pay them on Saturdays. He also took care of the wine and distributed it to the family. (He is here using that word in the sense of household.) He described the grotto in detail with the help of plans. (This was the place where workmen had claimed to have seen the Princess and Pergami lift the fig-leaves from statues of Adam and Eve.) His main point, not shaken by cross-examination, was that it was not possible to see the statues from the room in which the workmen were mould-ing the cornice because 'the communication is crooked and prevents the sight'. Perhaps not altogether unexpectedly, that strange peer Lord Blessington, who had a species of *menage-à-trois* with Lady Blessington and Count d'Orsay, asked for particulars of the fig-leaves. He was told that they were not fig leaves, but vine leaves and that they were made of tin: they were movable, and suspended by a brass wire. Giuseppe Giarolini was next called and corroborated what had been said about the impossibility of seeing the statues of Adam and Eve from the other rooms in the grotto. He provided the information that formerly the Villa d'Este had belonged to General Pino, under whom Pergami had served in the army. He made a serious charge against Rastelli who, as has already been stated, had been head-superintendent of the Princess's stables, and an important witness against her. The Queen's counsel were anxious to prove that Rastelli had offered people money to give evidence, but the counsel for the Bill objected to questions being put about conversations between Giarolini and Rastelli unless counsel could show that they arose from Rastelli's own evidence. The discussion of the point of law aroused great fire and fury among the peers. Lord Erskine, characteristically vigorous, argued the general point.

'If, then, Rastelli had intermeddled—he would not use a stronger word at present—but if he had intermeddled in getting evidence against her Royal Highness, the counsel had a right to inquire into that fact, and it was most important for their lordships. He attended there, from day to day, to do all in his power that the strict rules of law might be attended to as far as, in the situation in which they were placed, their proceedings could be assimilated to ordinary proceedings: but it was essentially necessary that all the light should be let in upon this dark transaction which they could let in: he lamented exceedingly that in this transaction they were at the present moment so much in the dark as to the Milan commission. . . . But when they knew that a commission had been appointed, that examinations had undoubtedly taken place, and that evidence so given originally was afterwards brought before their lordships, they ought to be informed of the origin and character of all this previous proceeding. What light had they upon the manner in which the witnesses became first known, and how they were brought to Milan, and examined upon this subject? What light had they upon any step in the proceeding before the case came to their lordships' bar? He, for one, had no light at all upon those subjects; and he ought to know, from examinations, cross-examinations, and every way in which light could be obtained. As to Rastelli, now was the opportunity of cross-examining him on points which had not been known before. The question now, therefore, was, how the contradictions to Rastelli, or the acts which he had done, could be brought before them. Either their lordships must assent to the request of the learned gentlemen at the bar, or Rastelli must be called back, as Majocchi had been. His opinion was, that it would be the better course to call back Rastelli: but was there not agency already admitted? Could any thing be clearer proof of agency—and, he would add, of corrupt and profligate agency—than the attempt to get a witness against her Royal Highness by saying that there were Englishmen at Milan who would see money paid to the witness in return? Was there a noble lord in that House who did not believe that the agency extended farther than they had traced by any inquiries or statements? If not, who could say that it was not necessary to have the whole of this profligate proceeding discovered, discussed, and well considered, before they formed any judgment upon the evidence in general? Before that was done, they could have no means of ascertaining the truth. When their lordships deliberated upon the general question now at issue, there must be nothing left dark, nothing must remain behind. He perfectly agreed that their situation was very different from that of ordinary trials. That was the great evil of the present proceeding, that it left the ordinary course of justice, and intrenched on the ancient constitution of the land. Care ought to be therefore taken by their lordships that this evil should not be magnified. Could he have any faith in the case as it stood at present before their lordships? Rastelli himself had admitted a corrupt agency—he said distinctly a corrupt agency, from the facts which were already in evidence. He said, therefore, that their lordships must in some way or other know further respecting the acts of Rastelli; they must know further, or they could not know the truth, or judge with safety in this case.'

It was decided that the question could be put and when examination was resumed Giarolini was asked whether he had any further conversation with Rastelli about witnesses.

'The first time I had conversed with him, I was coming from the States of the Pope, and I had a conversation with him in an inn, and afterwards I had conversation with him in other places; but we talked a little upon this subject, and then we talked upon other discourses; and another day we were coming out from the Custom House of Porta Tosa, and I was going out of the ramparts in the street of Circolazione of Milan, and we were then talking about witnesses; he told me that he had gone into my country about witnesses, and then, when he was in my country, he went to ask for one witness and that witness went to ask another, that other went to ask another, then they had drank together; and he has asked them whether they were willing to depose against her Royal Highness, and then he asked them, will you come to Milan with me; then they breakfasted at the Tredate coming from Cazzone, from Tredate they went to Musoc, there they dined; when they arrived at Milan they went altogether to the inn of St. Clement; when they were at the inn of St. Clement, Rastelli told the innkeeper to give them every thing they wanted for their victuals; then afterwards, one after another, he took them before Vimercati, and the other English that were there.'[1]

'On any of those occasions did Rastelli say that he had paid money to any of those witnesses?'

The Solicitor-General objected to the form of the question.

The Lord-Chancellor said they might ask whether Rastelli said any thing about paying money.

'Did Rastelli say any thing about his having paid money?'—'He told me had kept them seven days at the inn, and paid forty francs; that he had paid them forty francs each.'

When the peers were examining Giarolini there was an acrimonious but irrelevant altercation among them, which was started by Lord Lauderdale's question 'Do you recollect the bath-room at the Villa d'Este?' Brougham objected to the question and spoke of the delay if he was expected to bring over additional witnesses to meet the charges of another public prosecutor. Lord Lauderdale said that it was competent for any peer to put questions 'without being called a public prosecutor'. Lord Darnley—an impetuous Whig—then said: 'Their lordships, on this occasion, should recollect that they had taken upon themselves the anomalous functions of judges, jurors, and legislators. He had always understood it to be the duty of a judge or a juror to lean to the side of mercy, and in favour of the accused. Keeping in mind this understanding, he could not refrain from taking this opportunity of remarking, that, notwithstanding what had been said by some of their lordships of dignity and decency, of which he had heard so much, there were some to be found who appeared—instead of being impartial judges, and disposed to lean to the side of mercy—to have feelings of an opposite character. (The noble earl was here interrupted by loud cries of "Order".)'

Lord Redesdale, who was, it will be remembered, a lawyer

[1] The geography here is confused. He seems—allowing for changes in spelling—referring to places to the north-east of Milan. The nearest of the Papal States were south of the Po, and of Milan.

and a supporter of the bill, said that if allegations of partiality were to be made they applied, if at all, 'as well to the opposite side of the House as to his side; indeed, more so'.

Lord Holland, in a graceful speech (though it was a delicate one as he was an old political ally of Citizen Maitland, as Lauderdale was known in his Whiggish youth) brought the matter to its close. He said that 'he was as anxious as any body to see their lordships abstain from altercation. He begged that the learned lord (Redesdale) would not take their defence under his charge; for if his mode of defending the House against the charge of partiality was by imputing to his opponents unfair, unjust, and illiberal proceedings, it was the most unfortunate defence against partiality that he had ever listened to. It was wrong, he well knew, to impute improper motives to any noble lord; but he hoped that they would not feel hurt at an observation which he was going to make—namely, that both parties were as partial as they possibly could be. Nobody could possibly doubt that any noble lord possessed the right of calling up any witness who could either directly or indirectly give testimony respecting the bill. Neither could any body doubt that to such a witness any question could be put by them, even though in its nature it were not strictly legal. But his noble friend (Lord Lauderdale) had been the first to take objections against evidence which was not so, and the thanks of the House were due to him for so doing.[1] And therefore any party, or any of their lordships, had a right to object to the putting of questions leading to a new inquiry'.

Lord Holland's next intervention was less pacific. It transpired that Rastelli had been sent back to Italy, seemingly with the idea that he should reassure his compatriots that in spite of the Dover riots, when many of the witnesses had been hustled, they had not met with harm. Lord Holland said 'Gracious God! can your lordships—I ask it in the name of common sense and common feeling— can your lordships suppose that after such a proceeding as this, great

---

[1] This presumably refers to the cross-examination of Meidge Kress. Lauderdale interrupted Brougham to say that a cross-examination designed to undermine the credit of a witness with an understanding that there was to be a subsequent cross-examination was objectionable and destructive of all justice. His point of view was upheld by the Lord Chancellor. (See page 91.)

as is the reputation of your lordships, great as is the character of this House, which I have always been eager to uphold by every means in my power—can you suppose that we, who are subject to human failings and human infirmities, can stand in safety when opposed to the suspicion and the odium which such a proceeding must cast upon us? What is the case, my lords? Here is Rastelli, who was employed, by his own confession, as courier to the Milan commission—here is one of the witnesses who stated the most disgusting and unnatural fact that ever was mentioned in a court of justice[1]— here is this man, who is one of that description, regarding whom you were told that every step should be taken by the limited authority of this government (and there are some who wish that it were not so limited), to prevent them from being withdrawn from justice;— here is this very man, I say, upon whom suspicion now rests that he has been engaged in suborning witnesses for this prosecution, not merely escaping, but sent away by the government! If your lordships submit to be dragged through the mire in this manner—if, after having solemn promises made to you, you permit them not only to be evaded, but even to be counteracted by those who made them, then are your proceedings a mockery and a burlesque. You will taint, not merely your present proceedings, but all your future measures; you will taint this branch of the legislature, and will involve the country, already reduced to great distress from having blindly followed the counsels of these self-same men upon other points, in still greater distress, and will place its institutions in the utmost jeopardy and danger. He therefore said, with his noble friend (Lord Carnarvon), who had made such a solemn appeal to them on the point, that this matter ought to be set right, or that, considering all these circumstances as forming a *prima facie* case of the existence of a conspiracy to pervert justice, they would do well to get rid of the disgust and fatigue of this infamous proceeding.'

The discussion then proceeded more calmly and when the Prime Minister, in reply to questions, explained that Rastelli was sent back to Italy on the instructions of Mr. Powell it was decided that he

[1] Presumably an allusion to the position of the Princess's hand in the carriage when she was travelling with Pergami. Possibly Lord Holland had little direct experience of the criminal courts.

should be summoned to the bar of the House. John Allen Powell was a member of the firm of solicitors in New Square, Lincoln's Inn who was acting for the Bill. He had also been one of the members of the Milan Commission.

He explained that he had sent Rastelli back to Italy to reassure families of the Italian witnesses who had been alarmed as a result of the ill-treatment of those witnesses by the Dover mob when they landed. He said: 'If your lordships will allow me, I will give the explanation: Rastelli had been the courier who had conducted a great number of witnesses to Dover; those witnesses had been maltreated by the populace at Dover; they were afterwards sent into Holland. . . . I learned that various reports were propagated in Italy of the dangers which the witnesses for the bill ran, by coming over to this country. I had heard that reports were propagated in Italy that they had received great personal injuries. I had heard that the families of those persons who were here were exceedingly anxious upon the subject of their relations who were in this country. I had understood Rastelli to be acquainted with the greater part of the families of those persons, and I considered that it would be an act of humanity to those relations and friends, that some person who had seen the whole of those witnesses in this country, and who was acquainted with those families, should go over there with letters from the witnesses, and having himself been an eye-witness of their safety here, that he should report to those families what their situation really was, and by that means that he should put an end to the great anxiety which I thought those families must necessarily feel for their friends.'

After the peers had put many questions to Powell, Lord Lauderdale said that he thought it was inconsistent with the principles of law and abhorrent to him that the House should examine an agent about the steps which he took in his client's cause. Lord Ellenborough, while acknowledging the justice of these principles thought that the peers, as part of the state, had the right to examine a person even though he might be considered in some sense their own agent. The examination continued, and Powell explained that he had let Rastelli go because he reckoned that, travelling night and day, he should have been able to make the journey to and from Milan in twelve days. That would have left him a week in Milan and its neighbourhood to get in touch with the witnesses' families. Rastelli was not now present because he had been taken ill. Of the riots at Dover he added that one of the witnesses had never recovered, having been deaf ever since. After further questions about Powell's control over the witnesses Brougham made a dramatic intervention, in reply to the Lord-Chancellor who had asked the counsel whether they had any questions to submit.

Mr. Brougham.—'My lords, I wish to ask the witness one question. "Who is your client or employer in this case?"' (Cries of 'Order, order'.) The witness was directed to withdraw.

Mr. Brougham.—'I am sure your lordships will allow me to proceed, when I say that I wish to explain my object in making the inquiry. This question is put for no purposes but the purposes of justice, and in order to enable us the more effectually to perform our duty to the illustrious party for whom we appear. My lords, I submit that it is most important to us that we should be enabled to put this question to this witness, as the first one who has yet been called, in the course of these proceedings, that can give us the required information. Is it of no consequence to us (contending from day to day, as we have been, and engaged, as we at this moment are, without any specific party on the other side), in order that we may be able to fix that opposite party with his agent; is it of no consequence, I say, to ask the witness this question, so that we may procure that important evidence, which is not evidence unless it comes from the opposite party through his agent? My lords, if I knew who the party is against whom I appeared, *non constat* that I may not bring forwards a mass of evidence furnished by himself—namely, speeches, declarations, and acts of that opposite party. Again, my lords, whatever be the name of this unknown—this interesting unknown—your lordships see that, not knowing at present who this undiscovered being is—not knowing whether he have in truth "a local habitation and a name"—not knowing whether this shadow may not vanish into airy nothing, after he has eluded all sensible perception—I cannot fix him with any character. If I am told who he is, I may then be able to trace his lineaments, and at length to bring out the mighty secret who and what he is from his own mouth—if he have one. I know, my lords, that the rule of law is close on the subject of the professional confidence of agents. I do not deny it. But here there is no party. Prove to me who the party is, and I will not disturb the professional confidence of his agent. And who is the party? I know nothing about this shrouded, this mysterious being—this retiring phantom—this uncertain shape—

> *If shape it might be called that shape had none*
> *Distinguishable in member, joint, or limb;*
> *Or substance might be called that shadow seemed,*
> *For each seemed either . . . .*
> *. . . What seemed his head*
> *The likeness of a kingly crown had on.*[1]

If I could see it, I might interrogate it, and bring out of its mouth, if mouth it had, who and what it is, and whether it be a man. Yet under this shape, this "airy nothing"—and I know not whether it be one, or either, or neither, or both I am to face the adverse party; I am to be met at every turn, and in every part of the proceeding, by not being able to put a single question to this visionary personage. You must not put that question.'

The Miltonic comparison between King George IV and the powers of darkness is believed to have been suggested to Brougham by someone standing near him, identified as Spencer Perceval, son of the Prime Minister. Even if we are to make full allowance for the excitements of advocacy we should have to admit that the quotation, in its setting, was savage. Also it was damaging to Brougham himself. As Attorney-General to the Queen he was *ipso facto* within the bar and professionally a silk. At the Queen's death this ceased, and he reverted, with professional loss, to bombasine and the outer bar. The resentment of the King blocked his progress to becoming a king's counsel: it was six years before the King relented and Brougham was once again able to rustle in silk.

Perhaps Powell in the end had the best of things, when Gifford asked him if he had happened to be in the House when Brougham stated that he did not intend to cross-examine further any of the

[1] *Paradise Lost*, Book II.

witnesses for the bill. If Brougham really meant this, there was nothing objectionable in letting Rastelli go out of the country.

Joseph Planta, a member of the Foreign Office staff, was next examined to explain about Rastelli's passport. He said that in the

'This shape, this airy nothing'

Cruikshank cartoon from a William Hone pamphlet of 1820

Foreign Office they kept a number of passports ready signed by the foreign secretary, Lord Castlereagh, and Planta on his own responsibility granted one of these to Rastelli in his capacity as courier 'on the part of the prosecution'. (The last were Planta's words though 'promoters of the bill' would have been more literally exact.)

11

Panders from Milan

◆▭◦▭◆

The next stage of the evidence was devoted to proving that the witnesses against the Queen had been suborned and that they had been paid to give evidence on behalf of the promoters of the bill. The first witness to this accusation was Filippo Pomi, a carpenter who lived for 14 years at the Barona. That, it will be remembered, was Pergami's house not far from the Villa d'Este and sometimes called the Villa Pergami. He brought to the House of Lords the latest news of Pergami, who had driven with the Queen to Calais in June.[1] Pomi had seen him at the Barona in August. Before coming to the question of bribery he was questioned about the ball given by the princess. He said that one of the guests was called Antongina and that 'he has eighteen children between males and females'. They all came to the ball because the Princess wished to see this prodigious family 'coming from one father and mother'. An amusing exchange followed his description of the people attending the balls as 'all gentlefolks'.

'Do you know a person of the name of Maria Galletti?'—'Perhaps she may have come there.'

'Who is Maria Galletti?'—'I do not know her positively.'

'Does not she keep the public house called the St. Christopher?' —'You must have mistaken the name; it is not Maria Galletti.'

'What is the name of the landlady of the St. Christopher?'—'Rosina.'

[1] Pergami survived until 1841. He died after an apoplectic fit in a public house at Fossombroni near Urbino.

'How long has she lived there?'—'She has been landlady a long time.'

'Has she not been at those balls?'—'Yes, she came, but because she had been brought by those other girls; but she is a respectable woman, she is not a prostitute, (*trappola*).'

'Is she one of those persons whom you describe as the gentlefolks who used to frequent those balls?'—'Yes, she came, and came only once, this Rosina.'

'Is she one of the persons that you describe as gentlefolks, who came to the ball?'—'She was the mother of another girl who was used to go there; she was the mistress of this inn, called the St. Christopher.'

'Is there another inn at the Barona, besides the St. Christopher?' —'There is.'

'Who keeps that?'—'Pergami is the master.'

'Who keeps the house, who conducts it?'—'The innkeeper is there.'

'What is his name?'—'Giovanni Angelo Donnarini; it is now the son, but before it was the father, and he was called Antonio.'

'Did his wife and her sister use to go to those balls?'—'They came only once.'

'You said, that many gentlefolks went to the ball of the Villa Pergami; state the names of any of the gentlefolks whom you have seen there?'—'I cannot mention them.'

'Can you mention any of the ladies?'—'I might mention Marianna Donnarini, I might mention Giuseppa Donnarini; and there may be other persons who, if they were before my eyes, I might recollect their names.'

'Who is Marianna Donnarini, and where does she live?'—'At the Barona.'

'Who is she; is she a lady living upon her fortune?'—'A girl well brought up, and the flower of gentlefolks.'

'Is she not the daughter of the man who keeps one of the inns at the Barona?'—'Yes, she is the daughter of Antonio.'

But the crucial part of Pomi's evidence concerned some conversations with Rastelli.

'State, as nearly as you can, the exact words which Rastelli used when he told you that you should have a great present if you came to speak against the Princess?'—'He told me, "Pomi, if you like, you may make yourself a man"; I asked him in what manner; he answered: "You, who have always lived in this house, day and night, may have something to depose against her Royal Highness;" I said, that I had nothing to depose against that lady, who had always done a great deal of good.'

'Was Mademoiselle Demont present upon that occasion?'—'She was not.'

'Did Rastelli, at the time he made you this offer, mention the name of Demont to you?'

That question was objected to, and he was then asked: 'Was it upon this occasion, that Rastelli used the expression you have repeated, of making a good day's work?'—'Yes, it was on that occasion, that he was going about making recruits.'

'State all that Rastelli said about making a good day?'—'I cannot express it; I must only say that he told me, that on that day, when she came there to make that drawing, she had made a good day.'[1]

'Do you know a person of the name Riganti?'—'I do, he is a companion of Rastelli.'

'Where does Riganti live?'—'At the Porta Ticinese.'

'Of what Trade is Riganti?'—'He sells salt, tobacco, brandy, and other liquors.'

'Does he live at Milan?'—'He dwells out of Milan, at the distance of two gun shots.'[2]

'Has he ever asked you to come and depose against the Princess?'

This question was objected to by Copley because Riganti had not been a witness. On this and the kindred question whether a witness on behalf of the Queen could be examined to prove that one of the agents employed by the promoters of the bill had offered him a bribe, a long and involved debate took place before the questions were put to the judges. Lushington said that without examining Riganti and Rastelli, the Queen's counsel could not prove whether

[1] A drawing of the position of the rooms in the Villa.

[2] He presumably means that his shop was at the Porta Ticinese while his home was outside Milan. The Porta Ticinese is the famous gate built under the Visconti to the south.

they were agents of the Milan Commission or of any other person or body.'The part of prosecutor here seemed rather to be sustained by a joint-stock company than by an individual, compounded of the House, the Government and the notorious commissions of Milan. . . . If they rejected proof to show that individuals had gone over the whole of Italy, and indeed of Europe, committing subornation of perjury, it would convince the world that such conduct might be pursued with impunity.' Denman made the same point with greater vigour—'Unless my lips are to be sealed when I enter upon the defence of my illustrious client, I shall maintain, and I think it is but fair to give notice to all parties, that the most malignant and extensive conspiracy ever devised against the honour of a persecuted individual is the sole source and origin of the disgusting mass of corrupt evidence now upon the table of the House.'

Brougham was even more robust—'If he could be able to prove that witness after witness had been applied to by agent after agent, by saying "If you will come and swear certain facts against the Princess of Wales, you shall have so much reward"—if he could prove that an offer was made to this witness in these terms—"If you will say that you saw Pergami put his hands up the Princess's petticoats, you shall have such a reward"—if he could show that, with respect to other transactions, recourse was had to the same means, that individuals were offered rewards if they would swear to those falsehoods—to charges they had never heard of, until they heard them from the mouths of those panders of infamous evidence—if he could prove this, though he might not precisely connect each of those panders with his employers, the Milan commissioners!—if he could substantiate matter so important, he would assume, placed as their lordships were in a most extraordinary situation, as a house of legislature, with a bill of pains and penalties before them, that no man could deny but it would have very great influence in enabling them to form an opinion whether the bill should pass or not. Was there a noble lord sitting on the bill whose opinion would not be most materially affected by the last question?—Nay, he would say, whose mind must not be decided to throw out the bill, if a system of going about to bribe witnesses to tell those odious falsehoods against her Majesty the Queen should be made out by legal evidence, although it was not strictly made out to be the act of the Milan commissioners, or of his Majesty's ministers, who were his opponents now, and who were to be his judges hereafter? Could the Earl of Liverpool, or the Earl of Harrowby, and the other advocates of the bill, whom he only mentioned by name because they were his opponents—could they, or could any man, say that it was not important that those panders for false, foul, and filthy evidence, should be exposed?'

The Lord Chief Justice, giving the opinion of the judges on the point and describing it as 'a question entirely new, and of very difficult solution' decided against the counsel for the Queen. However, the Attorney-General, possibly feeling that the absence of Rastelli had put his opponents at a disadvantage, agreed to waive his objections and the Lord Chancellor also agreed to this, recording his opinion that the special circumstances of the case precluded this decision from being quoted as a precedent in courts of law hereafter.

After this decision Pomi was re-examined by Tindal.

'Do you know a person of the name of Riganti?'—'I do.'

'Do you know whether his name is Filippo?'—'I do, his name is Filippo.'

'Where does he live?'—'On the bank of Porta Ticinese.'

'What is he by trade?'—'He sells tobacco, salt, liquors, brandy.'

'Do you recollect his calling on you at any time?'—'He did not call upon me; but when I went into his shop, he always had something to say to me. I went to buy salt, tobacco, or something; and he told me, for he knew I belonged to the Barona, "Pomi, have you ever seen those jokes (*scherzi*) between the Princess and Pergami? now is the time to come forward, to gain something, to become a man." '

'Did he say any thing more upon that occasion?'—'He told me this; and I answered him, "No, I have seen no *scherzi*"; and he replied, "Oh, have you not seen Pergami put the Princess on the back of the donkey, and put his hands under her petticoats?" '

'Did you make any answer to that?'—'Yes, I told him that this was a perfect falsehood, for, instead of that, he paid her all possible respect and decency which was due to that great personage.'

'Was any thing more said?'—'Yes, at other times, whenever I went to his shop; so that I was obliged never more to go to his shop, for he annoyed me so much.'

Naturally enough the counsel for the Queen made great exertions to show that witnesses had been bribed to appear against the Queen and that there had been in Brougham's words 'a conspiracy' against her. The House agreed that the letters from Powell to Colonel Browne in Milan about Rastelli's return should be examined by a Secret Committee. This consisted of the Lord President (Lord Harrowby) and peers already familiar to readers of this book— namely Grey, Manners, Lauderdale, Erskine and Lansdowne. Lord Harrowby was one of the last survivors of the immediate circle of the younger Pitt. He has been well described as 'top of the second-rate men'. Also members of the Secret Committee were Rosslyn, who was a Tory and friend of the Duke of Wellington—a respected figure with 'his gallant, gentleman-like, old-soldier-like air', Arden, a relation of the Prime Minister Perceval, Amherst, a courtier and diplomat, who was appointed ambassador to China but was refused admission, and Lord Ross, which was the title by which the Scottish Lord Glasgow sat in the Lords; he was described as 'highly conservative'. The Committee reported to the House on the 39th day of the hearing—23 October. The letters between Powell and Colonel Browne were very much as stated in his evidence by Powell, and it was clear that Browne had emphasised the alarm of the friends of the witnesses; he admitted that very exaggerated reports were being believed, notably that Rastelli had lost an eye and that Sacchi had been murdered. Possibly these stories were spread by partisans of the Queen: certainly they deterred additional witnesses from coming to England.

As the witnesses on behalf of the Queen began to draw to a close there was a curious interlude on 21 October. The King of New Zealand and his Chamberlain came to watch the proceedings. They both wore black wigs and their faces were coloured and tattooed. The King's nose was a blaze of stars and planets, and Creevey was informed that the New Zealanders were much more profusely decorated *en derrière*. The start of the proceedings was greatly delayed while the peers collected at the bar to observe this remarkable king.

After a fisherman who with others took the Princess and Pergami from Como to the Villa d'Este had given evidence that he had never seen any endearments between the two, the Princess's chief Italian witness, Chevalier Vassali, was called. Examined by Denman he described himself as Equerry to the Queen of England, and said that before that, he was a captain in the dragoons, commanding a squadron in 'the late disbanded Royal Italian Army'. Cross-examined by Gifford he said that he had started as 'a simple soldier' in the Guard of honour of the King of Italy. (Napoleon was crowned as King in Milan Cathedral in 1805—appointing his step-son Eugène Beauharnais as viceroy.) He was in the service of the Princess in 1816, and again in 1818—and consequently was with her throughout the tour of Germany.

'Were you with her Royal Highness at Munich?'—'Yes.'

'Do you remember whether her Royal Highness dined with her suite, with the King of Bavaria?'[1]—'Yes.'

'Do you know whether Pergami dined at the table with the King?' —'I do.'

'Did he dine with the King?'—'He dined at the table of the King.'

'Do you know of any civility passing between the King of Bavaria and Pergami?'—'I have seen the King treat Pergami with the greatest affability.'

'Do you know whether there was any present given?'—'Yes.'

'Be so good as to mention what it was?'—'A golden snuff-box, surrounded with brilliants, and adorned with the name of the King.'

'Have you seen that snuff-box in the possession of Pergami?'— 'I have.'

'What was the name that was upon the box?'—'An M. and an I., which signifies Maximilian Joseph.'

'Was there any crown upon it?'—'No.'

He said that at the dance at the Barona he remembered the curate attending. The Princess retired to an adjoining room to play cards, chess or on the piano. He described the conduct of the dancers as 'most regular'.

---

[1] Maximilian I was the first king of Bavaria. He was the most sympathetic of the German rulers to Napoleon and his daughter married Beauharnais. He was unconventional, and enjoyed strolling about Munich *en bourgeois*.

He described the episode at Scharnitz. He and Pergami had gone to Innsbrück in the night, about the passports, and got back between two and three. The Princess was leaning—half lying on the bed—'She was covered with shawls or something like that.' According to him Pergami and others of the suite were in and out of the Princess's room. He was asked whether there were beds for members of the suite, and he gave a monosyllabic answer 'straw'. He confirmed the evidence given by a previous witness that Forti not Sacchi was the courier on the journey from Rome to Sinigaglia; he denied that he had ever seen the Princess in a *padovanello* which he described as a carriage for one person only, with two shafts and two wheels and without springs.

Cross-examined by Gifford he explained that there was much coming and going by members of the suite into the bedroom of the Princess at Scharnitz to tranquillise her mind that arrangements for the journey were being made and that the country-people were being organised to dig away the snow. In explanation of all this he added: 'A person is not easy, he is always in movement when he is obliged to wait upon a personage of that quality; a person is in eternal movement.'

At the end of Vassali's examination there was a discussion over the non-appearance of the Baron d'Ende from Carlsruhe to give evidence for the Queen. It may be remembered that great efforts had been made by the Queen's advisers to induce him to attend, and that a previous witness (James Leman) had said that the Baron having agreed to come, subsequently—and with tears in his eyes—said that he could not after all come, giving as a reason that he had received an express prohibition against coming. On the very day (5 October) on which the charge was made in the House of Lords, the Foreign Secretary, Lord Castlereagh, wrote to Mr. Frederick Lamb, the British Minister at Munich, telling him to go to Carlsruhe and make personal representations to the Grand Duke of Baden in the King's name, in protest against obstacles being put in the Baron's way to prevent his coming to give evidence. Castlereagh pointed out that Meidge Kress, a witness against the Queen, had been not only permitted but encouraged to go. She was also a subject of the Grand Duke. If these personal representations were unavailing, Lamb was to make a written representation 'pressing this request for the Grand Duke's favourable consideration as indisputably due to public justice'. Lamb went to Carlsruhe as soon as he had Castlereagh's letter, reaching there on 11 October, but his representations both spoken and written were unavailing. In reply the Grand Duke's minister, the Baron de Berstett, explained that 'I knew too well the fixed determination of his Royal Highness, never to take part directly in any thing which might relate to the solemn proceeding at this time before the tribunal of the House of Peers in England, to dare to propose to him to give any such orders to a person belonging to his court.' He went on to say that when previously Lamb had asked permission for one of the fourriers[1] to give evidence against the Queen, he had explained that it would be impossible to obtain the Grand Duke's consent. He distinguished between ordinary subjects such as Kress and members of the Grand-ducal court. Berstett then wrote to Baron d'Ende telling him that although the Grand Duke would never command him to go, 'You are perfectly at liberty to act, on the present occasion, as you should think proper.' Replying, Baron d'Ende said that he had heard once from M. Leman and that he had explained that the nature of his duties made it impossible for him to go to London. 'With respect to the tears,' he could only say he was astonished because the refusal was not made by himself but 'through one of my friends'. He firmly refused because he could only make so long a journey 'with the greatest danger' to his health, especially as he was about to undergo 'a rigid course of medical treatment'.

After several other witnesses had been called James Leman was again called to amplify what he had said about his attempts to secure the presence of Baron d'Ende. He gave convincing evidence that he had seen the Baron, explained that he had gone to his house and that when the Baron explained that he had been forbidden to come he appeared to be 'extremely vexed' and putting the young man's hand to his heart said 'Feel how my heart beats.' Brougham once again made a spirited intervention; he said 'he had now to call their attention to the various and insuperable difficulties interposed against the further prosecution of her Majesty's defence. He did not

[1] Literally a harbinger—here meaning a royal courier.

mean to cast blame on any person; the blame, in fact, was chiefly attributable to the proceeding itself. It was now, however, manifest that they could go no further with any chance of equal justice to the parties in this suit. Their lordships had seen that the Grand Duke of Baden did not by any means compel Baron d'Ende to make his appearance at their bar. He had indeed given him a *congé*—a word of ominous sound in the ears of a courtier—a word, the fearful import of which must strike a painful sensation in the hearts of some of their lordships: for a *congé* was, as many of their lordships knew, not so much a permission to go, as a permission never to come back: it was tantamount to saying—"never see my face again"; it was the word appropriated to the resignation of ministers, for ministers were of course never turned out: it was the word which, in France, sent a man to his country-seat never to return; and no doubt was of simi-larly dreadful import in a German ear. No wonder then that the chamberlain, as soon as he saw the terrific expression written in plain German characters, was taken extremely ill; he (Mr. Brougham) verily believed that the sickness was not feigned and that if Mr. Leman could have felt on this occasion also that part of his frame where his heart was lodged, he would have found a more violent palpitation there than when the worthy Baron had invited him to feel its throbs. But it was somewhat strange that none of the reasons which restrained the Baron from coming over had operated to prevent Kress, a witness for the prosecution, from leaving the terri-tories of the Grand Duke.[1] She was forced to come; that is, forced under the compulsion of Berstett. This, too, was done at the insti-gation of the Hanoverian government, the second branch amongst the authors of this prosecution, and the active employer of the Munsters, the de Redens, and the Grimms, and all the crew. But, as he had already said, he threw no blame on any of these parties; they had laboured in their vocation as well as others, and they were under a necessity of acting as they did. He had therefore now seriously and solemnly to appeal to their lordships' justice, to consider this subject as no light or trivial matter. It was in evidence before them that the ministers and agents of the British government abroad had not the

[1] The difference of course was that Kress was not a member of the Grand Duke's court.

power of running into places, and extracting evidence—material evidence for the vindication of Her Majesty, although it was with perfect ease that evidence against her might be obtained in the same quarters. He felt obliged again to repeat, that he threw no blame on any person; but he submitted, that from causes beyond the control and jurisdiction of that tribunal which he had now the honour of addressing, it was impossible to proceed further with any justice to the case of the defence. Undoubtedly their lordships must be of the same opinion, and sure he was, that the august monarch who now filled the English throne would be the last to desire any conclusion that should not work perfect justice to his royal consort.'

On the 39th day, Lord Lauderdale proposed that Lieutenant Hownam should be called in to produce the diploma of the Order of St. Caroline. This went in the following form.

Jerusalem, 12*th July,* 1816

By this present, subscribed by the own hand of her Royal Highness the Princess of Wales, and bearing her seal, her Royal Highness institutes and creates a new Order, to recompense the faithful knights who have had the honour of accompanying her on her pilgrimage to the Holy Land.

First—This Order shall be given, and worn only by those who have accompanied her Royal Highness to Jerusalem, except her physician Professor Mochetti, who by a simple accident could not follow her.

Second—The Colonel Bartholomew Pergami, Baron of Francina, Knight of Malta, and of the Holy Sepulchre of Jerusalem, equerry of her Royal Highness, shall be the Grand Master of this Order, and his children, males as well as females, shall succeed him, and shall have the honour to wear this same order from generation to generation for ever.

Third—This same advantage is granted to the Knight of the Holy Sepulchre, Mr. William Austin, and also his legitimate children, shall enjoy this honour for ever.

Fourth—This honour shall be personal for you, Mr. Joseph Hownam, captain of the British Navy, knight in the suite of her Royal Highness, created one of the Knights of this Order by this present, and at your death the cross and the patent shall be returned to the Grand Master.

Fifth—The Grand Master shall wear the cross round his neck, and the other knights shall be obliged to wear it at the button hole of the left hand side of their coats.

Sixth—The above mentioned Order consists of a Red Cross, with the motto 'Honi soit qui mal y pense;' and shall be called by the name of 'St. Caroline of Jerusalem.' The Ribbon shall be lilac and silver.

> (Signed) CAROLINE, Princess of Wales.
> Colonel PERGAMI, Baron of Francina, Knight of Malta, and of the Holy Sepulchre, Grand Master.
> (Addressed)—To the Knight Joseph Hownam, a Knight in the Suite of her Royal Highness, &c.

The Attorney-General and Copley both pointed out that the counsel for the Queen had 'unexpectedly raised' the question of a conspiracy and they asked that the peers would agree to a delay to enable Colonel Browne who, according to the Queen's lawyers, 'had been engaged in suborning evidence and even in purloining papers' to travel from Milan to give evidence. This was considered not unreasonable, but the prevailing feeling was that it would be a mistake to let the proceedings drag on. Lord Camden—a good-hearted Kentish peer—spoke up for Browne, saying that he had seen a great deal of service, had been 14 years a subaltern and had been wounded six or seven times. Lord Holland, generally the most genial of Whigs, thought that if peers felt justified in indulging in panegyrics, other peers might feel justified in giving their opinion of the transactions in which, from reading the minutes of evidence, the Colonel seems to have been engaged. The promoters of the bill accepted that Browne should not be called.

The Attorney-General then recalled Captain Briggs, the distinguished naval officer who was in command of the *Leviathan* when the Princess sailed from Genoa to Sicily in 1815. In his original evidence he had described how Captain Pechell, who commanded the *Clorinde* on which the Princess sailed from Sicily to North Africa, had complained that Pergami whom he first remembered waiting on the Princess was now to dine at her table In his fresh evidence Captain

Briggs described a conversation between himself and Lieutenant Hownam, when they were walking on deck on the *Leviathan* during the voyage with the Princess. 'I asked how it was that he (Pergami) was now admitted to her Royal Highness's table. Upon which he replied, that he was sorry it was so, he was sorry the Princess had admitted him, that he had entreated her on his knees, and with tears in his eyes, but to no purpose.' Remembering Hownam had denied this conversation, though he did not positively swear that it did not take place. After an abortive attempt to recall Hownam had been made by the Duke of Somerset who, having married a sister of 'the Red Deer', was presumably a partisan of the Queen, the evidence ended. It was 24 October—the 40th day of the proceedings. The Solicitor-General to the Queen then began his speech summing up the evidence on her behalf.

12

Copley answers Denman

❖⊰○⊱❖

Denman's speech, which occupied part of 24 October and the whole of 25 October, lasted for ten hours: it was extremely effective and powerful but, as will be seen, it contained two grave errors of judgment—one damaging to himself and the other inviting and receiving ridicule for his client. He began with a flourishing gesture of defiance, by saying that the evidence for the innocence of the Queen had satisfied 'the minds of all the people of England and those too of all the civilised nations in the world'. He rightly emphasised the Queen's considerable achievement in her journey to the Holy Land, and discounted the significance of the order of St. Caroline.

'When this was the first instance within six centuries of an European Princess visiting the Holy Sepulchre, there could surely be no crime if she, delighted with the adventure, and struck with the novelty of all around her, did that which the Dukes of Orleans and of Bourbon had done before her—institute an order of knighthood to reward those who accompanied her. He could hardly suppose that this could be visited with any peculiar severity against her Royal Highness, though it was the charge against her which had been best proved. Bacon had said, that "princes had many times made to themselves desires, and sate their hearts on toys, sometimes upon a building, sometimes upon erecting of an order." The illustrious lady, his client, was proved to have erected an additional wing to the Villa d'Este, which, he understood to be in the best of taste, and to do no discredit to her Royal Highness's judgment, however it might differ from some of those buildings which had been recently erected in this country.' (The last was an amusing gibe at the Pavilion at Brighton and perhaps at the King's cottage *ornée*—the Royal Lodge—in Windsor Great Park.)

He naturally spent some time in attempting to demolish the evidence against the Queen. One of the most damaging aspects of this was Demont's evidence about the state of the bed at Naples. He pointed out that it was after she had been recalled for re-examination that Demont had explained that it was her duty to make the beds at Naples—but only some weeks after their arrival there. Previously they had been made by Annette Preising, a personal servant of the Princess described by Denman as 'the chambermaid who could prove the marks'. He made much of the refusal of the crown to call her.

'He had heard it said, that it was always a matter of great difficulty to prove the fact of adultery itself. In general, a *corpus delicti* was a matter of inference from the circumstances of the case. He denied that in any case the fact could be inferred from such evidence as the present; but in no case could it be more clearly proved than in this, if it had ever existed. This chambermaid, who was so willing to swear against her mistress, must have had opportunities of knowing if it had occurred. Indeed this seemed to have been felt on the other side; and Demont, when she came to mend her evidence, spoke of having seen stains on the bed. If this were true, why had they not called the person who had made the bed for two months before? Why was not Annette Preising produced, whose evidence would have been most material to this point? Did their lordships suppose that those agents who had collected together a set of her Majesty's discarded servants, who had ransacked filthy clothes-bags, who had raked into every sewer, pried into every water-closet, who attempted to destroy all the secrecies of private life, who had wrung the feelings of a lady of rank and respectability by making her, at that bar, confess her poverty, and the embarrassments of her husband—who had interfered with private family concerns, so far as to produce a letter addressed by her to that husband;[1] did their lordships imagine that they who had resorted to such mean and filthy practices would have stopped short at producing such a witness as Annette Preising if they thought that she would have borne out the testimony of Demont? No: they rested upon that testimony, of which he would

---

[1] Lady Charlotte Lindsay. (See p. 141.)

say no more at that moment than that, if brought before any honest court of justice, it would have been scouted out.' He continued with a general indictment of Italian character—'Without charging any conspiracy now, he would venture to say, that if any place or country was to be selected or preferred as the scene of a conspiracy, and that the selection and preference were judiciously made, the scene would certainly be in Italy. It was there that the means presented themselves —it was there that cunning and artifice thrived—there that a price was openly set upon an oath—there that every infamous purpose might by bribery be carried into effect. They were now inquiring into the transactions of six years, and guided only by the light of Italian evidence. . . . It was remarkable that in all the numerous scenes described by our great dramatic poet, whenever he had occasion to paint the character of a man anxious to blacken the reputation of an innocent wife, he chose his scene in Italy.'

Naturally he made particular exertions over the evidence about the tent on the polacca. 'He now came to the polacca; and he could assure their lordships that it was with no small satisfaction he came to that part of the case; because he thought it was most perfectly clear that there was no more ground to suppose that any illicit connexion had taken place before her Royal Highness embarked on board that polacca, than there was for any one of their lordships to imagine that any female of his family, whom he had left at home that morning, had been guilty of such a crime, merely because she had an opportunity of doing so.' He went on: 'her Royal Highness the Princess of Wales goes on board the polacca without one single taint of suspicion', meaning that all the charges before this rested on false evidence.

He argued that if she had wanted to pass the night in the arms of Pergami she would have found it far safer to do this in her cabin instead of moving up to the tent on deck. (The reasons for this change were ostensibly the heat below, and the noise of the horses, and the allusion is to them in the first sentence of the following passage.)

'Was it to be believed that a circumstance of this nature—a trifling inconvenience—would induce her to stop the tide of irresistible passion, to withdraw from his secret and secure embraces, in situations where no eye could behold what passed, and to transfer herself to the deck, subject to the observation of the captain, in the neighbourhood of the steersman, and open to the remarks of every sailor in the vessel? Could it be supposed that she would, in such a situation, place herself under a tent, for the purpose of carrying on a guilty correspondence? A tent! O, no! any military officer who heard him would correct him and say, "This was not a close tent— it was not that close and small chamber, that confined and private recess, under which such acts could be performed."' He went on to argue that it was not a tent at all but the awning of the deck, hanging loosely around.

He went on to emphasise that the final proof of adultery on the polacca was lacking. Where was the *corpus delicti*? 'If there was any adulterous intercourse passing between her Royal Highness and Pergami, how happened it that with a chambermaid, anxious to discover so important a secret, the linen had not in this, as it had in other instances, betrayed that guilty intercourse? How was it in the intercourse which it was alleged had occurred in the polacca? There, it was true, there was not any, what he should call bodily linen, to betray it; but then there was the matting? Did it betray any marks of such intercourse? There was not even an attempt to exact such a fact from Demont.'

Moving on to events after the voyage on the polacca Denman worked himself into a great passion over the evidence of Rastelli —he spoke about the position of the Princess's hand in the travelling carriage—and Sacchi who had given evidence about the ball at the Barona. They had attempted 'to establish the most disgraceful facts that ever polluted the lips of man, and which he (Mr. Denman) should have thought no husband of the slightest feeling would have permitted to have been given in evidence against his wife, even if she had deserted his fond and affectionate embraces, much less if he had driven her into guilt by thrusting her from his dwelling; re-collecting that the more depraved he showed his wife to be, the more he established his own cruelty and profligacy; and the more imputations he cast upon her, the more he was to be despised for having deserted and abandoned her. He had heard examples supposed to be similar to the present quoted from English History, but he knew of no example in any history of a Christian king who had thought himself at liberty to divorce his wife for any misconduct, when his own misconduct in the first instance was the occasion of her fall. He had, however, found in some degree a parallel in the history of imperial Rome, and it was the only case in the annals of any nation which appeared to bear a close resemblance to the present proceeding. Scarcely had Octavia become the wife of Nero, when almost on the day of marriage she became also the object of his disgust and aversion. She was repudiated and dismissed on a false and frivolous pretext. A mistress was received into her place, and before long she was even banished from the dwelling of her husband. A conspiracy was set on foot against her honour, to impute to her a licentious amour with a slave, and it was stated by the great historian of corrupted Rome, that on that occasion some of her servants were induced, not by bribes but by tortures, to depose to facts injurious to her reputation; but the greater number persisted in faithfully maintaining her innocence. It seemed that, though the people were convinced of her purity, the prosecutor persevered in asserting her guilt, and finally banished her from Rome. Her return was like a flood. The generous people received her with those feelings which ought to have existed in the heart of her husband.'

This comparison with Nero (though there were superficial resemblances in the two cases) was widely and generally condemned. But not content with this Denman went on to quote what had been said by one of Octavia's servants to one of the people who had attempted to suborn her on behalf of the Emperor.[1]

It is believed that that profound scholar but unworldly man Samuel Parr suggested the comparison to Denman. In the future Denman, whose professional prospects of taking silk were blighted by the hostility of the King, had to submit a grovelling memorandum of apology. He wrote of his extreme sorrow that a quotation which he really intended to apply to Rastelli and Sacchi had been interpreted by the King as applying to himself, though the King was

---

[1] 'Octavia's body is chaster than your mouth.' The more precise anatomical comparison, which enraged the King, is perhaps best preserved in the Greek in which language it has been generally and decently disguised:

Καθαρώτερον, ὦ Τιγελλῖνε, τὸ αἰδοῖον ἡ τῆς δεσποινά μου τοῦ σοῦ στόματος ἔχει

THE KETTLE

ABUSING

THE POT.

𝔄 Satirical Poem.

BY THE BLACK DWARF.

Your most obedient Chaste Madam

Oh! you brute

"Sure such a Pair were never seen
So justly form'd to meet by Nature."

SEVENTH EDITION.

LONDON:

PRINTED FOR J. JOHNSTON, CHEAPSIDE;

AND SOLD BY ALL BOOKSELLERS.

1820.

Price One Shilling

not of course alone in this misinterpretation. The King agreed that Denman should take his place within the bar, but he absolutely refused ever to see him.

Arising out of the part which the Princess was supposed to have played in Harlequin and Columbine in the theatre at the Villa d'Este he made a general observation on the Princess's character which would seem to have been correct—'Upon this part of the case, as upon all the rest of the circumstances attempted to be made important on the other side, he had to observe, that undoubtedly there might have been on the part of her Royal Highness too much affability—too much familiar condescension—too much of a disposition to enjoy and to encourage all the innocent pleasures of life. But she possessed the peculiar talent, which very high rank was found often to possess, of indulging at times in the most familiar intercourse, without losing her claim to that respect—to that deference—to that attention which it belongs, not only to good subjects but to gallant and honest men to pay.'

Perhaps the most effective and widely quoted part of his speech was when he referred to her exclusion from the prayer-book at the death of George III. 'Her name was excluded from the Liturgy; but when it was forbidden that the prayers of the people should be offered up for her, their hearts made a full compensation for that odious exercise of unjust authority.'

In the following passage he defended the decision of the Queen's advisers not to call Pergami as a witness—

'From the beginning of the world no instance is to be found where an individual charged with adultery has been called to disprove it.[1] Yet, for the first time, we are to be compelled to put him to his oath! The answer is in a word—there is either a case against

---

[1] Counsel for the bill warmly criticised this part of the defence. The Attorney-General quoted a precedent of 1799 where in a divorce case the supposed adulterer was examined in support of the wife: Campbell *v.* Campbell.

Opposite: *The title page of this Cruikshank/Hone pamphlet of 1820 was inscribed:*

Nero and Octavia

us, or there is no case: if there is no case, there is no occasion for us to call a witness; and if there be a case, no man would believe the supposed adulterer, when he was put forward to deny the fact. On this subject the nicest casuists might perhaps dispute, with a prospect of success, on either side of the proposition; but I firmly believe that the feelings of mankind would justly triumph over the strictness of morality, and that a witness so situated would be held more excusable, to deny upon his oath so dear a confidence, than to betray the partner of his guilt. Even perjury would be thought a venial crime, compared with the exposure of the victim of his adultery. Surely, for the sake of dragging forward such a witness, the principles of our nature, and of the heart of man, are not to be repealed even upon this occasion, to which so many principles have been made the sacrifice.'

On the Duke of Clarence he made an attack which—if thinly veiled—was of the utmost severity.

'I know that rumours are abroad, of the most vague, but at the same time, of the most injurious character; I have heard them, even at the very moment we were defending her Majesty against charges, which, compared with the rumours, are clear, comprehensible, and tangible. We have heard, and hear daily, with alarm, that there are persons, and these not of the lowest condition, and not confined to individuals connected with the public press—not even excluded from your august assembly, who are industriously circulating the most odious and atrocious calumnies against her Majesty. Can this fact be? And yet can we live in the world, in these times, and not know it to be a fact? We know, that if a juryman, upon such an occasion, should be found to possess any knowledge on the subject of inquiry, we should have a right to call him to the bar as a witness. "Come forward", we might say, "and let us confront you with our evidence: let us see whether no explanation can be given of the fact you assert, and no refutation effectually applied." But to any man who could even be suspected of so base a practice as whispering calumnies to judges, distilling leprous venom into the ears of jurors, the Queen might well exclaim "Come forth, thou slanderer; and let me see thy face! If thou would'st equal the respectability even of an Italian witness, come forth, and depose in open court! As thou art, thou art worse than an Italian assassin! because, while I am boldly and manfully meeting my accusers, thou art planting a dagger unseen in my bosom, and converting thy poisoned stiletto into the semblance of the sword of justice!" I should fain say, my lords, that it is utterly impossible that this can be true; but I cannot say it, because the fact stares me in the face; I read it even in the public papers; and had I not known of its existence in the dignity of human nature, I would have held it impossible that any one, with the heart of a man, or with the honour of a peer, should so debase his heart and degrade his honour! I would charge him as a judge—I would impeach him as a judge; and, if it were possible for the blood Royal of England to descend to a course so disgraceful, I should fearlessly assert, that it was far more just that such conduct should deprive him of his right of succession, than that all the facts alleged against her Majesty, even if true to the last letter of the charge, should warrant your lordships in passing this bill of degradation and divorce.'

He ended with a richly deserved panegyric on Brougham, though the cause for which they battled was possibly over-grandiloquently described. 'We have fought the battles of morality, Christianity, and civilised society throughout the world; and, in the language of the dying warrior I may say,

> *In this glorious and well-foughten field*
> *We kept together in our chivalry.*'

He finished over-dramatically and—as it transpired—fatally for his client—'... and if your lordships have been furnished with powers, which I might almost say scarcely Omniscience itself possesses, to arrive at the secrets of this female, you will think that it is your duty to imitate the justice, beneficence, and wisdom of that benignant Being, who, not in a case like this where innocence is manifest, but when guilt was detected, and vice revealed, said—"If no accuser can come forward to condemn thee, neither do I condemn thee: go, and sin no more." ' All his life Denman bitterly regretted this ending. It is believed to have been impromptu as it of course ran counter to his whole argument that the Queen had not sinned. By this time the supporters of the King in the press had rallied and they were responsible for the variant on Denman's theme which certainly burst the bubble of her popularity.

Most gracious queen, we thee implore
To go away and sin no more;
Or if that effort be too great,
To go away at any rate.

Lushington followed and from the legal side his speech was perhaps the best. To histrionics it owed nothing. He simply ended: 'I leave her, not to the mercy, but to the justice of your lordships.' He meticulously went over the evidence against her, skilfully bringing out the improbabilities and inconsistencies. He began with a rather curious passage which suggested that his client was beyond the age of divorce.

'. . . and here he must observe, that though, through the whole of his professional life, he had been conversant with cases of adultery, he had to declare that this was the most extraordinary he had ever read or heard of. Indeed, such was the circumstance of this case, that he believed, he might safely say, not only that it was unprecedented, but that there was not a shadow of semblance to be found in all the records of the courts in which such cases were tried. It was not that it was a case of novelty with respect to the rank of the individual; it was not its want of analogy with other proceedings; it was not that the head of the government was the accuser; it was not that the government formed the very party who prosecuted; it was not all these things, uncommon and extraordinary as they were, which so particularly marked this prosecution; for these were circumstances which might have equally occurred in some other cases;—but that which first, and above all, distinguished the present case, was the age of the party accused. He was bold to say, without the fear of contradiction, that no precedent could be found in modern times where the husband sought a divorce by accusing a wife of 50 years of age. The absence of any case similar in this respect gave to the present a degree of improbability which, he confessed, appeared to him to deserve their lordships' serious consideration. This observation did not merely apply to wives separated from their husbands, and who had not lived together for many years; but, whether living together or separate, there was no instance on record of a prosecution for divorce by a husband against a wife who had attained the age, he would not say of 50, but even of 45.'

Although the speech of the Attorney-General, which began proceedings on 27 October, was not so crisp as Lushington's had been or so eloquently triumphant as Denman's it was a very shrewd analysis of the evidence against the Queen. At the beginning of his speech he alluded to the difference between his task and that of Denman and Brougham: ' . . . the path he had to pursue was a plain one, though it might be painful and tedious. He could not enliven it with the eloquence of his learned friends, nor scatter over it those flowers of imagination in which they had indulged. To them the field of ornament was open; all the brilliant illustrations of antiquity, and all that modern authors afforded, were in their power, and they could resort to them to captivate the feelings or adorn their orations. To them, as he had said, this field was thrown widely open, and they had entered it, and availed themselves of the advantages it afforded to the utmost extent. He was, on the contrary, condemned to call only simple facts, and lay them plainly and unadorned before their lordships.' The Attorney-General had to face a characteristic interruption from his opponents when he was being allowed a short interval to rest his voice.

Mr. Denman.—'I request that your lordships will wait a moment, that Mr. Brougham may be sent for, as he has a most important application to make to your lordships on a matter that has occurred within a few minutes.'

Mr. Brougham (who at that instant hurried up to the bar).— 'My lords, I should hold myself guilty of a dereliction of duty if I delayed for one moment longer than was necessary, while my learned friend was engaged in addressing you, to communicate what has come to my hands a few minutes since, when my learned friend was actually engaged, and could not be interrupted without impropriety. I have in my hand letters in the handwriting of Ompteda, and signed "*Ompteda, Ministre d'Hanover*," proving that he was, at the time of writing the letters, in correspondence with the household of her Majesty, and attempting to seduce her Majesty's servants; letting out, too, that he was endeavouring to seduce Mariette Demont. I am ready to prove the handwriting.'

The Attorney-General.—'I object to that as evidence in the first place; and, in the next place, I object that never was there an application of such a nature made at such a period.'

The Earl of Liverpool said, that 'whether or not this was evidence, or ought to be received, this was not the stage for receiving it'.

Mr. Brougham.—'My lords, if I had remained silent for one instant after I had received such a communication, I should be totally unjustifiable. It proves that I was right in my suspicions.'

When Gifford resumed he said (perhaps not incorrectly) that Brougham's excited intervention 'was one of the most extraordinary proceedings that had ever taken place in a court of justice'.

He made successful play with the contention of the other side that there could have been no impropriety under the tent on the polacca because neither the Princess nor Pergami were undressed. 'Did his learned friends know, (and if they did not, he could tell them) that in those countries it was not the custom to repose without their clothes. If they did not know it, they might learn it from the volumes of travels with which Dr. Holland had amused and delighted the world. In vol. i. p. 227, he said—"bed-chambers are not to be sought for in Greek or Turkish habitations. Their sofas are the places of repose for the higher classes, and the floors of their houses for the lower ranks . . . .; neither men nor women take off more than a small part of their dress, &c." . . . Not a single person of any description was called to contradict the Princess's sleeping under the tent with Pergami, and that sleeping, let their lordships recollect, when no possible reason but one could be assigned for its occurrence. He should therefore say, that in this case there was more than sufficient to establish the charge of adultery: if there were not such proof in this case, the House had done more than injustice in admitting as proof that which they had often deemed proof in others. That fact of sleeping in the tent, if taken alone, was enough, but it became indisputably conclusive when coupled with so many other circumstances which led to the same inference. Good God! unless this were proof of adultery, how else was it to be proved? His learned friends had said, where was the proof of any thing but their sleeping under the same tent, as if it were nothing to talk of a man or woman sleeping under the same tent, unless they were actually proved to have slept undressed on the same bed. Was it to go forth to the females of this kingdom that such a thing could innocently take place; if so, then there was an end to all delicacy of female feeling, there was an end to the fine moral sentiment of the females of this empire. He must again repeat, that if enough to establish the fact of adultery were not already proved in this case, then there was no hope of ever being able to establish that fact in any other.'

Gifford was severely critical of Carrington who, it will be re-membered, had left the Royal Navy at the instance of Sir William Gell in order to become his personal servant. Sarcastically he called him 'a witness of spotless purity, perfect integrity and entire veracity'. He said that Carrington was proved to have given false reasons why he had wanted to leave the Navy: 'he left the navy because he desired to be taken into the service of Sir W. Gell.'

Looking perhaps towards the bench of bishops Gifford said that the Princess's idea of going to the Holy Land 'might seem to have had its foundation in religious duties'. He went on 'it had been proved by Demont, that, during the whole time that she was in the household of the Princess of Wales, from the moment her Royal Highness set out from Genoa, even at the period when she was on the threshold of becoming Queen, that the celebration of divine service, according to the Protestant faith, was omitted. Their lordships would find, however, that, consistently with the other effects of the infatuated passion which governed her Royal Highness, she accom-panied that man on whom she bestowed so many marks of favour to places of worship which were conformable to his belief: but she neglected, and suffered to be neglected in her family, the worship of the established religion of this country, which, in her situation and rank, it was her duty, her imperative duty, to see regularly performed. But who was placed at the head of the order of St. Caroline, as grand master? Pergami; and, in the diploma, that man is, for the first time, styled Colonel, though he had never held any rank in the French army beyond that of quarter-master, which is only equal to that of sergeant in the British service. He is, however, made grand master of this order, and, ridiculous as the thing may be, this dignity is, by the diploma, to continue hereditary in his family, and to descend from generation to generation for ever.'

He stoutly defended Meidge Kress who, as he said, had been represented at public meetings outside as a woman 'infamous and undeserving of the slightest credit'. Alluding to her evidence about the stains on the bed at Carlsruhe he went on—'His learned friend, Mr. Denman, had stated that the manner in which this witness had given her testimony upon that point was such as convinced him of her falsehood. He had said that the blushes with which she had delivered it were the blushes of guilt, arising from a consciousness of the false-hoods which she was uttering, and not the blushes of modesty, arising from the disgusting details which she had to recite to their lordships. But, if their lordships were to judge of the validity of testimony by the manner in which it was given, he would maintain that this witness was entitled to the most implicit credit. Never had evidence been given in a more reluctant and unwilling manner: it was not an exaggerated statement of the facts—it was truth wrung out and extorted from her, and thus greatly enhanced the credit which was her due.'

The contrast between Gifford and Brougham in their style of advocacy was absolute. Gifford reminded the peers of Hownam's evidence about the Princess acting an automaton. He had been asked to describe this, and said that it was a woman who could be wound up to anything. We may picture the wonderful elaboration which Brougham would have evolved on such a theme. Gifford simply asked 'Need I dwell on the meaning of this?'

Copley concluded the reply of the promoters of the bill to the defence. His was a speech of the greatest force and in contrast with Gifford he threw back with vigour the insults and sarcasms of the Queen's lawyers. He explained at the beginning that he was not going over the ground already covered by the Attorney-General, 'the course which he meant to pursue was to select and lay before their lordships those facts which were not disputed . . . and they would see that a case was made out so clear, so complete, so distinct in all its parts as to carry conviction. ....' He started by examining Pergami's services which, according to the Queen's counsel were so high and extraordinary as to justify the confidential nature of his relationship to the Princess. 'He had listened, their lordships throughout the evidence had listened, for the smallest proof of these extraordinary services which were to justify this promotion: but to listen was in vain, for throughout the whole defence not the slightest evidence of such a description was offered; not the smallest attempt at proof in support of his learned friend's statement. The only thing said of Pergami's conduct by any witness was, 'his respectful obedience to her Royal Highness'. His respectful obedience, then, formed his claim to the honour of being made a Knight of Malta, a Sicilian Baron, and Grand Master of the order of the Holy Sepulchre. One of his learned friends at the other side had exclaimed, respecting the promotion of Pergami, "Oh, it resembles more the slow and progressive promotion of a man of merit struggling against the difficulties which impeded him, than the attachment of ardent and sudden love." What was there in the evidence to justify this exclamation? or, was there not everything, on the other hand, to show that the advance of the man was as rapid as it was extraordinary? ... His learned friends, whose copious power of classical illustration was so elegantly shown throughout their speeches, must remember the lines put by a dramatic author into the mouth of a Roman empress: "Threadbare Chastity is poor in the advancement of her creatures—Wantonness magnificent." ... The Princess engaged in her service the Countess Oldi. What were the qualifications of that lady for being the companion of her Royal Highness? They had it in evidence that her Royal Highness could speak so little Italian, that she was obliged to have Pergami with her when some alterations were going on in the garden, to communicate her directions to the workmen, as she herself could only speak a few words in Italian. The Countess Oldi did not understand a word of French; so how was it possible they could carry on any conversation together? How could one be a pleasing companion for the other? They had heard a good deal respecting the manners of this lady. Sir W. Gell thought her rather a good-looking modest lady. The Earl of Guilford sat next her at table: she was perhaps rather vulgar; but not particularly so; the precise shades of distinction could not be accurately marked. It was also remarkable that great care was taken that she was not to be known as the sister of Pergami. She was to attend the Princess, with whom she could not converse; but there was no introduction of this lady as a relation of Pergami. Why, if there was not some motive for the concealment, disguise this face? Why keep it a secret at first, from Demont, from Lieutenant Hownam, from Dr. Holland? None of these had the slightest idea of her relationship to Pergami. Of this man's family, it would be seen that, no less than 12 or 13 had been taken into the Princess's service: by his relatives and connexions her Royal Highness was beset on all sides, with one most remarkable exception, which their lordships could not fail to notice, and which had been already emphatically alluded to by his learned friend, the Attorney-General; it was, that Pergami's wife never made her appearance where the Princess took up her residence. All the rest of the family, and Pergami's child, were with the Princess; but the wife was kept at a distance; she never could partake of the hospitality of her Royal Highness's establishment; she was the only one of the family who was called to submit to every sacrifice without a murmur. How was it possible to reconcile all these facts with the statement of his learned friends opposite, that Pergami's fidelity as a servant was the sole cause of his advancement?'

He made a lively attack on Brougham, and at the close of his speech—to make certain that it was not forgotten—he repeated in what he called 'the fine language of Mr. Denman' the admonition to the Queen to sin no more. Of Brougham he said: 'During this case, by one of those slippery manœuvres for which his learned friend, Mr. Brougham, was so distinguished throughout the proceedings, with his arms extended forward with an air of apparent astonishment and momentary anxiety, he tendered a letter respecting Baron Ompteda, as if it had only that moment come to his hands. His learned friend, when he made this dexterous manœuvre, knew as well as any man that this letter could not be received in evidence; and yet, contrary to all decorum, to all propriety, he read the contents of that letter, which he knew as evidence was inadmissible. When his learned friend could not contradict the facts, he always made an experiment of his dexterity.'

Denman was very properly castigated for his references to Nero and Octavia. '... in a later stage of the proceeding, his learned friend, Mr. Denman, whom he had long known, and whose character he loved and admired, thought fit to say, that in the history of the world, in all the ages of either the ancient or the modern world, he knew of no parallel to this proceeding, unless in the annals of Rome, in the worst period of her history and under the worst and most infamous of her sovereigns. Her Majesty had been represented to stand at present in a situation similar to that in which Octavia was placed. Now how could he answer that allegation but by showing in what situation Octavia did stand? Octavia's father had been murdered by Nero; her brother had been murdered by Nero in her presence. She herself, as virtuous and spotless an individual as there was in the world was accused of a criminal intercourse with her slave. There was however, no semblance of truth in that charge; she had never advanced that slave to honours—had never slept in the same room with him. Yet, without evidence, she was convicted and sent into banishment. What then took place? A monster who had been employed by Nero to murder his mother, Agrippina, was applied to murder Octavia. The confession was made on oath, and the proofs of it were taken. Her veins were opened; but as they did not discharge quite enough of blood, she was thrown into a vessel filled with warm water; and her head was afterwards cut off and sent to Rome, to Nero. (A Peer.—'To Poppaea.')[1] That was to Nero. He knew not what to say to his learned friend, when he thought himself justified to say, in a court of justice, that this case of Octavia not only bears a resemblance, but is the only case in ancient or modern history to be compared to the present proceeding. When he had heard this comparison made, his blood thrilled with horror, and he hardly knew where he was, or who was speaking. But his learned friend, Mr. Denman, in making this comparison, had not even the merit of the invention: the idea had not originated with his learned friend; for he found in a newspaper, published some days before the speech of his learned friend was delivered, an advertisement of a work, entitled '*Nero Vindicated*'; and published by

---

[1] Poppaea was Nero's mistress, and subsequently his wife.

whom? By a man of whom he knew nothing himself; but who was well-known to the public—'Published by W. Hone, Ludgate Hill.'[1]

He drew attention to the reluctance of the Queen's advisers to call Pergami's sister—Countess Oldi. If Pergami had slept in his cabin on the polacca the Countess must have known it. '... she must have been the best witness on the subject. Why, then, had she not been called? She had been sent for. Mr. Vizard had her brought to this country. She was now in this country, and, no doubt, had been questioned. She was of course willing enough to assist the case, but she would not consent to state on her oath that which was not true.'

Copley himself was a man of gallantry, and he enjoyed demolishing the argument that everything must have been all right on the polacca because Pergami and the Princess were dressed. 'One very singular position had been taken on the other side—that the parties had never undressed; nay, Mr Brougham in one of his examinations had asked whether the Princess took off a stitch of her clothes (such was his word) during the whole of the long voyage? Yet the Princess had been lying all the time side by side with this "singular-looking, stout-built" man, and because her dress was not taken off, it was to be concluded that there had been no criminality. Was a proposition so monstrous ever urged before any tribunal, more especially before such a tribunal as this? Paturzo had sworn that he saw her looking out of the tent in a morning-gown, and it appeared that the dress of the other party was a loose Tunisian robe, and Dr. Holland had deposed that it was the ordinary mode of dressing. If such obstructions as these were effectual, what was to become of population? Formerly it had been said that a hooped and whale-boned petticoat was insufficient.

Oft have we known that sevenfold fence to fail,
Though stiff with hoops and armed with ribs of whale.

---

[1] William Hone 1780–1842. A reformer and philanthropist. He was very active at this time, publishing satirical pieces against the government. They were illustrated by Cruikshank, and the best known of them was called 'The Political House that Jack Built'.

This, too frequently

> *Gave way and bent beneath a fierce embrace.*

And was it credible that the Queen's morning-gown had made a stouter resistance?'

13

Nine Votes

The proceedings ended rather untidily on this day (30 October) with a further effort by Brougham to introduce Ompteda's letters, and the House adjourned till 2 November when the Lord Chancellor summed up. He started with one or two procedural points—'The ordinary course, in such cases, was after the allegations and proofs in their support had been laid before the House, for the person who had the honour to sit on the Woolsack to state his opinion. If any noble lord opposed that opinion, the question became a subject of discussion; but if no one dissented, it then followed, as a matter of course, that the noble lord who had taken charge of the bill should move that it be read a second time— . . . And here he must observe, that his duty was not to sum up the evidence, but to give his opinion upon it, and to state his reasons for that opinion. They all sat there in the character of judges and jurors. What they had to do was to communicate to each other their opinions, and to discuss grounds on which they were founded.' He went on to ask himself this question. 'Laying aside all testimony that could be suspected . . . does it or does it not support the allegation of an adulterous intercourse?' 'This was the course he had taken in viewing the case, and he was now about to deliver the opinion which, with the most painful and anxious attention, he had formed. He apprehended that, if their lordships looked at one or two cases or circumstances which had been proved—if they looked to a few facts which had been proved by witnesses quite above all suspicion, and on whom no suspicion had been attempted to be cast—they would then be able to pronounce an opinion on the charge of adultery.

Looking at the case in this point of view, it did appear to him, and it was with the utmost pain he said it, that he could draw no other conclusion than that there had been an adulterous intercourse.'

The evidence about the tent on the polacca seems to have been decisive with Eldon. He was also emphatic that there were many other people on board including Schiavini, Hieronimus and Countess Oldi who might have given evidence that the Princess and Pergami did not sleep together. He would ask if it were possible not to have had evidence of it. He thought that Flynn's failure to describe the sleeping arrangements on the polacca's homeward voyage, although he was able to recall every detail of those arrangements on the outward voyage, was a decisive point against placing too much reliance on Flynn's evidence.

'Considering that circumstance along with others which had come before them, could they doubt that the crime of adultery was committed in the tent? There was an observation in Mr. Hownam's evidence which deserved the consideration of their lordships. He stated that it was necessary that somebody should be along with her Royal Highness in the tent. If such a necessity existed, the fact must be known; and if it were known, why was there so much reluctance and difficulty in stating it? His lordship next adverted to her Majesty's being seen sitting on a gun, and also upon a bench on the deck of the polacca, with her arms around Pergami's neck—a circumstance which had been proved by Gargiulo and Paturzo, and which had not been contradicted by a single witness. Unless he misunderstood the nature of every divorce cause which had been before their lordships or the courts below during the course of his experience— and, unfortunately, there had been in that time a great deal too many —the inference which their lordships ought to draw, when they had the proof of two individuals sleeping under the same tent for five weeks together, and of familiarities subsequently taking place between them, especially if, in the language of the books, there had been the *tempus* and the *locus* for the *oscula* and the *amplexus*,[1] was, that the act of adultery had been committed by them. Had it not, then, been committed in this case? He thought it had: for, in cases of adultery, it was not so much whether the adulterous act was itself

[1] Time and place for the kiss and the embrace.

seen, as whether there were sufficient circumstances to lead a plain man to infer it.'

He went on to ask what reason there could be for Pergami sleeping inside the tent on the land journey to Jerusalem. 'She was surely sufficiently guarded without him; there was no squall of the sea there to incommode her, nor any heeling of the ship; and, therefore, the occurrence of the same event which had before taken place on board the polacca was a circumstance of such weight, that their lordships could not overlook it in coming to an opinion. The case, however, did not rest here: if their lordships would look to the contiguity of her Royal Highness's sleeping apartment to that of Pergami, they would find it to have commenced at Naples, and to have continued till their return from the long voyage. What could it mean? Let their lordships annex what meaning they pleased to it, still, he must ask, why were not the individuals who could have explained it called before them?'

Speaking of the Princess's visit to Carlsruhe and of Meidge Kress's evidence about the bed and what had been noticed he said, with enjoyable restraint, 'it was quite evident that something which was not right had occurred there'.

He ended with a glancing blow at Brougham because what he said was clearly prompted by Brougham's statement, in his opening speech for the defence, 'If your judgment shall go out against your Queen, it will be the only act that ever went out without affecting its purpose: it will return to you upon your own heads.' 'One word more', continued his lordship, 'as to what is passing out of doors, and then I have done. I take no notice of it, because I am supposed constitutionally not to be acquainted with it. But this I will say, let what may or will happen, that I shall here perform my duty. But your lordships have heard from the bar—what I was indeed sorry to hear from such a quarter, and what I never heard from it before—your lordships, I say, have heard an intimation, that, if you pass judgment against the Queen, you will most likely never have the power to pass another judgment. You have heard something like a threat held out to you. I declare, that such a mode of addressing a judge was never before conceived to be consistent with the duty of an advocate: but whether an advocate be right in using such language or not, you will allow me to observe, my lords, that it ought to have no effect upon you. You stand here as the great and acknowledged protectors of the lives, the liberties, the honours, and the characters of your fellow-subjects. That trust ought not to be imposed upon you for a minute, if you can be actuated by any improper bias or feeling. For myself, if I had not a minute longer to live, I would say to your lordships—"Be just, and fear not." I know the people of this country. If you do your duty to them as you ought, whilst you preserve their liberties and the constitution, which has been handed down to you by your ancestors, the time is not far distant when they will do their duty to you—when they will acknowledge that it is the duty of those on whom a judicial task is imposed to meet reproach, and not to court popularity. You will do your duty, and leave the rest to the wisdom and justice of God, who guides the feelings and sentiments of mankind, and directs the end and tendency of all human affairs. Having thus discharged my own individual duty, I leave it to your lordships to decide what is to be the fate of the bill now upon your lordships' table.'

Eldon was followed by another veteran of the law, Erskine, who, 14 years earlier had as Lord Chancellor countenanced and taken part in the Delicate Investigation. Considering his close, private friendship with the King he showed great courage in opposing the bill. Lord Campbell, who was always sparing with his praise, says of this: 'I particularly rejoice to think it was altogether worthy of him.'[1]

His main point before going on to analyse the evidence, was that the exclusion of the Queen's name from the Liturgy was a mark that she was deemed guilty before she was proven so. 'The scales of justice were not held even.' He went on to question whether the House of Commons would ever pass the bill. 'I am afraid of the consequences of the two Houses being at issue on the bill.' He thought it unjust to the Queen that the procedure had been by bill and not by impeachment. In view of what was to happen in the next few moments the following passage in his speech was highly impressive. 'I am now drawing to the close of a long life, and I must end it as I began it. If you strike out of it, my Lords, some efforts to

[1] Lord Campbell, *Lives of the Lord Chancellors*, 1847.

secure the sacred privilege of impartial trial to the people of this country, and by example to spread it throughout the world, what would be left to me? What else seated me here? What else would there be to distinguish me from the most useless and insignificant among mankind? Nothing—just nothing!—And shall I then consent to this suicide—this worse than suicide of the body, this destruction of what alone can remain to me after death—the goodwill of my countrymen? I dare not do that. Proceedings of this kind, my Lords, have never been countenanced but in the worst times—and have afterwards not only been reversed, but stigmatised. You were justly reminded at the bar, that they were ordered by succeeding Parliaments to be taken off the file and burned, —"to the end that the same might be no longer visible in after ages!" But upon that I desire to repeat a sentiment which I remember to have expressed in struggling against arbitrary prosecutions in former times[1]—that instead of directing these records to be burned, they ought rather to have been blazoned in our Parliaments, and in all our tribunals, that, like the characters which appearing on the wall were deciphered by the prophet of God to the Eastern tyrant, they might enlarge and blacken in our sight to terrify us from acts of injustice.'[2]

He then proceeded to analyse the evidence and 'his voice suddenly ceased. The pause was not particularly noticed at first, as it appeared as if his Lordship were looking over the minutes placed on the table before him; but after some time had elapsed without his resuming his speech, some of the peers became alarmed, and rose from their seats to gather round him. The anxiety of the House was now aroused as he fell forward senseless on the table. There were cries of "Open the window" and "Some water". The Lord Chancellor and the Earl of Liverpool evinced the greatest concern, and proceeded immediately to Lord Erskine's assistance ... but his speech and colour were gone. ... it was found that he was suffering from a violent temporary cramp in the stomach.' The peers thought that the end of the great lawyer was to resemble that of Chatham, who collapsed while speaking in the Lords, and after a few days died.

[1] He is referring to the political prosecutions in the 1790's.
[2] This passage is taken from Campbell *op. cit.*

Campbell characteristically adds 'and it certainly would have been well for his reputation'.

The debate was opened by speeches from peers who, for the most part, had made their sympathies known by questions to the witnesses. Lord Lauderdale made the expected examination of the evidence which bore unfavourably on the Queen; Lord Rosebery opposed this 'severe measure': Lord Redesdale 'taking the whole of the evidence from beginning to end, felt that it was, in its most material parts, entitled to confidence': Lord Grosvenor, the builder of Belgravia and a man of taste, attempted a burst of eloquence: 'Their lordships should look to the signs of the times. They would find that nature had rendered them as visible in the physical world, as their own judgment must have shown to them in the moral one. They had read in Scripture that the stars would run from their courses, that the moon and sun would alter their appearance. When the Attorney-General in this case levelled (acting, doubtless, from his instructions—and, so acting, some viewed him as acting innocently) the foul barbs from his quiver against the person of his Queen, his attack commenced in storms;[1] and when the hour of her Majesty's counsel arrived to make in her behalf their unanswerable defence, the sun emerged in all the blaze of his brightness from the heavy obscurity of an eclipse. Their lordships, in looking at the present agitated state of the public mind, must see that the moral clouds, charged with thunder, were collecting over their heads: let them, therefore, disperse them, by abandoning this fatal bill. Then, indeed, their moral horizon would resume its clearness. Let them, then, put an end to this bill—a breath had created it, and a breath could destroy it; nothing would disseminate wider joy than such a decision —a joy which would not only pervade England but all Europe.' Lord Harewood, in a confused speech, appeared to think the Queen's guilt proved but preferred to vote against the bill. Lord Donoughmore made a resounding speech against the Queen, and in his conclusion made eulogistic references to the King. He asked what right any man had to suppose that the Lords would not uphold their character for integrity as a court of justice: 'What right, then, had any man either within or below the bar to suppose for an instant

[1] He is referring to the thunderstorm on the opening day of the case.

that they would not continue to uphold that character? Had anything been done by them to show that they would be guilty of injustice? Had there been nothing in the conduct of the illustrious person at the head of the government, in the management of the war, and in the bringing it to a glorious conclusion, which entitled him to the gratitude and redoubled loyalty of his subjects? The most arduous and difficult part of that war had fallen to his lot: he had presided at the helm of its affairs, and the triumphs which he had gained would reflect an immortal lustre over the military reputation of this country.'

Lord Grey—though what might be called a reluctant partisan of the Queen—swayed opinion with a highly distinguished speech. He made a detached and broad-minded examination of the evidence. He certainly offered an original suggestion for the Queen's favour to Pergami: 'Although it might appear paradoxical, he considered that there was something in Pergami's situation which furnished less ground for suspicion than would have existed had he been a person of superior rank. When it was recollected that sovereigns were, in situation, as much above the rest of mankind as a person on a lofty mountain was above the passenger on the plain beneath him, it would not create surprise if it sometimes happened that they acted as if they had lost sight of the proportion which existed between themselves and those below them. Besides, they claimed the right, as well as possessed the power, to exalt individuals from the lowest stage in society to the most distinguished rank and the highest honour. He agreed with his noble and learned friend on the woolsack that the advancement of Pergami differed very much from that of individuals who, after long years of exertion, worked their way to distinction either in the bar or the church, the army or the navy. He likewise thought with him, that it was one of the noblest points in the British constitution, that it placed no bar in the road to promotion before any individual. Still he could not forget that all history, both ancient and modern, and especially our own history, was pregnant with examples of persons elevated from the lowest to the most exalted stations from no other motive than caprice and favour; and, as was said by a noble friend of his, it was seldom found that those who obtained that good fortune did not let in some part of their family to partake of it.'

Grey's examination of Majocchi's evidence was damning. 'What should he say of Majocchi's want of recollection, under which he had sheltered himself, upon points which it was impossible for him not to remember? He was asked "were there any sheets on the bed?" which he had before sworn he had been in the daily habit of making. His answer was, "I do not remember." He was asked whether he knew where the other livery servants slept, and he replied again, "I do not remember"; that too when he had described the arrangement of the different bedrooms with great accuracy in 15 or 16 different places. Under those circumstances, did he not stand so disqualified as a witness, as to render it impossible for any man, who really wished to do justice, to attach the slightest credit to an assertion of his? Did their lordships recollect the manner in which he had supposed to hearing the creaking of the bed through two decks— a question by which he (Earl Grey) had been so disgusted, that he could not conceive what infatuation could have led the learned counsel to put it. Had they forgotten the glee with which Majocchi had recounted the use to which he said that the bottle found in the carriage was applied? Surely they could not: for it showed a malignant spirit in that witness, which, till that time, he had thought could not have existed in a human creature.'

He went on to recall how Sir William Gell and Mr. Keppel Craven had sworn that the Princess had not appeared at Naples 'in a state of indecent nakedness'; and Sir W. Gell, from that knowledge of antiquity by which he was distinguished, had been able to refer them to the model from which her Majesty's dress had been taken, and which proved, to the satisfaction of every candid man, that it was quite the reverse of nakedness and indecency. Their lordships, if they looked to the dress of some of their own wives and daughters, would find that their dresses, in the vagaries of modern fashions, had often led to much more shameful and indelicate exhibitions than that upon which, as a foundation, the whole fabric of this abominable conspiracy had been built. Though no suspicion of guilt had ever arisen from such exposures, he trusted that the ladies of this country, warned by the experience of her Majesty, would abstain from them in future. If the present proceeding had no other effect than that of correcting the indelicacy of certain modern fashions, it was likely to do good; for he must tell the sex in general, that the more abstemious in displaying their charms the more likely they were to attract and captivate. In a language that had lately been familiar to most of their lordships he would say, *Quanto si mostra meno, tanto piu bella.*'

Though a rather reserved man Grey closed his speech with an allusion to his own career and his own political loyalties. 'He had lived through extraordinary times, big with events that found no parallel in the history of the world. In the course of those events he had been much engaged in political discussion; and all he could say of his own labours was, that it had been his endeavour, as far as human infirmity would permit, to act with a free and impartial uprightness. The attainment of power had never been the principle by which he was governed; if it had been, he, perhaps, should not so long have been excluded from office. He had been, notwithstanding, and still was, the object of much reproach; but he had uniformly endeavoured to resist the undue extension of the power of the crown, without invading its undoubted right. The prerogatives of the crown were not given merely for its own splendour, but for the protection of its subjects, who had as deep an interest as the King himself in their continuance and preservation. Many national calamities might be the result of this measure, but after what he had now said, he could retire with a sound spirit, and an untroubled conscience, and spend his remaining years—and few they necessarily must be—in the confident hope that he should leave to his children the reputation, the character, and the example of an honest man. He fairly avowed, that in the outset his prejudices and feelings were unfavourable to the Queen: he did think it possible that a case would be made out that would compel him to vote, however reluctantly, in support of the bill; but as it now stood, viewing it first as a question of guilt or innocence, and, next, as a matter of political expediency, he was bound to declare that he could never lay down his head in tranquillity in future if he did not to his utmost resist its progress. He must therefore give the only vote he could reconcile to his honour and his judgment; and laying his hand upon his heart, with the deepest sense of the solemnity of the occasion, conscientiously and fearlessly, before God, pronounce—Not Guilty.'

The Prime Minister followed Grey. His extreme fairness throughout the proceedings deserves to be recorded, and won the admiration
even of partisans of the Queen.[1] He prefaced what he had to say
about the evidence by this warning 'whatever any noble lord might
think of all the allegations, no person ought to vote, and he desired
no person would vote, for the second reading, who did not believe
that the adulterous intercourse had been proved by sufficient and
satisfactory evidence'. He was quite willing to admit that there was
a great mass of contradictory evidence. But he asked whether there
ever had been a great case where the evidence was not a mass of
contradiction. He cited the Douglas peerage of 1769 and the Angle-
sey peerage claim of 1771 as comparable cases. Each of them turned
to an extent on feminine virtue. He explained this with the reason
that 'without perhaps any intention to commit deliberate perjury,
the witnesses on both sides became partisans'. He went on: 'If in the
course of his argument, he rejected a great deal of the testimony,
it was not because he disbelieved it, but because he was ready
to give her Majesty the advantage of all hesitation arising from
contradiction.'

He made much of Pergami's speedy rise. He said that he 'was
among the last of mankind to say that any man in the country was so
low, so poor, or so degraded, that talent, virtue, or even good
fortune might not raise him to a station of eminence;[2] but did any
man ever hear of a courier in six months becoming Baron Francina
and a Knight of Malta? What had he done to merit this distinction?
From what danger had he rescued his royal mistress?'

He was satirical over the order of St. Caroline. 'Pergami, Baron
Francina and a Knight of Malta, was made grand master, and all
his issue, male as well as female, were to succeed to that title from
generation to generation for ever. W. Austin, on the other hand,

[1] The only thing remembered by one of the last people to survive who had
been present at the proceedings, was that Lord Liverpool wore the garter round
his trousered leg.

[2] Here Lord Liverpool may have been thinking of his own father who, when
he was rebuked in the House of Commons for a pompous manner, which ill-
became a gentleman, replied: 'I have risen by industry, by attention to duty, and
by every honourable means I could devise.' (Quoted in L. Namier, *Structure of
Politics at the Accession of George III.*)

the *protegé* of the Queen, had only the rank of a knight, with succession to his legitimate children. From this might be gathered the religious and moral character of the institution.'

About the tent on the way to the Holy Land—that was the double tent—he made a very reasonable comment. 'There the parties were enclosed within the same tent, whilst in an outer tent slept Carlini and Theodore. Now if Pergami was considered so much better as a protector, why was he not placed in the outer tent? Was it not in human nature that some circumstances must occur which could not have been endured—he would not say by a woman of any delicacy, but by one gross in the extreme—without there had been the most intimate connexion between the parties? . . . But then it was said, that when her Royal Highness entered the tent, it was after travelling, and when she was worn out with fatigue and exhaustion. That told both ways. For if there were any circumstances in which a delicate woman would least desire the presence of a male observer, it must be under those so described.'

And towards the close of his speech he asked a pertinent question: 'He remembered that a case which occurred a few years ago, of a criminal intercourse between a lady and her servant, occasioned no very inconsiderable sensation in the public, in consequence of the difference of rank between the parties. The crime was very naturally considered much aggravated, and the lady still more degraded, by having descended to an intercourse with her own servant. How much more would not such a feeling prevail in the present case?'

After several peers had expressed anxiety over the divorce clause Lord Ellenborough spoke. He had in many questions to witnesses shown himself hostile to the Queen. He explained that he had expected that her guilt would be proved by evidence 'clear, unsuspicious, untainted and irresistible' so that its realisation would 'produce a material change in the opinion of the public'. He would vote against the bill chiefly because of 'the strong and almost universal feeling which existed against it'. But he was not able to pass over the Queen's conduct 'without censure'. He went on 'The Queen of England was a public character; . . . All that was required of her was that she should be a correct model and example in this respect; and in this respect it was that the present Queen utterly failed. Every unprejudiced man who had heard the evidence, every man who lived at all in the world, would admit that the Queen was one of the last women whom he would wish his wife to resemble— one of the last whom the father of a family would propose as an example to his daughters. It was obvious, then, that she could not adequately perform the offices belonging to her station: but then the question assumed a new aspect, when it was considered that these functions were inherent in her as Queen, and when it was proposed to deprive her of them. To him it appeared clear that another course was open, and that none could be more constitutional than to address the King on the conduct of any high public function- ary; none more natural than, in a case like this, to state in that address the substance of the evidence which, in conformity with the royal message, they had taken, and then to state their own conclusion, that the Queen's conduct had been derogatory to her high rank, inconsistent with the delicacy of female virtue, and such as to cast an indelible suspicion on her honour and character. By this means the national manners and virtue might be preserved as effectually as by the bill itself. There was also a parliamentary mode of restraining the Queen in the exercise of her prerogatives, by limiting her allow- ance. He did think there was an absolute necessity, if they wished to pay due respect to female virtue, for visiting her with some censure. Female virtue was one of the great points of superiority which we enjoyed over other countries. It was of the highest importance in maintaining our superiority in other respects. What was the love of country but the love of home? And how could the love of home exist without domestic confidence? It was important to the national character not to suffer the Queen's conduct to pass without observation, not to suffer it to go forth to Europe that the fact of her sleeping for five weeks under the same tent with a menial servant created no suspicion in this country. He had heard of English Princesses who likewise had their paramours—a Mortimer, a Leicester, or an Essex—men of high birth and distinguished qualities —men unlike in every particular to the base object about whom they had heard so much.

> *Lust, thro' some certain strainers well refin'd,*
> *Is gentle love, and charms all womankind.*

But lust and love were indeed very different passions, and where was the love here? Love for the fellow-servant of Majocchi! What could be his topics of conversation? Drawn, he must presume, from an experience gathered in the stable, and from the society, at best, of the upper servants. He must say that he viewed the Queen's conduct towards this man with unqualified and unutterable disgust.'[1]

Lord Erskine, beginning with a reference to his 'severe indisposition', continued his speech from where it had been interrupted by his collapse. 'He would not proceed to address their lordships, as if he were a judge in a court of law; and he was extremely glad to see a number of the learned judges present on this occasion. He was afraid, from the nature of the speech he was about to deliver, that he would not be able to attract their lordships' attention. He could not give to his address the characteristice warmth of senatorial eloquence, because, as he assumed the character of a judge, he must speak coolly and dispassionately.'

He was severe on Demont, who had sworn on oath to the Queen's 'disgusting acts' although she had told Madame Martigny that it was 'all calumny'. 'This woman's testimony was, then, of no value. Unless the laws of England were subverted—unless all he recollected of law was a fiction—unless all his experience misled him—unless the experience of all the authorities, living or dead, which he had consulted was in error—Demont was no witness at all. . . . This infamous witness, for so he was now entitled to call her, swore that the Queen returned early from the Opera, that the bed where she generally slept was unslept in that night, and that a large bed, in which Pergami slept, was disturbed, as if two slept in it. Every syllable of this was completely contradicted, and by witnesses who could not have been mistaken, and who were beyond the reach of suspicion.'

Towards the end of his speech he became more impassioned and more personal than might have been expected from a judge. 'This case was not only supported by perjury, and perjury alone, but the character of that perjury proved the perfect innocence of her Majesty. The witnesses against her, when they left the service of the

[1] A decade later Lord Ellenborough was to divorce his own celebrated wife on the ground of her adultery with Prince Schwartzenburg.

Queen, called her a pattern of every virtue. But if this *furor uterinus*, which that infamous scoundrel, Sacchi, swore to, had existed— if any symptoms of licentious conduct on the part of her Majesty had appeared amid all the spies that beset her, exposed to the machinations of a conspiracy of all the powers of Europe—would it not appear as evident and clear in the proof as any fact ever appeared in a court of justice? Yet, thus beset and exposed, she had done nothing, she had said nothing, which any man living could appeal to as clear ground of any inference against her. . . . In preserving the King's life, or promoting any object connected with his happiness, he was ready to sacrifice his own life—to do any thing but violate his duty. His duty he would not violate: his principles he never, never would desert. He then adverted to the evidence respecting the tent on the deck, and the use of it in the day-time. There was no proof at all upon this subject. He had had as strong passions as any man, and had been as apt to indulge in gallantries; but he could confidently say that the circumstances detailed in evidence, in this part of the case, were unnatural—incredible—impossible. If he were that moment entering into eternity, he would lay his hand on his heart, and say he could not believe that the Queen, covered with all the filth of adultery which had been sworn to, had instituted an order in commemoration of having visited the tomb of the Saviour of mankind: this last fact had affected him very deeply, and most differently from the design of the evidence for the bill. Did it affect any one else so? He spoke for himself. What interest had he in opposing this bill? All his feelings were the other way. He had never even seen this unfortunate Princess, before she appeared on her trial in that House, except once. But he stated facts and arguments which would convince twelve honest men in every court of law in this country, if the laws of England were not subverted and forgotten.'

His habits of gallantry were perhaps illustrated by two further points in his analysis of the evidence. 'Adverting to the evidence respecting the stains on the bed-cover, he submitted that the testimony carried with it its own refutation; for if her Majesty had her clothes on at the time, then these stains could not have reached the bed; and if her clothes were off, it was not surely likely that she would have lain above the bedclothes without any covering whatever. In either way that the case was put, the fact appeared equally incredible. This Demont, or rather this demon, who, as a witness, was dead and buried, had been raised again to patch up the charges at Catania. The supporters of this bill, though compelled to acknowledge that the case had failed, as far as it rested on her testimony, had assumed nevertheless that her testimony relative to the alleged transactions in Catania was worthy of credit.

> *The times have been*
> *That when the brains were out, the man would die,*
> *And there an end: but now they rise again,*
> *With twenty mortal murders in their crowns,*
> *And push us from our stools.*[1] . . .

It ought also to be borne in mind, with reference to this case of the polacca, that in hot climates there could be no enjoyment in such a situation; and, therefore, the object of such an arrangement could only be society and protection.'

Passing from such topics he closed his speech with dignity. He was apparently in a state of great exhaustion and declared that 'he should not have been happy if he had given a silent vote on this momentous occasion. Had he even been assured that the present was the last time he should ever address their lordships, and he certainly was not in good health, he should still have felt himself impelled by an imperious sense of duty to come down to the House to express the opinion he entertained.'

One of the oddest speeches came from the reactionary Duke of Newcastle—the founder of the Newcastle scholarship at Eton. He confessed that from family circumstances—his wife had had a child —he had been unable to be present for the examination of witnesses or the speeches of counsel for the defence. None the less he thought that the Queen had been guilty of degrading and disgraceful adultery: he would vote for the bill and the infliction of the full penalties.

In a series of speeches which followed, the prevailing feeling was possibly expressed by Lord Grantham—'I feel myself bound to

[1] *Macbeth*, Act III, scene 4.

say "Not Content" [to the second reading of the bill] but I can not put my hand on my heart and say "Not Guilty".'

Lord Blessington, an earl, in speaking against the second reading, drew attention to the severe cross-examination of Lady Charlotte by Copley—'she, the daughter of a prime minister, and the sister of an earl. If such were the conduct pursued towards this lady, what sort of examination would the Countess Oldi have undergone at their lordships' bar?'

A former prime minister, Lord Grenville, said that he had been convinced by events on the polacca and by the total absence of any excuse for them; he was effectively answered by a moderate speech from Lord Rosslyn. Then the vote was taken at 3 o'clock on 6 November. Each peer, beginning with the Barons, was asked to say 'Content' or 'Not Content'. There voted 123 'Contents' and 95 'Not Contents'—a majority for the Second Reading of 28. The prospects for the bill after this slender majority are perhaps best summed up in a word used by Creevey—'fatal'. He added "eleven bishops voted for it and the Archbishop of York alone against it."

At the opening of the proceedings on 7 November Lord Dacre— he was formerly well-known as Thomas Brand, a radical member of the House of Commons who was nicknamed Firebrand—introduced a protest from the Queen. This was probably prepared by Brougham and contained thrusts against those peers who had voted and been members of the Secret Committee and those who had voted though attending irregularly.

'THE PROTEST

' *Caroline Regina.*

'To the Lords Spiritual and Temporal in Parliament assembled.

'The Queen has learnt the decision of the Lords upon the bill now before them. In the face of parliament, of her family, and of her country, she does solemnly protest against it. Those who avowed themselves her prosecutors have presumed to sit in judgment upon the question between the Queen and themselves. Peers have given their voices against her who had heard the whole evidence for the charge, and *absented* themselves during her *defence*. Others have come to the discussion from the *Secret*

Committee with minds biassed by a mass of slanders, which her enemies have not dared to bring forward in the light.

'The Queen does not avail herself of her right to appear before the committee; for to her the details of the measure must be a matter of indifference; and, unless the course of these unexampled proceedings should bring the bill before the other branch of the legislature, she will make no reference whatever to the treatment experienced by her during the last 25 years.

'She now, most deliberately, and before God, asserts that she is wholly innocent of the crime laid to her charge; and she awaits, with unabated confidence, the final result of this unparalleled investigation.'

The Duke of Newcastle voiced his indignation about the jibe against him, saying that he had not thought their lordships were jurymen. Poor Lord Somers felt obliged to explain that he had had to be absent for parts of the case and his hearing not being very good he had moved close to the bar; he added that he had never attended any judicial proceeding 'in which he was more perfectly convinced of the guilt of the party'. He added that those were the grounds on which he had given his vote. After debate the House consented to receive the protest, 'though justly' taking exception to the offensive parts of it. The House then went into committee, Lord Shaftesbury being in the chair. After considerable debate various adjustments were made in the preamble to accord with the evidence.

The House then turned to the difficult question whether the divorce clause should remain part of the bill. The Archbishop of York, a metropolitan and in rank and distinction of mind one of the great prelates of his age, spoke first. Although, as Creevey noted, he was the only bishop to vote against the bill, he was to preach the sermon at George IV's coronation. He said that he had often heard it said that a regard for public morals required the passing of the bill. 'In what way, he begged to know, could the general interests of religion be promoted by the public dissemination through the country, and the introduction into every private family, of those offensive and disgusting particulars with which their lordships had been nauseated throughout this protracted investigation?'

On the divorce clause he said: 'I know not where any mention is made in the word of God of a religious expediency that could justify this measure . . . I must look on the word of God, and on that only, as the guide of my conduct.'

The Archbishop of Canterbury (Manners Sutton) discoursed on what was said in the gospels about divorces; 'They are expressly declared to be lawful by Our Saviour himself.' He then led his listeners into the intricacies of theology when he said 'it was impossible to believe that that was not intended which was expressed, though that which was not expressed might be intended'. The Bishop of London, the accomplished Howley who was to be the next Archbishop of Canterbury, agreed with Manners Sutton and could not agree with Harcourt.

The Archbishop of Tuam, Power le Poer Trench, a masterful, fighting bishop spoke of S. Matthew chapter 5 verse 32 and then turned to the second chapter of the prophet Malachi. The awkward point about the verse from S. Matthew was that the King by 'putting away' his wife could, in the sense of that verse, be held to have caused her to commit adultery. He quoted Malachi: 'For the Lord, the God of Israel, saith that he hateth putting away.' With an engaging frankness the Archbishop explained that nothing except the fine to which he would have been liable had made him attend. 'He had been forced away from important duties—duties which no man on earth but himself were entitled to perform, and which had therefore remained suspended for the last three months.'

Lord King, a strange peer, an economist of note but erratic in his opinions, who disliked the Church, drew attention to the lack of conformity of opinion (which the Church demanded and on which it prided itself) among the prelates on this topic. He suddenly went back in history to the far-off past when the Queen was at Blackheath, where he said that she was guilty of indecorum with the Prime Minister (Liverpool) and games of blindman's buff with the Chancellor of the Exchequer (Vansittart). 'They never took place' growled the Prime Minister. Unabashed, Lord King said that he could not state the exact time but that it must have been before the regency, in the days when 'the noble earl was looking for means to get into office'. 'Never, I assure the Noble Lord' said the Prime

Minister. When the vote was taken 129 voted in favour of keeping the divorce clause and 62 against.

There was then a desultory debate on the Third Reading—the adherence to the divorce clause had caused singular confusion—and when the vote was taken on the fifty-third day, Friday 10 November there voted 108 in favour and 99 against. As soon as the figures were known Lord Dacre sprang up to present a petition from the Queen. Lord Liverpool interrupted him. 'Had the Third Reading been carried by as considerable a number of peers as the Second had been, he and his colleagues would have felt it their duty to persevere with the bill.' But in view of the narrow majority 'it was his intention to move that the bill do pass this day six months'—the parliamentary device for shelving a measure. This was carried *nemine contradicente* and, as the official report says, 'almost by acclamation'. 'The Bill is gone, thank God! to the devil', wrote Creevey.

The Lord Chancellor made a wise comment on the result in a private letter to his daughter. 'I thought it wholly inconsistent with the dignity of the House of Lords to close the most solemn inquiry ever entertained in that House by doing nothing. The bill should have been rejected or passed. But to have upon our journals four different resolutions, all founded upon our avowed conviction of her guilt, and then neither to withdraw those resolutions, nor to act upon them appears to me perfectly absurd, and, both to the country and to her, unjust. To her surely it is so.'[1]

The vote and the consequent decision to drop the bill coincided with the verdict of the public. Whether it coincided with the evidence, to which the peers had patiently listened, is a matter of individual opinion. One thing at least was outside dispute—the Queen's behaviour in Italy had completely lacked dignity and decorum; with her train of Italian servitors she had dragged in the mire the good name of the English royal family and—to an extent—the reputation of the country. How the King and the Government could have best dealt with that situation is again a matter of opinion, but it is outside dispute that the method which they chose was unwise. She who was said to have carried on a licentious, disgraceful and adulterous intercourse with an Italian courier was triumphant. She

[1] Horace Twiss, *Life of Lord Eldon*, 1844, vol. III 399–400.

was in her room in the House of Lords, when the news was broken
to her and she said, in her brazen way: 'There Regina still in spite
of them.' Jubilation followed her carriage all the way from Westminster to Brandenburg House. For three days the town was illumi-
nated. A flag flying from a public house at the corner of Half Moon
Street and Piccadilly was much remarked. A gallows proper was
depicted on ground argent: below was written: 'Whats that for?
Non mi ricordo.' On 29 November the Queen celebrated her
triumph by going in state to St. Paul's to offer thanks to God for
her deliverance from her enemies. The company inside the Cathedral
was somewhat mixed, and the dignitaries of the Church were
noticeably absent. But there was no mistaking the enthusiasm of
the London crowd which was enormous and exultant. Although
few observers realised this at the time, it was the last flaming blaze
of this curious conflagration. Ten weeks later the King, who had not
been able to show himself in the capital, went in state on consecutive
nights to Drury Lane and Covent Garden. He was rapturously
acclaimed both inside the theatres and on his way to and fro. Five
months later, on 19 July, the King was crowned, and the Queen,
attempting to force her way into the Abbey, was turned away and
greeted by the London crowd with cries of 'Shame, shame' and 'Go,
go'. A fortnight afterwards on 7 August she was dead. Some said
that she had died from a broken heart as a result of her reception at
Westminster Abbey, others that she had died from that inherited
affliction of the bowel which had killed her namesake and great
grandmother—the most illustrious Queen-Consort in English
history. She lies in the vault of the cathedral church of Brunswick,
surrounded by members of her illustrious family, and on the lid of
her coffin are written words chosen by herself: 'Here lies Caroline
of Brunswick, the injured Queen of England'. And perhaps in
choosing the word 'injured' she was not thinking only of wrongs
done to her by the King, the Government and the House of Lords
but of a lack of understanding from her own following. Did she not
herself say of the proceedings in the House of Lords 'Nobody cares
for *me* in this business. This business has been more cared for as a
political business than as the cause of a poor forlorn woman.'

The Bill of Pains and Penalties

A Bill to deprive her Majesty Caroline Amelia Elizabeth of the Title, Prerogatives, Rights, Privileges, and Pretensions of Queen Consort of this Realm, and to dissolve the Marriage between his Majesty and the said Queen.

WHEREAS in the year one thousand eight hundred and fourteen, her Majesty, Caroline Amelia Elizabeth, then Princess of Wales, and now Queen Consort of this realm, begin at Milan, in Italy, engaged in her service, in a menial situation, one Bartolomo Pergami, otherwise Bartolomo Bergami, a foreigner of low station, who had before served in a similar capacity:

AND WHEREAS, after the said Bartolomo Pergami, otherwise Bartolomo Bergami, had so entered the service of her Royal Highness the said Princess of Wales, a most unbecoming and degrading intimacy commenced between her Royal Highness and the said Bartolomo Pergami, otherwise Bartolomo Bergami:

AND WHEREAS her Royal Highness not only advanced the said Bartolomo Pergami, otherwise Bartolomo Bergami, to a high situation in her Royal Highness's household, and received into her service many of his near relations, some of them in inferior, and others in high and confidential situations about her Royal Highness's person, but bestowed upon him other great and extraordinary marks of favour and distinction, obtained for him orders of knighthood, and titles of honour, and conferred upon him a pretended order of knighthood, which her Royal Highness had taken upon herself to institute without any just or lawful authority:

The Bill of Pains and Penalties

AND WHEREAS her said Royal Highness, whilst the said Bartolomo Pergami, otherwise Bartolomo Bergami, was in her said service, further unmindful of her exalted rank and station, and of her duty to your Majesty, and wholly regardless of her own honour and character, conducted herself towards the said Bartolomo Pergami, otherwise Bartolomo Bergami, and in other respects, both in public and private, in the various places and countries which her Royal Highness visited, with indecent and offensive familiarity and freedom, and carried on a licentious, disgraceful, and adulterous intercourse with the said Bartolomo Pergami, otherwise Bartolomo Bergami, which continued for a long period of time during her Royal Highness's residence abroad, by which conduct of her said Royal Highness, great scandal and dishonour have been brought upon your Majesty's family and this kingdom.

Therefore, to manifest our deep sense of such scandalous, disgraceful, and vicious conduct on the part of her said Majesty, by which she has violated the duty she owed to your Majesty, and has rendered herself unworthy of the exalted rank and station of Queen Consort of this realm, and to evince our just regard for the dignity of the crown, and the honour of this nation, we, your Majesty's most dutiful and loyal subjects, the Lords Spiritual and Temporal and Commons in Parliament assembled, do hereby entreat your Majesty, that it may be enacted;

AND BE IT ENACTED by the King's most excellent Majesty, by and with the advice and consent of the Lords Spiritual and Temporal and Commons in this present Parliament assembled, and by the authority of the same, that her said Majesty Caroline Amelia Elizabeth, from and after the passing of this Act, shall be and is hereby deprived of the title of Queen, and of all the prerogatives, rights, privileges, and exemptions appertaining to her as Queen Consort of this realm; and that her said Majesty shall, from and after the passing of this Act, for ever be disabled and rendered incapable of using, exercising, and enjoying the same, or any of them; and moreover, that the marriage between his Majesty and the said Caroline Amelia Elizabeth be and the same is hereby from henceforth for ever wholly dissolved, annulled, and made void to all intents, constructions, and purposes whatsoever.

Index

Index